RUSSIA

KAZAKHSTAN

UZBEKISTAN

KRAINE

TURKEY

SYRIA   IRAQ
ISRAEL JORDAN
68

KYRGYZSTAN
75

TURKMENISTAN

AFGHANISTAN
78

•74
MONGOLIA

NORTH
KOREA
SOUTH
KOREA
84

JAPAN

86

GYPT

SAUDI
ARABIA

IRAN

PAKISTAN

UAE   67

OMAN

NEPAL   77
76   BHUTAN
        BANGLADESH

CHINA

•83

85   TAIWAN

ERITREA   YEMEN

DJIBOUTI

DAN

SOMALIA

OUTH
UDAN   66
ETHIOPIA

UGANDA
72

KENYA

INDIA

MYANMAR
79 • 80
THAILAND
CAMBODIA

LAOS

82
VIETNAM

PHILIPPINES

81   SRI
     LANKA

BRUNEI

MALAYSIA
SINGAPORE

TANZANIA

MALAWI

MBABWE   MADAGASCAR

•70

INDONESIA

TIMOR-
LESTE

PAPUA
NEW GUINEA

SOLOMON
ISLANDS

VANUATU   FIJI

92 •

AUSTRALIA

87 •• 88

90

93 •

91 • 89 •

100
98 •   • 99

94 • 95

97
96

NEW
ZEALAND

RIDE

RIDE

CYCLE THE WORLD

CONTENTS

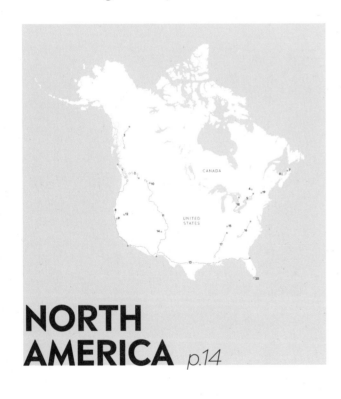

**CENTRAL
AND SOUTH
AMERICA** *p.60*

**NORTH
AMERICA** *p.14*

EUROPE *p.90*

4

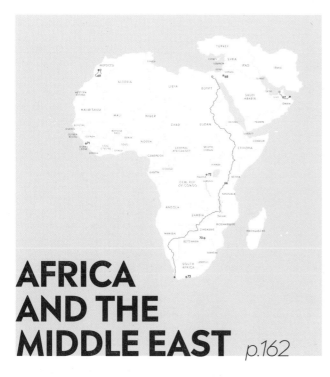

AFRICA
AND THE
MIDDLE EAST *p.162*

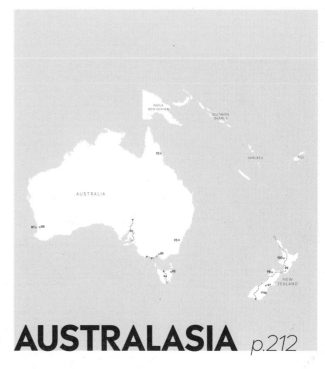

AUSTRALASIA *p.212*

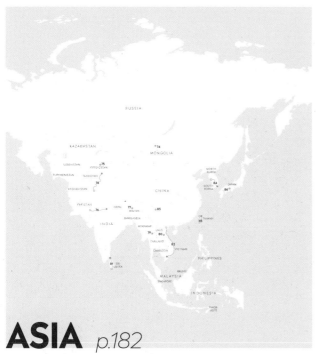

ASIA *p.182*

Riding along the
Old Ghost Road
single-track trail
in New Zealand

INTRODUCTION

Exploring the world by bike is pure freedom. Nothing beats the feeling of jumping in the saddle and heading off to discover diverse landscapes and new cultures, all completely under your own steam. That's why we've created *Ride*.

Covering 100 of the world's most incredible cycling routes, this book will take you on an adventure across the world, from Ecuador's remote back country to laid-back Melbourne. The rides featured have been selected by our expert writers—who include among their number intrepid bikepackers and talented bike racers—and enthusiastically approved by our cycling-obsessed team. Of course, the big hitters are covered—among them the iconic Alpe d'Huez and stunning Cabot Trail—but we've also included some less-pedaled rides, from bikepacking through the Mongolian steppe to cycling Africa top

to bottom. There's plenty of variety, meaning that whether you're a lycra-clad roadie, a mud-loving mountain biker, or someone new to two wheels, there's a ride for you.

The book is handily organized by continent, so wherever you're headed you can find the best rides available. Even better, each route has practical information to help you plan your trip, including distance, total ascent, and road surface, plus tips on the best sights to see and snacks to devour along the way. We've also included elevation profiles, so you can—quite literally—see the ups and downs of the route.

Whether you're planning your first big ride or an epic bikepacking adventure, this book will have you itching to get pedalling. So what are you waiting for? Grab life by the handlebars and cycle the world.

PRACTICAL INFORMATION KEY

 DISTANCE    TOTAL ASCENT    ROAD SURFACE

Top Gliding along
smooth pavement on
a road bike

Bottom A pair of
mountain bikers rolling
down a dirt trail

CHOOSING A BIKE

*Hankering to head off on a cycling adventure but not sure which bike to choose?
We've got you covered. Here's a quick guide to the four main types of bike, so
you can easily pick which is best for you.*

Road

Light and agile, road bikes are designed for speed. Narrow
tires and lightweight frames make them efficient at rolling
along paved surfaces, helping riders achieve maximum
speed for minimum effort. A road bike doesn't handle
rough terrain very well, but if you're staying on smooth
surfaces it should comfortably manage a wide range of
recreational rides. While some models may accommodate
a rack and panniers, most aren't really built to carry
luggage beyond a small saddlebag, so you'll need to travel
light or have your bags transported for multiday rides.

Mountain

"MTBs" can go almost anywhere off-road, however
rough, thanks to their robust frames and wheels, big
tires, and (usually) suspension. Wide, flat handlebars
and an upright riding position help maneuverability,
as do high-power brakes. They're less efficient to pedal
on smooth surfaces, so are best suited for forest roads,
towpaths, rocky trails, and dirt tracks. For bikepacking—
remote off-road touring—an MTB can be turned into
a pedalable packhorse by using specially shaped bags
attached to the frame and handlebars.

① Dropped handlebars allow
riders to hunker down into
an aerodynamic, forward-
leaning riding position for
greater efficiency.

② Frames need to be light and
rigid. Carbon fiber is the usual
material of choice for top-end
bikes, but titanium is a sought-
after alternative. Aluminum
alloys are a popular, less
expensive option.

③ Brakes are either rim
brakes, which grip the wheel
rim, or disc brakes, which
clamp a small rotor fixed to
the hub; hydraulic disc brakes
are the most powerful.

① Suspension forks absorb
shocks from rough surfaces but
add weight; they can usually
be locked if you need to do any
road riding. Some MTBs have
rear suspension, too.

② Gears include very low
ratios for easy hill climbing—
perhaps as low as two pedal
revolutions for every one of
the back wheel. Range is more
important than the overall
number of gears.

③ Tires are big and often set
at low pressure to help smooth
out rough surfaces. They also
feature bumpy or ridged
patterns for traction in mud.

Top A gravel bike fitted with front and rear panniers for touring

Bottom A foot-powered recumbent bike laden with luggage

Gravel and Touring

There are many bike types between road and MTB, each suited to a particular mix of surfaces and amount of luggage. Sturdy gravel bikes are built with alloy or steel frames to optimize comfort and speed on roads and lighter off-road trails. Low gears help with climbs and strong brakes with descents. Most models can be fitted with rear racks for panniers, though some cyclists use bikepacking bags. Traditional touring bikes are similar, but are designed for maximum comfort, heavy loads (handling steadily even with front and rear panniers), and a more leisurely pace.

Recumbent

They come in various forms, but whatever their number of wheels, pedal position, or steering system, recumbents allow you to recline in comfort, feet to the front, rather than sit upright on a saddle. They're efficient to pedal and their lower profile reduces wind resistance, meaning that riders can cover big distances quickly, even while heavily laden—though uphills are laborious. Recumbents are a boon for those with back issues or limited mobility, and can be adapted to suit the circumstances of almost any user: some can be cranked and steered solely by hand, for example.

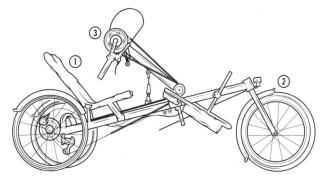

① Mudguards prevent your wheels spraying you with water and dirt. They may appear on a gravel bike (clip-on ones give flexibility), while a touring bike will almost always have them.

② Rear racks let you hang panniers and strap more luggage on top; most riders find backpacks uncomfortable for touring. Some bikes can also be fitted with front pannier racks.

③ Handlebars often have drops, like road bikes, but with a more upright riding position; some cyclists prefer straight or butterfly (figure-eight-shaped) bars for more comfort.

① Seats, usually mesh, support the rider's body in a reclined position. By taking weight off the hands and backside, and avoiding sore necks, they enable long distances to be covered in comfort.

② Wheels differ in size and number. Many recumbents use a three-wheeled setup—such as two at the back and one at the front—for stability.

③ Arm-powered recumbents are known as handcycles. The hand pedals drive either the front or rear wheels, simultaneously propelling the bike and controlling the steering.

PREPARING FOR YOUR RIDE

Advance planning is essential before setting off on any cycle ride—especially if you're organizing a longer trip or heading to a remote region. So, to help you get trip-ready, we've put together some handy pointers on preparing for your next ride.

Maintenance

Learning how to fix punctures and adjust your brakes (including replacing the blocks), as well as keeping your chain and cogs clean and lubricated, should get your ready for coping with the vast majority of situations. On longer trips, the most likely mechanical issues are broken spokes and skipping gears. If you can deal with those, you'll be pretty much self-sufficient: every other problem will either be straight-forward to solve on the road (tightening up something loose, say) or likely to need a bike shop anyway (a badly buckled wheel, for example). Puncture-proof tires can be a great investment to avoid dealing with flats.

Responsible Cycle Touring

Cycle touring is by nature one of the most sustainable and lowest-impact forms of travel. If you plan to do any wild camping, check the local rules before setting off and be sure to leave no trace while there: you should inconvenience nobody and leave nothing behind.

Essential Kit

On any ride, it's worth carrying a small multitool (which usually includes hex keys and screwdrivers), a bottle of chain lube, and a basic puncture repair kit (including compact pump and spare inner tube)—together, these should allow you to fix most issues. For a hotel- or hostel-based trip, rear panniers are usually sufficient in terms of luggage. Cycle-camping can be cheaper and offer greater flexibility—and may be the only option for adventurous journeys—but all the supplies (lightweight tent, sleeping bag and liner, food, water, and cooking gear) might require extra

Fixing a puncture
at the side of the road

Stay Safe

Don't overexert yourself, and finish before dark; 40 miles (60 km) a day is usually plenty.

Carry plenty of water and food—the next open shop might be a day's ride away.

Keep valuables in a barbag you can easily take with you when parking the bike.

Good maps are vital for avoiding dangerous highways: back roads are often more interesting anyway.

Driving standards vary worldwide, especially at night or on truck routes. Check blogs and websites for local advice.

Planning the route
with a paper map

front panniers and bungees for strapping things atop the rear rack. Alternatively, you could use bikepacking bags fastened to the bike frame and handlebars.

Navigation
Paper maps are simplest, and easiest to read, but the miracle of GPS means you're never lost. Bar-mounted systems are available, although a smartphone can work just as well. Use an app that can download maps and work offline, however, or rely on costly mobile data—assuming you can get a signal. Gadgets gobble electricity so be sure to take a power bank; some bikes boast on-the-go recharging through hub dynamos, or even solar panels.

Transportation
Most airlines take bikes as checked luggage (sometimes with a hefty surcharge). You typically have to remove the wheels and bag or box it—make sure you pack your

bike securely, as damage in transit is not unknown. Ferries almost always take bikes just wheeled on, as do some intercity and international trains. Alternatives are to hire or buy at your destination, invest in a folding tourer, or courier your bike.

Further Reading
The following websites are all excellent resources for tips on planning a cycle tour.

bicycletraveler.bicyclingaroundtheworld.nl
Free online magazine to get you dreaming.

bikepacking.com
Comprehensive info for off-road adventures.

tomsbiketrip.com
Advice on choosing bikes, supplies, and routes.

travellingtwo.com
Insights from a couple who traveled around the world by bike.

womencycletheworld.org
Inspiring cycling stories and blogs from a female perspective.

To download GPX routes for the rides featured in this book, plus access to our Strava Club and other great cycling content, head to *dk.com/ride*.

NORTH AMERICA

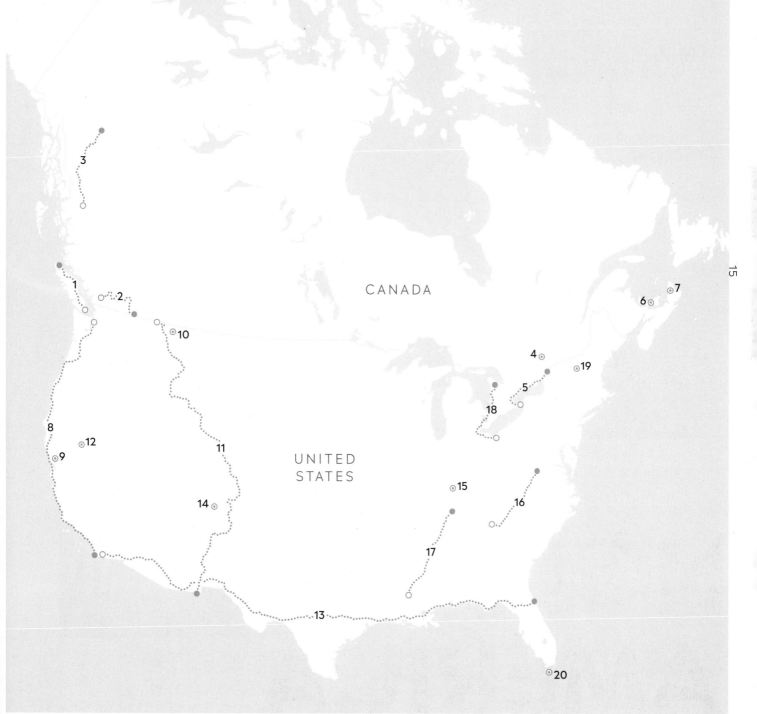

1

Vancouver Island

VICTORIA TO PORT HARDY, CANADA

Dive into unspoiled wilderness on a ride along the length of Vancouver Island. Heading off the beaten track, this adventurous route showcases both the area's incredible natural beauty and its wondrous wildlife.

Port Hardy

Port McNeill

393 MILES (633 KM)

29,839 FT (9,095 M)

PAVED / GRAVEL

16

Sitting on Canada's west coast, Vancouver Island doesn't just host British Columbia's cultured capital, it's also home to some of the country's most impressive flora and fauna. On this ride, you'll cycle through dense forest, past shimmering lakes, and alongside sandy shores, inhaling the clean air and listening to the sounds of rustling leaves and chittering birdsong. There'll be a few dips into the island's main cities and ports, where you can stock up on supplies and treat yourself to some home comforts, but most of the time you'll be completely surrounded by wilderness.

The route follows a combination of long-distance cycling trails, gravel logging roads, and scenic main roads, the majority of which are largely traffic-free (other than the occasional logging truck). From

the island's capital, Victoria, the famous Galloping Goose trail—part of Canada's Great Trail System, a colossal initiative to link up trails across the country—leads you directly out of the city center and into lush nature within minutes. Heading "up island" (local vernacular for anywhere north of Victoria), the route becomes gradually more remote as you delve deeper into the wilderness via forested tracks; hours can pass by without the interruption of the sound of a motor.

Riding out of Victoria on the Galloping Goose Trail

ELEVATION PROFILE

3,000 ft (914 m)

0

0   393 miles (633 km)

CAMPBELL RIVER offers plenty of opportunities for wildlife watching. From the marina, you will likely see bald eagles hunting in the tidelines and some curious harbor seals.

17

REFUEL

Nanaimo Bars

The famous Nanaimo bars—no-bake, rich, and creamy layered brownies—originate from Vancouver Island's central city of Nanaimo, and almost any bakery or café you visit on the island will serve up their own homemade squares. You definitely deserve a treat after all that cycling.

Johnstone Strait

Elk Falls Provincial Park

Campbell River

Practise some *shinrin-yoku* (forest bathing) in the lush rain forest of **ELK FALLS PROVINCIAL PARK**, north of Campbell River.

Courtenay

Cumberland

Spend a day riding on the well-maintained singletrack surrounding **CUMBERLAND**, a new mecca for mountain biking.

VANCOUVER ISLAND

Port Alberni

Lake Cowichan

Take a day off the bike and swim, kayak, or waterski on the glittering **LAKE COWICHAN**. You can also spend the night at its shoreside campsite.

Victoria

Explore **VICTORIA**, the capital of BC, before starting your journey. The city is rich in museums, restaurants, and markets.

0 ·········· km ·········· 40
0 ·········· miles ·········· 40

18

Left An orca surfacing in Johnstone Strait, off Vancouver Island's northeast coast

Soon, your first climb rises on the horizon, a series of short but steep undulations. Most of the ascents on this route come early on, so you can feel good at this point to already have one of the hardest sections behind you. Dropping downhill, you'll pass by the small inland community of Lake Cowichan, perched on the edge of its eponymous lake; cycle alongside the deep-blue waters, surrounded by tree-clad mountains.

Quiet logging roads along emerald corridors take you deeper into the island, leading you to Port Alberni, a small town

that thrives on recreational fishing and cold-water surfing in the nearby Pacific Rim National Park. From here, you'll pedal north on gravel roads toward the center of the island, lured onward by the white peaks of Strathcona Provincial Park looming ahead of you.

This section of the ride takes you across the spine of Vancouver Island, but it's not as hard-going as you might think. The stretch of logging roads through the alpine scenery of the island's center is one of the most pleasant on the whole route. Wildflowers erupt in color alongside the path, and deep-green forest flanks the sides of grand mountains. You will likely encounter some of the locals—deer, elk, and black bears, that is. There are few human inhabitants found here. At the end of this leg is the small town of Cumberland,

> ## Quiet logging roads along emerald corridors take you deeper into the island

Top Tip

Mosquitoes can be a real pain—be sure to bring along some repellent.

nestled in the dramatic Comox Valley, a booming hub of mountain biking, where you can take a break at the local microbrewery or bike-themed pizzeria.

Heading onward, you'll flow toward the coast via the faster, direct paved road along the shore. Keep a keen eye on the waves for harp seals, otters, and even orcas. There are plenty of spots to park the bike for a moment and dive in for a swim—if you can handle the cold.

The northern half of Vancouver Island is a true wilderness that few visitors ever make it to, especially under human power. Wildlife sightings abound on land and in sea and sky, and the small communities you pass through celebrate the indigenous heritage of the island. There is a true feeling of remoteness to this section, and a sense of the cleansing power of

nature. Expect long, quiet miles with no interruptions from the modern world.

Port Hardy is the final destination on your journey, and a wonderful place to finish. You can replenish with the daily catch in one of the pubs by the marina before snuggling into a warm, clean bed—a wonderful and welcome luxury after your journey through the wilderness.

MAKE IT LONGER
Ferry Excursions

It is well worth extending your ride to visit some of the small islands that are connected by car ferries along the eastern coast. Sointula, a 30-minute trip from Port McNeill, boasts regular "orca traffic" and offers a number of accommodations options.

Centre An aerial shot of a spectacular suspension bridge in Elk Falls Provincial Park, one of the stops on the route

Right A fiery sunset over the small town of Port McNeill

0 ···· km ···· 30
0 ···· miles ···· 30

Sip and savor award-winning Okanagan wines at one of the 40 boutique wineries found along the **NARAMATA BENCH**.

Take your time riding over the trestle bridges at **MYRA CANYON**, which offer great views of the surrounding landscape.

Brookmere

Lake Okanagan

Myra Canyon

Summerland

Naramata

Princeton

Penticton

Beaverdell

CANADA

Hope

Coquihalla River Gorge

Rock Creek

Midway

Cross the raging Coquihalla River Gorge via a series of bridges and then roll through the spectacular **OTHELLO TUNNELS**.

2

Kettle Valley Rail Trail

MIDWAY TO HOPE, CANADA

Uncover a slice of railway heritage on the Kettle Valley Rail Trail. Following an old train line, this easygoing route beautifully blends incredible engineering and spectacular landscapes.

300 MILES (483 KM) 10,675 FT (3,254 M) GRAVEL

Cycling this historic trail, you'll be astounded that it was ever built; carved over three mountain ranges, the refurbished railway line is an amazing feat of construction over challenging yet beautiful terrain. Leaving tiny Midway, you'll ride through a forested landscape toward Myra Canyon, crossing this deep chasm via 18 wooden trestles. Chugging on through dark, chiseled tunnels,

you'll reach the Chute Lake Lodge; this once-rundown railway workers' bunkhouse has been restored and is now a great spot for lunch. Back on the bike, a sweeping descent offers views of the sparkling Okanagan Lake—keep your eyes open for the elusive Ogopogo, cousin of the Loch Ness Monster. You'll then roll through the vineyard-clad landscapes of Naramata and on to sunny Penticton, nestled between two lakes. Easy riding among emerald hills leads to the grand finale at the Coquihalla River Gorge. Here, you'll pedal through a last engineering marvel—the Othello Tunnels, five passages carved in a straight line through solid rock.

ELEVATION PROFILE

6,500 ft (1,981 m)

0

0   300 miles (483 km)

20

At **JADE CITY**, visit one of the world's most remote jewelry stores and buy some jade from the family who mine it from the surrounding hills.

Watson Lake

Jade City

The former gold-rush town of **DEASE LAKE** is the biggest settlement along the highway and a great place to stock up on supplies.

Dease Lake
Gnat Pass
Iskut

CANADA

0 ·········· km ·········· 150
0 ·········· miles ·········· 150

Gitanyow
Kitwanga

Turn left as you ride up the hill out of Kitwanga to visit the historic village of **GITANYOW**, home to British Columbia's largest concentration of standing totem poles.

3

Cassiar Highway

KITWANGA TO WATSON LAKE, CANADA

Visit the ghosts of the gold rush as you follow their route north toward the Yukon. You'll camp beside deep-blue lakes, watch black bears at play, and experience one of the last great wildernesses.

If you want the whole world to yourself, the Cassiar Highway is the perfect route. This undulating road passes through just a couple of tiny settlements as it meanders along river valleys, avoiding the worst of the climbing while never straying too far from the spectacular towering peaks that separate British Columbia's remote interior from the Pacific Coast.

You'll need to pack bear spray and mosquito repellent, but it's more than worth it for the wildlife you'll see along the way, including bears, moose, mountain goats, and the herd of caribou that live near the top of Gnat Pass—the high point of the ride. Here and there you'll pass the remnants of more prosperous times, when miners and prospectors swarmed into the Canadian interior in search of gold. Cabins lie in ruins along an old telegraph line and an abandoned railway stretches off into the deep-green forest. This ride is so remote that the modern world will come as quite a shock when you turn onto the much busier Alaska Highway at the end of your journey.

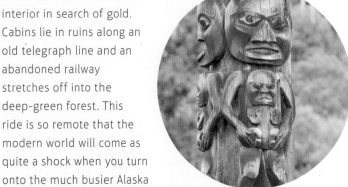

ELEVATION PROFILE

6,500 ft
(1,981 m)

0

0   464 miles (746 km)

⊖ 464 MILES (746 KM)

⊗ 18,975 FT (5,784 M)

⊖ PAVED

4

Capital Pathway

OTTAWA RIVER PARKWAY TO
GATINEAU PARK VISITOR CENTRE, CANADA

Enjoy a leisurely ride through one of the most bike-friendly urban areas in North America, rolling from downtown bustle, via countless historic sights, to a tranquil green haven.

You don't need to be a hardcore cyclist to enjoy this ride—flat and largely car-free, it's suitable for everyone, whatever your level of fitness and experience. Following a central section of the Capital Pathway—a 373-mile (600-km) network of cycle paths in the Ottawa-Gatineau region—the route runs from the heart of Ottawa in Ontario to the region's most popular green space, Gatineau Park in neighboring Quebec.

You'll start your ride on the leafy banks of the Ottawa River. Looming over you is Parliament Hill, home to the stately Neo-Gothic federal government buildings and the Peace Tower, which resembles London's Elizabeth Tower, home of Big Ben. Following the water, you'll pass by the end of a huge set of locks connecting the Ottawa River with the Rideau Canal—an engineering marvel and UNESCO World Heritage Site. Before you pedal onward, look up the canal to spy the castlelike Hotel Fairmont Château Laurier, which looks like it has been plucked straight from the pages of a fairy tale.

Have your camera at the ready as you cross the breezy Alexandra Bridge to reach the French-speaking city of Gatineau; it offers excellent views of downtown Ottawa to the left and the Canadian Museum of History complex to the right—the latter's eye-catching architecture was designed to symbolize the Canadian landscape.

From here, you'll wander into the ever-popular Gatineau Park. This conservation area's varied landscapes, including forests, wetlands, and lakes, provide a fascinating contrast to the bustling cities you've just pedaled through. It's also bursting with wildlife, so keep your eyes peeled for beavers and white-tailed deer as you cycle—you might even spot black bears and wolves. Rolling up to the visitor center, you can hop off your bike and explore on foot, or keep following the Capital Pathway deeper into this vast park.

Gatineau Park
Visitor Centre

0 ·······km·······0.5
0 ···········miles···········0.5

Following signs for the Ottawa River Pathway, which forms part of the Capital Pathway network

⊖ 6 MILES (9 KM)

⊘ 230 FT (70 M)

⊖ PAVED

ANOTHER WAY
Rideau Canal Pathway

If you'd prefer a shorter ride, try this gentle 4-mile (6.5-km) route. From the Hotel Fairmont Château Laurier, it winds along the scenic Rideau Canal Pathway, passing flower-filled parks and gardens, before finishing at Dow's Lake. Here you can grab a bite to eat or head out onto the water aboard a kayak or stand-up paddleboard.

The **CANADIAN MUSEUM OF HISTORY** charts 20,000 years of human history in Canada and beyond. The highlight is the world's largest indoor collection of totem poles.

Take a detour to the lively **BYWARD MARKET** to pick up a BeaverTail. A local speciality, this long, flat, deep-fried doughnut is covered with sweet toppings.

Alexandra Bridge

Canadian Museum of History

ByWard Market

GATINEAU

Rideau Canal

OTTAWA

Parliament Hill

Plaza Bridge

Ottawa River Parkway

Admire the locks of the **RIDEAU CANAL**, which was completed in 1832 and links Ottawa with Lake Ontario and the St. Lawrence River.

Carry your bike up a short flight of steps to **PLAZA BRIDGE** for the finest view of the Hotel Fairmont Château Laurier's dreamy towers, turrets, and stained-glass windows.

ELEVATION PROFILE

650 ft (198 m)

0

0   6 miles (9 km)

Take a side trip to **TORONTO ISLAND**. Hop on the ferry from Bay Street to cycle this pretty island's boardwalk and enjoy great views of the city.

GANANOQUE is "Canada's Gateway" to the Thousand Islands —more than 1,800 islands in the St. Lawrence River, between the US and Canada. Take a break here and enjoy a sunset kayak tour.

South Glengarry

Cornwall

The welcoming town of **CORNWALL** is a great place to take a break, thanks to its thriving local culinary scene, excellent craft brews, and delicious farm-fresh produce.

CANADA

Gananoque

Kingston

Toronto
Rouge River
Oshawa

Lake Ontario

Niagara Falls

0 ···· km ···· 50
0 ···· miles ···· 50

5

Great Lakes Waterfront Trail

NIAGARA FALLS TO SOUTH GLENGARRY, CANADA

Fall in love with Ontario's waterways. Stretching from Niagara Falls to the Quebec border, this route takes you past world-famous falls, powerful rivers, environmentally important wetlands, and one very great lake.

450 MILES (723 KM) 6,932 FT (2,113 M) PAVED / DIRT

You're never far from the water on this picturesque ride, which follows a section of the 2,237-mile (3,600-km) Great Lakes Waterfront Trail. Beginning at the iconic Niagara Falls, pause to feel the mist on your face as torrents of water plummet downward, before wandering alongside the wide Niagara River toward Lake Ontario.

You'll spend much of your ride tracing the shoreline of this vast body of water, passing by Toronto's skyscrapers, an incredible 28 beaches, and countless biodiverse wetlands, where you can spot beavers and herons. It's not all lakeside riding, though. At the mouth of the Rouge River, you'll bike up to bluffs overlooking Lake Ontario— from here, it's easy to see why Iroquois call it the "Lake of Sparkling Waters." The last section of the ride tracks the St. Lawrence River, offering views of the emerald islands that rise out of its inky waters. As you roll toward the Quebec border, reflect on your new connection with Ontario's waterways.

ELEVATION PROFILE

650 ft (198 m)

0

0   450 miles (723 km)

MAKE IT LONGER
Branch Trails

The main Confederation Trail route runs from Tignish to Elmira, but there are several branch trails on which you can explore more of the island. An easy extension is the 6-mile (10-km) spur down to Souris, where you can stroll along the boardwalk and visit the quaint seaside shops, then hit the beach at Basin Head Provincial Park.

6
Confederation Trail

TIGNISH TO ELMIRA, PRINCE EDWARD ISLAND, CANADA

Go beyond the pastoral postcard and discover one of Canada's most enchanting regions on a relaxed rail-to-trail ride that takes you tip to tip across Prince Edward Island.

Built on the former PEI Railway corridor between Tignish and Elmira, the Confederation Trail draws thousands of cyclists to Canada's smallest province each year. Why? The easy riding, for one: the rolled stone dust trail is very well maintained and signed, and the gradient rarely exceeds 2 percent, which makes it perfect for beginner cyclists and family adventures. The serene setting, for another: you can't help but tune out the world, and tune into the smells of spruce and pine, the distant lapping of the sea, and your own thoughts. Then there's the easy access to off-trail experiences: spend the morning pedaling and the afternoon trying your hand at clamming, listening to live music, walking among the rare parabolic sand dunes of Greenwich National Park, visiting iconic lighthouses, or gorging on chocolate-covered potato chips, an island delicacy. And last, but by no means least, there's the friendly island welcome, which is guaranteed to make you feel right at home from the moment you arrive.

170 MILES (274 KM)   4,298 FT (1,310 M)   GRAVEL

Before you set off, take a peek at **TIGNISH**'s striking lighthouse, colored white, red, and black.

ELEVATION PROFILE

650 ft (198 m)

0

0   170 miles (274 km)

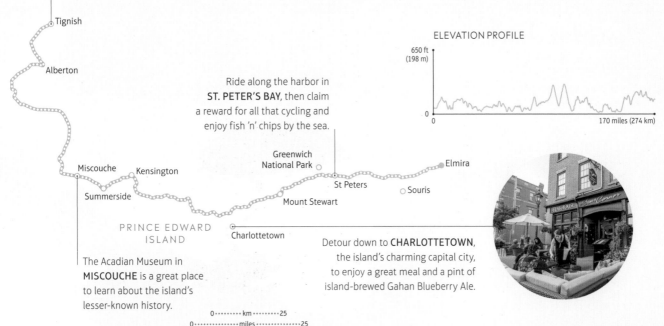

Tignish

Alberton

Miscouche   Kensington

Summerside

PRINCE EDWARD ISLAND

Charlottetown

Mount Stewart

Greenwich National Park

St Peters

Souris

Elmira

Ride along the harbor in **ST. PETER'S BAY**, then claim a reward for all that cycling and enjoy fish 'n' chips by the sea.

The Acadian Museum in **MISCOUCHE** is a great place to learn about the island's lesser-known history.

Detour down to **CHARLOTTETOWN**, the island's charming capital city, to enjoy a great meal and a pint of island-brewed Gahan Blueberry Ale.

0 ·········· km ·········· 25
0 ·········· miles ·········· 25

NORTH AMERICA

In **CHÉTICAMP**, visit Les Trois Pignons (the Museum of the Hooked Rug and Home Life), an Acadian cultural center, with both antique and contemporary hooked rugs. The traditional rug-hooking demonstrations are fascinating.

MARGAREE VALLEY is the best spot on the island for salmon and trout fishing. Fittingly, it's also home to Nova Scotia's oldest fish hatchery, as well as the fascinating Margaree Salmon Museum.

White Point

Skyline Trail

Neils Harbour

Ingonish Ferry

Chéticamp

CAPE BRETON ISLAND

Margaree Valley

For some well-earned zzzs, spend the night at Castlerock Inn in **INGONISH FERRY**. It overlooks the magnificent vista of Middle Head Peninsula, the Atlantic Ocean, and the mountain range of the Cape Breton Highlands.

0 ········· km ········· 20
0 ········· miles ········· 20

Baddeck

IN FOCUS
Inspired Artworks

Cape Breton Island is home to many artisans inspired by both the beauty of their natural surroundings and the area's Celtic heritage. Many of their studios and workshops can be found along the Cabot Trail, including those of kiltmakers, weavers, metal sculptors, leather workers, jewelry designers, and rug hookers.

Before you start your ride, visit the Alexander Graham Bell Historic Site in **BADDECK**. This museum features displays relating to the Scottish-born inventor's work in the field of hearing-impaired education (his mother was deaf), which led to his invention of the telephone.

26

7

Cabot Trail

BADDECK, CAPE BRETON ISLAND, CANADA (LOOP)

If you're looking for a ride with views, look no further. Looping around the north of Cape Breton Island, the stunning Cabot Trail takes in some of Canada's most beautiful scenery.

183 MILES (294 KM)

11,187 FT (3,410 M)

PAVED

Top Tip
This route is at its best in autumn, with a full palette of brilliantly colored trees.

Every turn on this jaw-dropping ride reveals ever-changing postcard-perfect scenery. One day you might be cruising along an undulating coastline, taking in stunning views of emerald-green hills, secluded coves, and sparkling ocean. The next you could be wheeling along wooded trails leading to glistening turquoise lakes, pedalling through rolling farmland where herds of shaggy Highland cattle graze, or cycling alongside winding rivers where salmon are leaping their way upstream.

It's not just the landscape that's varied, though—the terrain is constantly changing, too. Sometimes it's flat, sometimes hilly, and—very occasionally—there are some challenging steep ups and downs. But despite this, the cycling is manageable, and there's always a pay-off after a big hill, whether it's a delicious meal or more drop-dead-gorgeous vistas.

The Cabot Trail is as much about the scenic stops en route as it is about the ride itself. Hop off your bike in Cape Breton Highlands and spend an hour or two hiking through a forest canopy dappled with light,

keeping your eyes peeled for moose and black bears. At White Point, the windiest place in Cape Breton, see the waves fly 20 ft (6 m) into the air before crashing against the rocks. Or take a quick detour to ride to the end of the Skyline Trail and look down at the deep-blue ocean—if you're lucky, you might even see whales spouting. There are plenty of quaint towns to explore along the way, too, where you can stop in to buy handcrafted goods from talented artisans, or spend the evening at a charming inn dining on locally sourced meals, including steaming seafood chowder and freshly made lobster salads.

But no matter where you stop, the route always lures you back with its promise of ever-more-spectacular scenery around the next corner.

Cycling along the spectacular northern coastline of Cape Breton Island

ELEVATION PROFILE

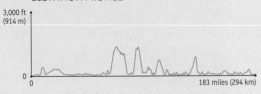

3,000 ft
(914 m)

0

0   183 miles (294 km)

The road winding along Big Sur, a rugged stretch of California's coastline

8

Pacific Coast

SEATTLE, WASHINGTON, TO
SAN DIEGO, CALIFORNIA, US

Riding alongside the Pacific Ocean, you'll pedal from the rain forests of Washington to the palm trees of California via one of the world's most spectacular coastal roads.

1,578 MILES (2,540 KM)   107,316 FT (32,710 M)   PAVED

28

The Pacific Coast Highway may well be the perfect bike tour. It's long and hilly enough to challenge you physically, but, as a well-trodden tourist route, it's also got the infrastructure to ensure you're never far from comforts like food, shelter, or a bike shop.

You'll start your journey among the islands and inlets of the Pacific Northwest, pedaling through evergreen forests toward the rugged Oregon shoreline. Crossing into California, you'll pass giant redwoods and rolling vineyards, as the landscape gradually fades from green woods to golden desert.

On the way you'll sample Portland's microbreweries, sip coffee in San Francisco, people-watch in Los Angeles, and explore countless towns and villages. Route 101 is popular with drivers, too, but a generous shoulder and well-signed bike paths ensure there's plenty of room for all.

ELEVATION PROFILE

3,000 ft
(914 m)

0

0   1,578 miles (2,540 km)

Top Tip

There's a strong northerly wind along the Pacific Coast, so make life easier, and ride it in a southerly direction.

Spend a day in **SEATTLE** before you head off—ride on the monorail, take in the views from the top of the Space Needle, and fuel up for the journey ahead at the famous Pike Place Market.

Ring your bell, wave at your fellow cyclists, and explore the community of **PORTLAND**. It's America's most bicycle-friendly city, with over 300 miles (480 km) of bike paths.

DEPOE BAY is the best place along the Oregon coast for whale-watching—grab your binoculars, train your eyes on the horizon, and look out for the telltale plumes.

UNITED STATES

Get ready to feel very small as you pedal along the **AVENUE OF THE GIANTS**—the redwoods here are some of the tallest and oldest trees in the world.

Marvel at the force of nature on **GLASS BEACH** near Fort Bragg, where the ocean waves have turned tons of discarded glass bottles into smooth, multicolored pebbles.

SANTA CRUZ's pier is a great place to take a break from the bike and enjoy a stroll—watch the sea lions bask or take a ride on the 100-year-old Giant Dipper, if you're brave enough.

Seattle
Portland
Depoe Bay
Newport
Yachats
Bandon
Avenue of the Giants
Leggett
Glass Beach
Mendocino
Marin Headlands
San Francisco
Pigeon Point
Santa Cruz
Big Sur
San Luis Obispo
Santa Barbara
Gaviota
Los Angeles
Carlsbad
San Diego

30

Follow the bike path across the golden sands of **VENICE BEACH** in Los Angeles, dodge the skateboarders and roller bladers, and pause to watch a game of beach volleyball.

0 ·········· km ·········· 200
0 ·········· miles ·········· 200

There's no better place for a little rest and relaxation than **SAN DIEGO**'s beaches. Put your feet up on the golden sands of Coronado or try surfing on Pacific Beach.

The Pacific Ocean makes its presence known right from the very start of this ride. You'll spy it as you pedal round Seattle's leafy headlands and feel its cloudy breath even as you ride inland, following the Columbia River down toward Portland. Eventually, you'll meet it face to face as you speed into Lincoln City, and from then on it's a constant reassuring companion on your right—you can't get lost, as long as you stay within earshot of its crashing waves.

For the first few days the ride skirts the cliffs, coves, and sandy beaches of the Oregon coast, passing through seaside towns like Lincoln Beach and Newport, kindly spaced to ensure you'll always find coffee or ice cream when you need it. Here the road is undulating rather than hilly, guiding you up to the many viewpoints—the section around Yachats will delight with its windswept basalt headlands. Farther south you'll find yourself wanting to call it a day in Bandon, to eat fish and chips among its white sand dunes.

As you drift toward the California border, the weather gets warmer, although the rich green forests that line the coast suggest there's still a good chance of rain. The road cuts inland for a while, guiding you through shady avenues of the biggest trees in the world, before heading back to

Going for a day cycle along one of the many sandy beaches that line the Oregon coast

the coast after Leggett, over a climb that dwarfs even the giant redwoods. Enjoy screeching round the hairpins as you speed down through the forest to rejoin the Pacific, arriving onto a section of road that hugs the coast so closely, it feels like there's nothing between you and the waves.

The next section is more challenging, winding its way in and out of a series of steep gullies—but you'll be rewarded with the charming Victorian town of Mendocino, which boasts some of the finest cafés in Northern California. The land around you is now golden rather than green, although the famous San Francisco fog may remind you of the mists of the Pacific Northwest.

Your legs will be aching as the halfway point draws closer, but even the promise of a much-needed pit stop won't detract from the glories of the Marin Headlands, a famed mountain biking area with winding roads and views out over the ocean, the city, and the Golden Gate Bridge. The bike path across this iconic structure is your grand entrance into San Francisco.

IN FOCUS
Mountain Biking in Marin

Modern mountain biking began in Marin County in the 1970s, when a group of friends began launching themselves down Mount Tamalpais on modified bicycles known as "klunkers." The first downhill mountain bike race was held here—it was named "Repack," since the riders had to repack the grease in their coaster brakes after it burned out on the descent.

Sandy beaches abound, and if you're lucky you'll get to spy sea otters playing in the waves and colonies of elephant seals basking on the sand.

Finding your way out of San Francisco is easy enough—just locate the ocean, keep it on your right, and you'll soon be on your way south, along a coastline that's busier than the wilder stretches of Oregon, but no less beautiful for it. Sandy beaches abound, and if you're lucky you might spy sea otters playing in the waves and colonies of elephant seals basking on the sand. And, at Pigeon Point, you'll pass the tallest lighthouse on the West Coast.

It's perhaps too soon for a day off, assuming you had one in San Francisco, though Santa Cruz will tempt you, with its laid-back student vibe, bustling beachfront, and oddities such as a museum dedicated to surfing. Either way, now you have the Pacific Highway's crowning glory to look forward to. The road around

Big Sur is more often than not included in lists of the world's most scenic drives, so the hordes of vehicles and tourists won't surprise you. You may join them as they pause at every viewpoint for a selfie, or you may cycle past, smugly thinking about the equally beautiful—but far less crowded—stretches of coastline you've seen farther north.

The road gets quieter and hillier from this point, as the vast golden-brown mountains of Southern California rear up to your left, and you start to see the effects of the drought that afflicted this region between 2011 and 2017. The road meanders inland for a day or so to visit San Luis Obispo, then descends back to the coast in spectacular style at Gaviota, for a relatively flat run into Santa Barbara, where you may wish to make an extra loop to take in the pink towers of the Old Mission, founded by Spanish Franciscans in 1786.

A pair of elephant seal bulls fighting over a mate at Piedras Blancas beach in California

Above Sunrise over the cliffs and pier in Gaviota Beach State Park

Right The exterior of the historic Old Mission in Santa Barbara

There's a busier stretch between Santa Cruz and the metropolis of Los Angeles, but once you've worked your way past the mansions and beach houses that line the Malibu coast, you'll find the bike path of your dreams, leading you straight across the golden sands of Venice Beach. It's a far more memorable arrival into the City of Angels than landing at LAX or driving down one of the city's many freeways.

There are more bike paths south of LA, as you continue through the sprawling surf towns of Oceanside and Carlsbad, closing in on the Mexican border, with one final climb over the cliffs of La Jolla. San Diego, with its parks, beaches, and mouth-watering food scene, is the perfect place to spend a few days recovering at the end of this mammoth ride, before heading home—or, if you're hooked, getting back on the bike and carrying on into Mexico, to continue the adventure.

MAKE IT LONGER
An Olympic Loop

To avoid the urban sprawl south of Seattle, take a ferry across the Puget Sound and do a loop of the Olympic National Park before beginning your southward journey. This thinly populated peninsula is packed with snowy peaks, old-growth rain forest, and over 70 miles (110 km) of rugged coastline. Keep your eyes carefully peeled for a glimpse of the elusive black bear.

9

Point Reyes Loop

MILL VALLEY, CALIFORNIA, US (LOOP)

Experience the drama of California's coast on an exhilarating circuit north of San Francisco. Navigate craggy headlands, glide along wave-lashed shores, and cruise through quaint towns.

62 MILES (100 KM)

3,950 FT (1,203 M)

PAVED

Towering redwoods, hilly headlands, the sparkling Pacific Ocean—the views on this loop will set your spirits soaring. Beginning north of San Francisco's iconic Golden Gate Bridge and the rugged Marin Headlands, the road skirts old-growth redwoods before following the coast's sheer cliffs and rocky coves. This circuit covers more than 3,937 ft (1,200 m) in elevation but coffee roasters and bakeries will keep you fueled up at a handful of towns en route.

As you cycle north along the Shoreline Highway, the road is flanked by green hills on one side and the blue Pacific on the other. After you soar past Bolinas Lagoon, a broad wetland, the road leaves the ocean behind en route to Olema, a former logging outpost, and Point Reyes Station, whose dairy farms produce some of San Francisco's favorite cheese. Meadows and forests line the inland leg back to Mill Valley, a town tucked between marshland and redwood forests. Here, rest your legs at a coffee shop and ponder your next cycling route along the surf-splashed Californian coast.

ELEVATION PROFILE

1,500 ft (457 m)

0

0   62 miles (100 km)

34

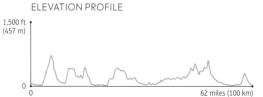

Snap a shot of historic St. Mary's Church, nestled in **NICASIO VALLEY**. Built in 1867 from redwoods, it has a white-washed exterior and lush setting.

Point Reyes Station

Nicasio Valley

Olema

UNITED STATES

San Anselmo

Linger awhile by **STINSON BEACH**, a popular escape for San Franciscans seeking to sunbathe or play beach volleyball. There are a couple of great family-run diners in town, too.

Bolinas Lagoon

Mill Valley

Muir Woods

Stinson Beach

MUIR WOODS offers you the chance to crane your neck at old-growth redwoods. Less than 4 miles (6 km) on, secure your bike and take the stairs to the breezy lookout above Muir Beach.

Muir Beach

0 ······ km ······ 5
0 ······ miles ······ 5

The Loop

Exit **EAST SIDE TUNNEL** for a view that explodes in size from a scooped green valley to scads of peaks.

Lower St Mary Lake

THE LOOP, a large switchback, gives you your first real taste of scenery—views swoop down to the valley and up to rugged peaks.

St Mary

East Side Tunnel

Logan Pass

St Mary Lake

0 ·········· km ········· 6
0 ·············· miles ·············· 6

UNITED STATES

Lake McDonald

Mark your arrival at **LOGAN PASS**, the route's apex, with a photo next to the Continental Divide sign.

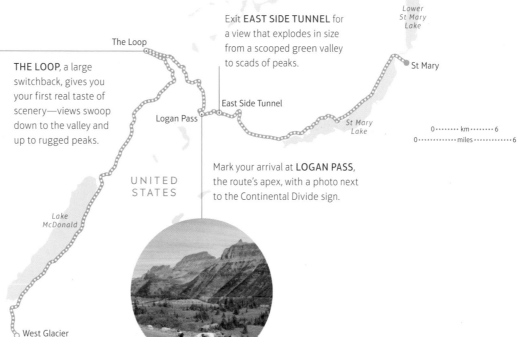

○ West Glacier

10

Going to the Sun

WEST GLACIER TO ST. MARY, MONTANA, US

Twisting through Glacier National Park, this dramatic route climbs over the Continental Divide. Expect gawk-worthy views of glacier-carved landscapes that get bigger and better the higher you go.

Top Tip
The road is closed to vehicles in spring, but cyclists can ride up as far as snowplowing allows.

50 MILES (80 KM) 4,287 FT (1,307 M) PAVED

From West Glacier, the route spins along the flat shore of Lake McDonald before lazily ascending a valley corridor squeezed by soaring peaks. The riding is easygoing here—but don't be lulled into assuming the ride will stay gentle. Soon, the skinny road pitches upward into a 6 percent gradient on the long, continuous grind to the Continental Divide. As you ascend, glaciated valleys deepen below, while above steep mountainsides rise into jagged peaks. As you climb higher, more peaks pop up and several glaciers appear in the distance. The road's design intentionally shows off the stunning landscape: tunnel portals frame peaks, stone bridges cross tumbling waterfalls, and the pavement slices along vertigo-inducing cliff edges. The route tops out at Logan Pass, a wildflower meadow with mountain goats and bighorn sheep. From here, you'd better have good brakes for the flying descent around Going-to-the-Sun Mountain down to turquoise St. Mary Lake.

ELEVATION PROFILE

6,500 ft
(1,981 m)

0

0   50 miles (80 km)

11

Great Divide Mountain Bike Route

ROOSVILLE, MONTANA, TO ANTELOPE WELLS, NEW MEXICO, US

As far as epic mountain bike rides go, the Great Divide is hard to beat. Bisecting the rooftop of America, it's a challenging route that provides a back-country riding experience like no other.

2,400 MILES (3,862 KM)

138,615 FT (42,250 M)

GRAVEL / DIRT

The Great Divide is a true wilderness cycling adventure. Following the Continental Divide—a mountainous boundary that splits the US into east and west and determines whether water flows to the Pacific or the Atlantic—it takes you down the spine of the Rockies from Canada to Mexico. On the way, you'll cycle through deserts, deep forests, and high mountain passes, and pedal past abandoned mining towns, plush ski resorts, and remote luxury hunting lodges—encountering the full spectrum of wildlife, culture, history, and weather the United States has to offer.

The route was stitched together by the Adventure Cycling Association in the mid-1990s. Aiming to create a predominantly off-road trail that followed the Continental Divide as closely as possible, they admirably met their lofty agenda. The end result features a lung-pounding 26 crossings of

the mountainous watershed and includes historical routes ingeniously linked to contemporary forest trails, four-wheel-drive tracks, and fire roads to produce a continuous off-road masterpiece. You'll ride trails pioneered by Lewis and Clark during their expedition to charter the west and retrace the derelict narrow-gauge mountain railbeds of yesteryear. And you'll get a taste of authentic cowboy life as you cycle along former Pony Express delivery routes and cattle-herding trails in lands that haven't changed for millennia.

Top Tip

Weather-wise, the route is best between late June and mid-October, but be aware that it can snow at elevation at any time.

ELEVATION PROFILE

13,000 ft
(3,962 m)

0

0   2,400 miles (3,862 km)

Traveling through an open meadow in the Rocky Mountains

Keep your head up and enjoy the scenery despite the climbing. **RED MEADOW LAKE** is the first of many beautiful lakes you'll get to see on this ride.

Soak up the mountain vibe in **WHITEFISH**, a world-renowned ski resort, and celebrate getting your first 100 miles (160 km) under your wheels by treating yourself to a three-course meal.

Roosville

Red Meadow Lake

Whitefish

Helena

Butte

Yellowstone National Park

Grand Teton National Park

Take time out of the saddle to enjoy the spectacular **YELLOWSTONE NATIONAL PARK**, the world's first national park . Explore its thermal springs, nature, and rich history.

UNITED STATES

37

Breckenridge

Reward yourself with a plush hotel room and a rest day in **BRECKENRIDGE**, a resort town rich in gold-rush history. It will be a welcome break from trailside camping and gas-station breakfasts.

Indiana Pass

Abiquiu

Pull in for an eponymous baked treat at the Pie-O-Neer café in **PIE TOWN**. The cherry pie and ice cream are legendary, and the calories will be much needed.

Pie Town

Silver City

Antelope Wells

IN FOCUS
Adventure Cycling Association

The Adventure Cycling Association *(adventurecycling.org)* is a not-for-profit membership organization that exists to encourage people to undertake adventures by bicycle. Since its inception in 1973, it has mapped over 50,000 miles (80,000 km) of long-distance cycling routes across the US and run campaigns to make cycling safer for everyone. You can find out more and buy detailed route maps on its website.

0 ········ km ········ 200
0 ········ miles ········ 200

NORTH AMERICA

Top Tip

This route is remote, so always carry several days' worth of supplies and make the most of any chances to stock up.

Your adventure begins in the mountains, lakes, and tall forests of Montana. Though the climbs are undeniably tough, the beautiful surroundings are worth the effort. The riding here is remote and you'll routinely spend successive days without seeing another person. You won't be lost for company though; critters such as grizzly bears, mountain lions, moose, and elk all call these forests home.

As you pedal south, the route clips the northwest corner of Idaho before heading into Wyoming. Here, the landscape changes and as the trail crisscrosses the Continental Divide the climbs get longer—a lot longer. You'll pass by the stunning Grand Teton National Park and later cross the old wagon routes once used by the early pioneers seeking their fortunes in the west.

The Colorado Rockies provide the real climbing. This section entails many hours on long drawn-out ascents, winding your way through sweet-smelling aspen woods and flower-speckled alpine meadows. In southern Colorado the route reaches its fabled peak, 11,910-ft (3,630-m) Indiana Pass, where you'll experience the enervating effects of high altitude, the awe of epic thunderstorms, and the comforting knowledge that you've crested the zenith.

As Colorado gives way to New Mexico, the scenery changes once more. The trail deteriorates and the terrain becomes more arid. Mesas and volcanic formations jut out of the desert floor, creating a surreal, Mars-like landscape. There's little surface water here and your search for it will turn to fervor as you continue to the Mexican border and your journey's end. Watch out for the rattlesnakes on this last stretch: they can have a penchant for striking out at tires.

Understand that the Great Divide is an awesome challenge—in every sense. The route is dramatic. The skies are big. And the climbs are huge. Whether you attempt a record-setting ride, or opt for a more pedestrian pace, it will test your stamina, equipment, and resolve to their limits. But rest assured, the beauty and sheer distance will leave you enraptured.

MAKE IT LONGER

Anniversary Extension

The original Great Divide route begins in Montana, but in 2018—to celebrate the 20th anniversary of the trail—an extension up to Jasper in Canada was added. Beginning your ride from this alternative starting point will add 590 miles (950 km) to your journey.

Top Pedaling through Grand Teton National Park, surrounded by spectacular scenery

Bottom left Two cyclists pausing to check the map as they traverse the Great Divide Mountain Bike Route

Bottom right Cycling along Marshall Pass Road in Colorado

12

Lake Tahoe

STATELINE, NEVADA, US (LOOP)

It's clear why this route has been dubbed America's most beautiful bike ride. Tracing the sparkling shore of Tahoe, North America's largest alpine lake, it offers soul-stirring views and restful detours.

73 MILES (118 KM)
4,100 FT (1,250 M)
PAVED

Shimmering coves and evergreen forests line the road around Lake Tahoe, which leads cyclists from Nevada to California and back again. This state-straddling circuit is big on views: see the lake's dazzling blue expanse on one side of the road, and razor-edged cliffs and sugar pines on the other.

The route is undulating, but it won't exhaust you. That's because you'll be stopping along the way to ogle views of the Sierra Nevada mountains, idle by restful lake beaches, and take plenty of detours. Towns like South Lake Tahoe and Tahoe City beckon you to stop by. Their cafés and restaurants have an unmistakably Californian charm: they're cozy, laid-back, and packed with hikers and bikers talking adventures over macchiatos.

It's possible to cycle this loop in either direction but traveling clockwise puts you closer to views of the lake. Hardened riders can sweat their way around within six hours, but Tahoe is a route worth lingering over. Allow the entire day so you have time for coffee stops, a leisurely picnic at Emerald Bay, or boat-spotting from Cave Rock.

Cycling up one of the tree-lined switchbacks near Lake Tahoe

Starting in Stateline in Nevada, the road heads southwest and almost immediately crosses over into California. Beyond South Lake Tahoe, the route wiggles between Cascade Lake and Lake Tahoe until making a zigzagging ascent. Relax: your exertions are soon rewarded by views of Emerald Bay, whose glassy waters look almost tropical against the rocky beach.

It's an easier cruise onward to turquoise Rubicon Bay and Tahoe City, with its pleasant beach and excellent spread of cafés, bars, and restaurants. The toughest climb is on the lake's eastern shore, up to Spooner Lake. There's a park entrance fee but it's worth it if you want to secure your bike and wander a while by the aspen-fringed shores. After all, you're only one more easygoing hour of cycling away from the finish line.

ELEVATION PROFILE

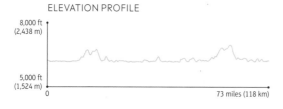

8,000 ft (2,438 m)

5,000 ft (1,524 m)

0   73 miles (118 km)

40

See the lake's dazzling blue expanse on one side of the road, and razor-edged cliffs and sugar pines on the other.

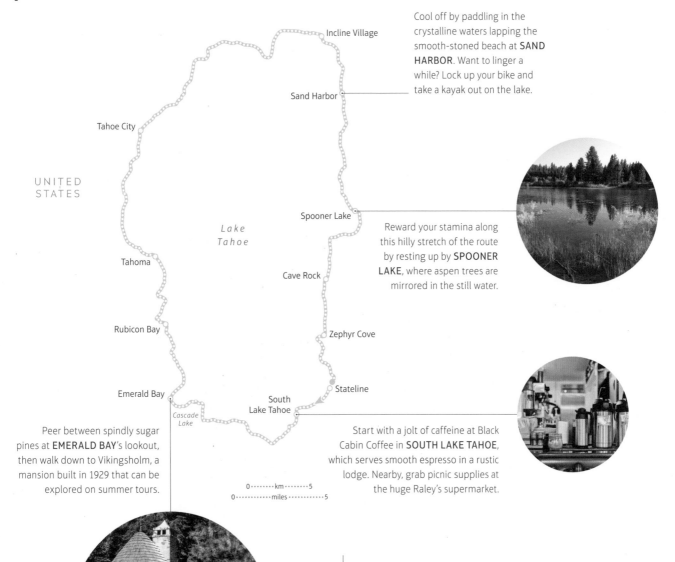

Cool off by paddling in the crystalline waters lapping the smooth-stoned beach at **SAND HARBOR**. Want to linger a while? Lock up your bike and take a kayak out on the lake.

Reward your stamina along this hilly stretch of the route by resting up by **SPOONER LAKE**, where aspen trees are mirrored in the still water.

Peer between spindly sugar pines at **EMERALD BAY**'s lookout, then walk down to Vikingsholm, a mansion built in 1929 that can be explored on summer tours.

Start with a jolt of caffeine at Black Cabin Coffee in **SOUTH LAKE TAHOE**, which serves smooth espresso in a rustic lodge. Nearby, grab picnic supplies at the huge Raley's supermarket.

Incline Village

Sand Harbor

Tahoe City

UNITED STATES

Lake Tahoe

Spooner Lake

Tahoma

Cave Rock

Rubicon Bay

Zephyr Cove

Emerald Bay

Cascade Lake

South Lake Tahoe

Stateline

0 ⋯⋯⋯ km ⋯⋯⋯ 5
0 ⋯⋯⋯⋯ miles ⋯⋯⋯⋯ 5

REFUEL

Jake's on the Lake

Roughly halfway along the route, Tahoe City has several food options but the best is Jake's on the Lake (*jakestahoe. com*). Waterfront seating allows diners views of glittering Lake Tahoe, with the snow-streaked Sierra Nevada mountains rising behind. Just as appealing is California produce like sea bass, Dungeness crab cakes, and vegan bowls brimming with tofu and macadamia nuts.

Two cyclists rolling through cacti-filled Saguaro National Park in Arizona

Top Tip
The Southern Tier is best ridden in early autumn or late spring, to avoid contending with summer heat or winter snow.

13

Southern Tier

SAN DIEGO, CALIFORNIA,
TO ST. AUGUSTINE, FLORIDA, US

Snaking alongside the Mexican border and around the Gulf of Mexico, this is the most southerly route across the US. Saddle up for the ride of your life as you pedal from the Pacific to the Atlantic.

2,778 MILES (4,470 KM) 45,825 FT (13,967 M) PAVED

Established by the Adventure Cycling Association, the umbrella body for cycle touring in the US, the Southern Tier is a fascinating tour that takes in all of the best bits of the southern United States. It's got the food: think tacos, gumbo, steaks, and grits. It's got the culture: from American Indian heritage in New Mexico to French-influenced Louisiana. And, with swamp, woodland, deserts, and mountains, it's certainly got the landscapes. It's hard to believe that the route is all contained within a single country, such is the variety it packs in.

This is a ride that doesn't do things by half: on the road you can expect big skies, big distances, big cars, and even bigger food. The Southern Tier's sheer scale can be somewhat daunting, but don't be put off—while the first half features some strenuous ascents in the west, the second half flattens out for a more gentle finish in the east. It's also possible to do this ride in relative comfort, with cheap motels in every town offering the relief of a cozy bed after a long day in the saddle. Or, if you don't mind hauling a tent, there are plenty of well-equipped campsites where you can bunk down en route. Just bear in mind that you'll need to plan your stops carefully, as gaps between settlements can be very long, especially in the section through Texas.

> It's hard to believe that the route is all contained within a single country, such is the variety it packs in.

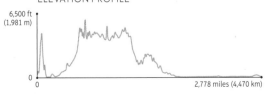

ELEVATION PROFILE

6,500 ft
(1,981 m)

0

0   2,778 miles (4,470 km)

43

Starting out on the Californian coast with the ocean lapping at your wheels, the route passes through almond groves before climbing up into the sun-baked hills. Once over the mountains, you'll fly downhill into the terra-cotta sea of the Arizona desert, where the scenery opens up under cobalt skies. The official Southern Tier route takes you north from here toward Phoenix, but by detouring south toward Tucson, you avoid the big city and can instead explore the cacti-filled Saguaro National Park.

Entry into Arizona also marks the beginning of your ascent to the watershed of America. Known as the Continental Divide, this imaginary line separates the country's river systems, with water west of here flowing downhill to the Pacific and water to the east flowing all the way to the Atlantic. Crossing a high-altitude plateau that stretches over 600 miles (965 km), you'll zigzag back and forth across the actual dividing line a number of times, traversing the mountains over rolling terrain that's thankfully never too steep.

Every so often you'll be reminded of your proximity to the Mexican border, as you encounter the fence that separates the US from its southern neighbor. Signs warn of illegal smuggling and the white jeeps of the border patrol are never far from view.

REFUEL
Po-Boy Perfection

From jambalaya to gumbo, crawfish to boudin sausages, Louisiana is home to some delicious food. A highlight for the hungry cyclist is a po-boy: a delicious sandwich served on crusty French bread, filled with anything from roast beef and gravy to crawfish or oysters. Such is the appeal of the snack that New Orleans even has a festival in its honor—the Oak Street Po-Boy Festival, held every year in mid-November—where local traders compete to offer the most inventive fillings.

Soak up American Indian culture in New Mexico: the **GILA CLIFF DWELLINGS NATIONAL MONUMENT**, at the edge of the Gila Wilderness, is especially worth a visit.

San Diego

Tucson

Saguaro National Park

Gila Cliff Dwellings National Monument

El Paso

Marfa

Marvel at the classic desert landscape of **SAGUARO NATIONAL PARK**, near Tucson. Saguaro cacti are native to this area of the US, and look like the backdrop to an old Western movie.

Flashing lights frequently appear in the skies around **MARFA**, Texas—some people attribute them to UFOs, but scientists say they are reflections of car headlights and campfires.

44

Bourbon Street, an icon of the
French Quarter in New Orleans

Before you know it, you'll enter the
longest, emptiest stretch of your ride:
the grassy plains of Texas. Known for
cowboys, barbecue, and country music,
the Lonestar State is a land where everything is super-sized. Brace yourself: the
next state is 1,000 miles (1,600 km) away.

Although the biggest climbs are
behind you, the hills and headwinds of
Texas keep the journey interesting. It
might feel like it's going on forever, but
you'll eventually reach the coast (for the
first time since California) and the border
with Louisiana. The route hugs the shore
as it heads towards the Cajun capital of
New Orleans, allowing you to explore the
bayous and the creole culture. The houses
on stilts (for protection from flooding) highlight that you're now in hurricane country.

The final stretch of the ride takes you
across the Florida Panhandle and toward
the fabulous beaches of the Atlantic Coast,
via alligator-infested swamps and bear-
filled forests. As you roll toward the ocean
in the Florida sunshine, take a moment to
reflect on all the mountains and miles
you've covered on your journey. But don't
dally for too long because there's only one
way to celebrate arriving back on sand
after crossing an entire continent: with a
headlong dive into the refreshing waters
of the ocean.

Party all night in buzzing **NEW
ORLEANS**. Kick off proceedings
at the Sazerac Bar, named for
the city's most famous cocktail: a
feisty combination of rye whiskey,
absinthe, bitters, and sugar.

Keep your eyes peeled for the
alligators that roam the swamps
around **GAINESVILLE**, Florida.
For guaranteed sightings from
the safety of a raised boardwalk,
try Sweetwater Wetlands Park.

UNITED
STATES

Austin

Pensacola

New Orleans

Gainesville

St Augustine

0 ·········· km ·········· 250
0 ················· miles ················· 250

Top Tip

There's only one way to head back into Durango: take the train. Bikes are permitted, but it's best to book a ticket in advance.

Admire the old Wild West wooden architecture of **SILVERTON**, a former mining town established in the late 19th century.

At 10,915 ft (3,327 m), **MOLAS PASS** is the highest point of this route. Pause here to savor the mountain views.

Inhale the fragrance of pines and wildflowers as you ride through forests on the ascent to **COAL BANK PASS**. You might also spy elk and bears.

Silverton

Molas Pass

Coal Bank Pass

UNITED STATES

0 ·········· km ·········· 10
0 ·········· miles ·········· 10

Durango

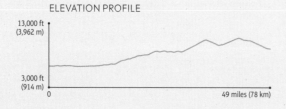

14

Iron Horse

DURANGO TO SILVERTON, COLORADO, US

Inspired by a race against a historic steam train, the Iron Horse is a formidable cycle through snowcapped mountains—your lungs will be puffing in overdrive.

49 MILES (78 KM)   6,000 FT (1,829 M)   PAVED

In 1971, avid amateur cyclist Tom Mayer challenged his brother Jim—a brakeman on the Denver & Rio Grande Western Railroad between Durango and Silverton—to a race between steam engine and bicycle. Tom's two-wheeled transportation proved triumphant, and his feat went on to spawn the annual Iron Horse Classic, in which cyclists compete to beat the still-functioning steam train.

But you don't have to enter the race to enjoy this route's 6,000 ft (1,829 m) of breathtaking climbing. Just pedal away from Durango's meadow pastureland on Highway 550 (also known as the Million Dollar Highway) and feel the screaming build-up of lactic acid over nearly 40 miles (64 km) of continuous ascent into a bowl of snow-topped jagged mountains. The rapid sweeping descent that follows may not be for the fainthearted, but it hurries you into Silverton: an authentic mining town of wooden buildings that has scarcely changed since the late 19th century. Look out for the old Iron Horse as you put on your brakes at Silverton train station.

ELEVATION PROFILE

13,000 ft (3,962 m)

3,000 ft (914 m)

0   49 miles (78 km)

Kentucky Bourbon Trail

LOUISVILLE TO LEXINGTON, KENTUCKY, US

You don't have to like bourbon to enjoy this ride—though it definitely helps. Set off on a tour between distilleries to experience the best of the Kentucky countryside.

A bronze statue of "master distiller" Booker Noe at the Jim Beam Distillery

188 MILES (303 KM)

7,375 FT (2,248 M)

PAVED

Pedaling through bluegrass country, riders are constantly surrounded by all the things that make Kentucky bourbon special— cornfields stretching for acres, clear water trickling down limestone cliffs into underground aquifers, white-oak forests, and that sweet scent of corn mash coming from the distilleries themselves.

This route stops at no fewer than ten distilleries, so the lure of the next bourbon stop is usually enough to get most riders over the seemingly nonstop rolling hills. Some stretches of road are so devoid of traffic that you'll see more rickhouses— large warehouses where barrels of bourbon are aged—than cars. Lycra-clad cyclists are still a rarity in some of these spots, so expect a few bemused looks from folks wiling away the day on their front porches.

Don't worry about getting too drunk to ride; samples are too tiny for that. The trick is working out how to carry all the souvenir bottles on your bike.

If you're unfamiliar with the intricacies of tasting bourbon, **ANGEL'S ENVY** should be your first stop. "Distillery guardians" will teach you how to identify and savor the spirit's subtle nuances.

Get an inside look at the workings of the **JIM BEAM DISTILLERY**, one of the largest whiskey makers in the world.

Dine at the **BOTTLE AND BOND KITCHEN AND BAR** in Bardstown, where you can dig into the best fried chicken in the state.

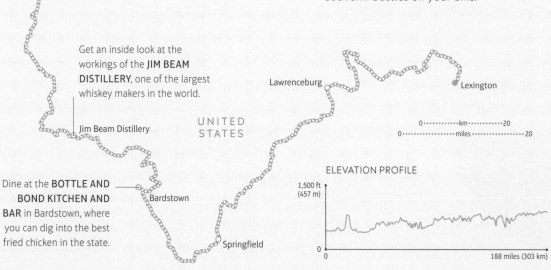

Louisville

Jim Beam Distillery

UNITED STATES

Bardstown

Springfield

Lawrenceburg

Lexington

0 ·········· km ·········· 20
0 ·········· miles ·········· 20

ELEVATION PROFILE

1,500 ft (457 m)

0

0

188 miles (303 km)

NORTH AMERICA

Waynesboro

0 ·········· km ·········· 50
0 ·········· miles ·········· 50

Apple Orchard
Mountain

**CHATEAU MORRISETTE
WINERY** is one of the
oldest wineries in Virginia.
Pull in for a tour, a tasting,
and a little lunch.

Chateau Morrisette
Winery

Blue Ridge
Music Center

Stone Mountain State Park

Detour into **MOUNT
MITCHELL STATE PARK** via
a 4.5-mile (7-km) spur.
There you can summit
the tallest mountain in
the eastern US, standing
6,684 ft (2,037 m) high.

Linn Cove
Viaduct

Blowing Rock

Stop at the **BLUE RIDGE MUSIC
CENTER** to enjoy its free daily
concert of bluegrass music, a
genre born in these hills.

Mount Mitchell
State Park

Cherokee

Asheville

Waterrock
Knob

Before you descend down
into Cherokee, pause at
WATERROCK KNOB—this
stunning viewpoint offers
almost 360-degree views over
the surrounding mountains.

REFUEL
Barbecues and Brews

Plan a rest day (or two) in Asheville, North Carolina,
a city with renowned breweries and acclaimed chefs.
Buxton Hall Barbecue will give you a taste of regional
cuisine with its whole-hog barbecue and chef's
treatment of down-home sides (traditional and simple
side dishes that perfectly complement the richness of
the barbecue). Hi-Wire Brewing, meanwhile, serves up
everything from thirst-quenching IPAs to rich porters.

48

Blue Ridge Parkway

WAYNESBORO, VIRGINIA, TO CHEROKEE,
NORTH CAROLINA, US

*Follow the crest of the Blue Ridge Mountains on an iconic
route that takes you through the rolling hills of Virginia
and the high peaks of North Carolina.*

49

469 MILES (755 KM) | 48,602 FT (14,814 M) | PAVED

Picture 469 miles (755 km) of smooth road unmarred by a single traffic light, stop sign, or roundabout. Around every curve awaits yet another beautiful vista: deep, river-cut gorges; mountains that lie across the land like a rumpled quilt, their peaks growing blue and hazy with distance; clouds scuttling across the vast dome of sky, casting shadows across the ridges and valleys below. This is the Blue Ridge Parkway, or "America's Favorite Drive," a ribbon of asphalt built to satisfy the country's insatiable desire for a road trip. Today, it satisfies a grand total of 15 million visitors—tens of thousands of whom are cyclists—every year.

You'll find few patches of flat ground here; the parkway is either climbing or descending for mile after relentless mile, gaining 48,602 ft (14,814 m) in elevation

Top Tip

There are limited facilities along the route, so join an organized tour that offers food and lodgings.

Pausing to look over forested mountains
on the Blue Ridge Parkway

as you travel southbound. Climbs are long, thigh-burning affairs, and the longest— a 13-mile (21-km) push from the lowest point on the parkway to the highest spot in Virginia—will test the endurance of most riders for two solid hours. Thankfully, the gradient's never too steep, making for elbows-tucked, hands-off-the-brakes descents that give you a chance to catch your breath; as you fly down, you'll also be treated to refreshing breezes and eye-popping overlooks around each turn.

ELEVATION PROFILE

6,500 ft
(1,981 m)

0

0   469 miles (755 km)

Cycling along a tree-lined section of the Blue Ridge Parkway in Virginia

Almost equally split between the states of Virginia and North Carolina, the Blue Ridge Parkway presents two different personalities: Virginia's open, rolling terrain, and the roller-coaster hills and skyscraping peaks of North Carolina.

Through Virginia, you're in for lengthy but gentle climbs and even gentler curves as the scenery—the bucolic American countryside at its best, dotted with pastures, farms, and hayfields—unfurls around you. It's an inspirational landscape, giving birth to both bluegrass and country music—a story that's more fully told at the Blue Ridge Music Center near Galax.

After Milepost 217—the midpoint of the ride—the route crosses over the state line into North Carolina. There, the land-scape begins to shift. The first 7.5 miles (12 km) retain the ease and grace of Virginia's wide river valleys and rolling hills, but on the horizon, the fins of North Carolina's highest peaks rise as if in

challenge to riders. Ascending into the mountains, you'll pass by dramatic gorges and deep valleys, where tumbling waterfalls feed lowland rivers and morning mist gathers to form lakes of cloud. In the shadow of Grandfather Mountain, you'll ride through the curves of the Linn Cove Viaduct—slowing down only to savor the view from this elevated roadway that seems to hang in mid-air. Additional over-looks and viewpoints provide previews of the curves and climbs ahead, as well as a welcome opportunity to catch your breath—and you'll need to. As you ride deeper into the range, the parkway rises to a blistering crescendo, taking you past the highest mountains in the eastern US. Finally, you crest the Blue Ridge and settle in for a long coast to the route's end.

Cycling the Blue Ridge Parkway is a feat of endurance, as the steady climbs will push you to your limits. The route will also force

Almost equally split between the states of Virginia and North Carolina, the Blue Ridge Parkway presents two different personalities

you to test your logistical skills—there are few places to stay along the way, other than campgrounds, and fewer places to eat, so you'll need to plan ahead. But these practical considerations pale into insignificance when compared with the freewheeling joy of miles-long downhills and the rewarding views that will spur you on around every turn. So saddle up, find your pace, and settle in: the Blue Ridge Parkway is calling, and it's time to heed its cry.

Skyline Drive

At the north end of the Blue Ridge Parkway is Shenandoah National Park, home to the famed Skyline Drive. Warm up with a ride on this 105-mile (169-km) scenic road before setting off along the parkway—it will give you an inspiring taste of the long ridgelines and mountain meadows to come.

The curving Linn Cove Viaduct, sweeping around the edge of Grandfather Mountain

17

Natchez Trace Parkway

NATCHEZ, MISSISSIPPI,
TO NASHVILLE, TENNESSEE, US

Running through three states, the Natchez Trace Parkway takes riders on a journey past memorable historical and musical landmarks, and into some of the most gorgeous scenery east of the Mississippi River.

449 MILES (722 KM)   15,289 FT (4,660 M)   PAVED

52

A scenic byway managed by the National Park Service, the Natchez Trace Parkway is one of the most popular long-distance routes for cyclists in the US. The scenery is beautiful, it's nearly impossible to get lost, and the route is relatively safe. Thanks to a fairly low speed limit (50 mph/80 kmph) and a ban on commercial traffic, most road users are out for a relaxing jaunt through the countryside.

Some sections of the Natchez Trace are two-lane roads, while others are four lanes divided by a huge median. The road surface is typically pristine. Flat to gently rolling hills dominate the terrain in the south, gradually increasing in elevation as you travel farther north—by the time you enter Tennessee, it's seemingly one long climb after another. Thankfully, gradients typically fall below 5 percent, meaning it's completely manageable for most casual riders. Cycling from south to north gives

you more of a tailwind, though the route can be done the opposite way if you'd prefer to tackle the hilliest sections first.

Much of the Trace is lined with gorgeous forests of pine, maple, and oak trees, which become even more beautiful in autumn as the fall colors burst into view. If you haven't worn out your legs on the ride, you can delve deeper into these woodlands along one of the short hiking trails that branch off the road, leading to scenic natural treasures like Sunken Trace and Jackson Falls. Near Franklin, Tennessee, the massive 1,600-ft (488-m) Double Arch

Colorful autumn foliage along the Natchez Trace Parkway

ELEVATION PROFILE

1,500 ft
(457 m)

0

0   449 miles (722 km)

Take a few pedal strokes off the Trace to experience the **WICHAHPI COMMEMORATIVE STONE WALL**. Tom Hendrix took 30 years and almost 8.5 million pounds (4 million kg) of stone to build the wall in memory of his American Indian great-grandmother.

Many food stops in Tennessee double as music venues. Enjoy a sandwich and a serenade at **PUCKETT'S GROCERY** in Leiper's Fork.

Nashville

Leiper's Fork

Jackson Falls

Wichahpi Commemorative Stone Wall

Muscle Shoals

Tupelo

UNITED STATES

0 ·······km ······· 100
0 ······· miles ············· 100

Swap your cycling footwear for Blue Suede Shoes when entering **TUPELO**, Mississippi. Visit the museum at Elvis Presley's birthplace and visit the Tupelo Hardware Company, where a young Elvis bought his first guitar.

Sunken Trace

Natchez

REFUEL
Loveless Café

The northern terminus of the Natchez Trace is so close to the Loveless Café *(lovelesscafe.com)*, you can practically smell the biscuits from the parkway. How good is the fried chicken? They haven't changed the recipe for nearly 70 years.

Bridge offers panoramic views of the foliage for miles in nearly every direction—just be sure to stay clear of the edge on a blustery day.

History buffs might spend more time off the bike than on, as the Trace passes by multiple ancient American Indian sites, Civil War battlefields, and the final resting place of famed explorer Meriwether Lewis. Music lovers might be excited to visit Nashville, but the route has plenty of other fun stops for audiophiles, including Elvis Presley's birthplace in Tupelo, Mississippi, and (with a slight detour) Muscle Shoals, Alabama, where Aretha Franklin, Wilson Pickett, and the Rolling Stones recorded some of their biggest hits. You might be exhausted after a day of riding the Natchez Trace, but there are too many things to see and do for you to put your feet up in a hotel room. You can relax on the journey home.

Lake Huron

Owen Sound

Contemplate the symbolism of the **BLACK HISTORY CAIRN** in Owen Sound, which is built out of stones from places with a direct connection to slavery or the abolition movement.

Kincardine

Goderich

CANADA

Built in 1851, **SANDWICH FIRST BAPTIST CHURCH** in Windsor is the oldest active Black church in Canada. It was a busy terminal on the Underground Railroad due to its proximity to a river crossing.

Sarnia

The **UNCLE TOM'S CABIN HISTORIC SITE** was once the home of the Dawn Settlement, which provided a refuge and vocational school for former enslaved people.

Dresden

Detroit

Lake St Clair

Ann Arbor

Windsor

North Buxton

Explore the **BUXTON NATIONAL HISTORIC SITE**, which includes an 1852 log cabin, an 1861 schoolhouse, and a replica of the Buxton Liberty Bell.

Adrian

Lake Erie

0 ·········· km ·········· 50
0 ·········· miles ·········· 50

Toledo

UNITED STATES

Oberlin

Before setting off from **OBERLIN**, pay a visit to the Oberlin Heritage Center for an introduction to the history of the Underground Railroad.

IN FOCUS

Detroit's Role in the Railroad

It is estimated that 100,000 people utilized the network of the Underground Railroad during its years of operation, and as many as 30,000 of that number are thought to have dared to escape from the US via Detroit. This makes the roads that led to the historic Detroit River bordering Canada the most frequented and significant in the Underground Railroad history.

Underground Railroad Detroit Alternate

OBERLIN, OHIO, US, TO OWEN SOUND, CANADA

Connecting sites of importance along the Underground Railroad through Detroit, this historical ride offers an insight into the bravery of enslaved people trying to reach freedom and those who helped them.

Top Tip
The Detroit Greenways Coalition (*detroit greenways.org*) is a great source of information on cycling in Detroit and Windsor.

556 MILES (895 KM)

10,991 FT (3,350 M)

PAVED

The Underground Railroad—a network of clandestine routes used by enslaved African Americans to escape to freedom in the northern US and Canada—flourished from the late 18th century to the end of the Civil War in 1865. It was a significant early expression of the American civil rights movement, bridging the divides of race, religion, sectional differences, and nationality, and spanning state lines and international borders.

In 2007, the Adventure Cycling Association commemorated this important chapter of US history with the creation of the Underground Railroad Bicycle Route (UGRR), stretching 2,016 miles (3,244 km) from Mobile in Alabama to Owen Sound in Ontario. Designed around a course

described in the "Follow the Drinking Gourd" song, the route incorporated historic sites visited by freedom seekers while making their way north. It proved hugely popular with cyclists and was expanded in 2011 with the addition of the UGRR Detroit Alternate. This shorter route begins in Oberlin, Ohio, taking in key sites around Detroit before crossing the Canadian border to finish in Owen Sound.

Looking out over the skyscrapers of the lakeside city of Detroit at sunset

ELEVATION PROFILE

1,000 ft
(914 m)

0

0   556 miles (895 km)

The UGRR Detroit Alternate is as varied and tough as its subject matter. The early stages in Ohio and Michigan are for the most part fairly gentle, while the second half through Ontario features some steep climbs. For several sections of the route you'll be pedaling along quiet rural trails, but in others you'll need to be prepared for some serious urban cycling.

Setting off from Oberlin—home to Oberlin College, one of the first colleges in the US to allow entry to African American students—the ride gets off to a steady start, skirting around the edge of Lake Erie and on into Michigan. Many of the cities you pass through were just small towns and villages at the time of the Underground Railroad, but records of the activities here are supplied by historical markers along the route. In Adrian, you'll uncover the story of abolitionist Laura Haviland, whose family farm became the first Underground Railroad stop in Michigan, and in Ann Arbor you'll find the home of the Reverend Guy Beckley, where Caroline Quarlls—the first person to escape slavery via Wisconsin's Underground Railroad network—took refuge on her journey from St. Louis to Canada.

The UGRR Detroit Alternate is as varied and tough as its subject matter.

As the route weaves steadily closer to the Canadian border, it brings you into Detroit. The city was an important destination for freedom seekers and became a pivotal place to cross into Canada. Take time here to visit the Second Baptist Church— formed in 1836, it is the oldest African American church in the Midwest. It was also an important stop on the Underground Railroad, and freedom seekers were often sheltered in the building's basement until it was safe to cross the Detroit River.

The river lies at the heart of this section of the route through the city, and with good reason: it was the scene of at least one-quarter of all the Underground Railroad escapes from the US during the Civil War. As you pedal along the riverfront, look out for the Gateway to Freedom statue by sculptor Ed Dwight, which depicts a group of Underground Railroad users fleeing enslavement; on the opposite bank, in Windsor, is a companion monument called the Tower of Freedom, portraying their arrival in Canada. It's not possible to cycle over any of the bridges

The Gateway to Freedom monument, next to the riverfront in Detroit

Above The interior of Josiah Henson's house at the Uncle Tom's Cabin Historic Site

Right Weavers Creek Falls in Harrison Park, Owen Sound

here, so your own border crossing is via bike-friendly shuttle bus. Windsor's Olde Sandwich Towne area is home to several notable sites tied to the Underground Railroad, and it's worth pausing here to explore before climbing back in the saddle.

As you pedal deeper into Ontario, the route becomes more rural. Highlights on this stretch include the Buxton National Historic Site in North Buxton, commemorating the Elgin Settlement established by former slaves, and the Uncle Tom's Cabin Historic Site in Dresden. The latter was the home of Josiah Henson, the inspiration for the title character in Harriet Beecher Stowe's 1852 anti-slavery novel *Uncle Tom's Cabin*.

A final descent brings you sweeping down into Owen Sound, the northernmost terminus of the Underground Railroad and the final stopping point for your own journey. Mark the end of the ride with a visit to the Black History Cairn in Harrison Park, where the city's Emancipation Festival is held every August. Originating in 1862, this event celebrates those who made the Underground Railroad possible—a fitting subject to reflect on, as you contemplate all you've learned about the perilous journey from slavery to freedom and the quest for justice and dignity.

ANOTHER WAY

Ripley Routes

If you'd prefer a shorter ride, the Adventure Cycling Association has established three Underground Railroad-related routes in Ripley, Ohio, that can be done in a single day. The Ripley Loop takes in the scenically situated Rankin House, one of the state's most active Underground Railroad stations.

Explore the picturesque college town of **MIDDLEBURY**, visiting the Vermont Folklife Center to admire local crafts, and the Henry Sheldon Museum to get a feel for 19th-century New England life.

FORT TICONDEROGA, an 18th-century star fort overlooking Lake Champlain, makes a good side trip from Shoreham—it can be easily accessed via ferry.

Lake Champlain

UNITED STATES

Vergennes

Middlebury

East Middlebury

Falls of Lana

Shoreham

Lake Dunmore

Fort Ticonderoga

Orwell

Brandon

Hop off your bike just above **LAKE DUNMORE** for the short hike up to the Falls of Lana, a series of cataracts that cascade some 98 ft (30 m) down the hillside.

19
Champlain Triangle

BRANDON, VERMONT, US (LOOP)

Coast along the peaceful byways and back roads of Addison County in Vermont's rural Champlain Valley. It's a winsome region sprinkled with covered wooden bridges and Dutch-gabled timber barns, guarded by the forested ridges of the Green Mountains.

The broad, bucolic Champlain Valley, a swathe of somnolent farm belt stretching between the Green Mountains to the east and New York State's Adirondacks to the west, is quintessential New England: fertile, picturesque, and positively aflame in autumn, when maples carpeting its hillsides blaze crimson and gold. It's also a dream for cyclists: Vermont hosts the second-smallest population of any state, and its gently winding back roads are suitably quiet, punctuated by friendly villages where historical inns offer

toothsome hospitality. To cherrypick the area's highlights—the photogenic bridges, the perky market towns, the waterfalls, and glittering Lake Champlain—take a tour through Addison County. Pedal away from the Victorian clapboard houses of Brandon and roll north through leafy landscapes toward the historic towns of Middlebury and Vergennes, before heading south to bijou picket-fence burg Shoreham alongside Lake Champlain. From there, it's a pleasantly meandering ride east back to Brandon or—if you've been entranced by New England's charm—simply choose another maple-lined road and keep going.

ELEVATION PROFILE

1,000 ft (305 m)

0

0   107 miles (172 km)

⊖ 107 MILES (172 KM)

⊘ 5,250 FT (1,600 M)

⊖ PAVED / GRAVEL / DIRT

58

20
Overseas Heritage Trail

KEY LARGO TO KEY WEST, FLORIDA, US

Turquoise waters, pristine beaches, and refreshing ocean breezes: take in the tropical beauty of the Florida Keys on an island-hopping adventure that follows an old train line to reach the southernmost point in the US.

Tracing the route of the former Florida East Coast Railway, the Overseas Heritage Trail links together 50 of the islands that make up the idyllic Florida Keys. Cycling from Key Largo to Key West—often on bike paths that run parallel to the scenic Highway One—you'll travel along a route thick with palm trees and tropical vegetation, hopping from island to island via historical rail bridges that stretch over the

Caribbean-like waters. The best of these is Seven Mile Bridge, an engineering marvel that offers jaw-dropping views of the ocean.

Expect to be lured off your bike by mangrove-lined bays, seaside towns, and sandy shores lapped by balmy waters—it's definitely a good idea to build some beach time into your schedule. But there's reason to keep pedaling: at the end of the road lies Key West, the southernmost point in the US, with the promise of margaritas, conch fritters, and delicious Key lime pie.

Top Tip
Contact a local outfitter such as Florida Keys Bike Ride *(floridakeys bikeride.com)* for help with logistics.

ELEVATION PROFILE

300 ft
(91 m)

0

0   107 miles (172 km)

⊖ 107 MILES (172 KM)

⊘ 98 FT (30 M)

⊖ PAVED / GRAVEL / DIRT

Explore the underwater world of **KEY LARGO**, famed for its dive sites.

UNITED STATES

Key Largo

0 ·········· km ·········· 20
0 ·········· miles ·········· 20

Dine oceanfront at **LAZY DAYS RESTAURANT** in Islamorada, where you can bring your fresh catch to the kitchen or try Florida dishes such as cracked conch and Key lime butter.

Islamorada

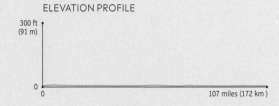

Pull up to Mile Marker 0 in **KEY WEST** for a photo, then head a few blocks away to the Southernmost Point Buoy, an iconic spot to snap another picture.

Marathon

Hawks Cay Resort

HAWKS CAY RESORT is a perfect place to have a luxe Keys experience. Spend a day (or two) soaking up some sun and getting on the water for fishing or paddleboarding.

Seven Mile Bridge

Key West

NORTH AMERICA

MEXICO

CUBA
◎ **25**

BELIZE
◎ **21** ◎ **22**

GUATEMALA HONDURAS

NICARAGUA
◎ **23**

◎ **24**

COSTA
RICA PANAMA VENEZUELA

GUYANA

SURINAM

27◎

COLOMBIA

○
ECUADOR **26**

●

PERU

○
30

●

31
◎

BRAZIL

◎ **28**

BOLIVIA

○
29

●

PARAGUAY

URUGUAY
CHILE

ARGENTINA

◎ **32**

○
33

●

CENTRAL AND SOUTH AMERICA

21

Sierra Norte

OAXACA DE JUÁREZ, MEXICO (LOOP)

*Complemented by the fine culinary fare of Oaxaca, this loop into the
Sierra Norte takes you on a two-wheeled tour of the region's rugged
mountain beauty and biodiversity.*

67 MILES (108 KM)

10,614 FT (3,235 M)

PAVED / GRAVEL / DIRT

62

Let's be honest: a visit to Oaxaca is as much about the food as it is about the cycling. Very much the culinary capital of Mexico, Oaxaca will appeal to any pedal-powered foodie with a penchant for chili, afternoon mezcal, or even a cup of locally roasted coffee straight from the nearby mountains.

Speaking of mountains, that's exactly where this route is bound—up and up into the Sierra Norte. Leaving behind the *bon vivant* vibes of beautiful Oaxaca de Juárez, it spirals its way skyward from 4,921 ft (1,500 m) to over double that—10,663 ft (3,250 m)—and back down again, over a distance of some 67 miles (108 km). You can try tackling it in one epic day, but splitting it into two is far more fun. After all, there's no shortage of delights to be appreciated, especially when it comes to flora. Oaxaca abounds with plants that change in size and form depending on elevation. As hard-fought yards are accrued, giant agaves give way to towering pines

A cyclist riding through a rocky
stream in rural Oaxaca

and glades of old-growth oaks, mottled with lichen and draped with bromeliads.

Either camp out or travel light, taking advantage of accommodations in the Sierra Norte's mountain communities. Be sure to stop for a restorative glass of *agua de jamaica*—hibiscus water—and dig into a hearty *tlayuda*. These large and crispy corn tortillas are baked on a skillet, coated with a black-bean purée, and laced with Oaxacan *quesillo* (cheese), fresh vegetables, chorizo, or *huitlacoche*—a corn fungus.

One of the highest points of this route, a mountaintop known as La Cumbre, is also a hub for a thriving enduro mountain biking scene. Rest assured, though, that

ELEVATION PROFILE

13,000 ft
(3,962 m)

3,000 ft
(914 m)

0   67 miles (108 km)

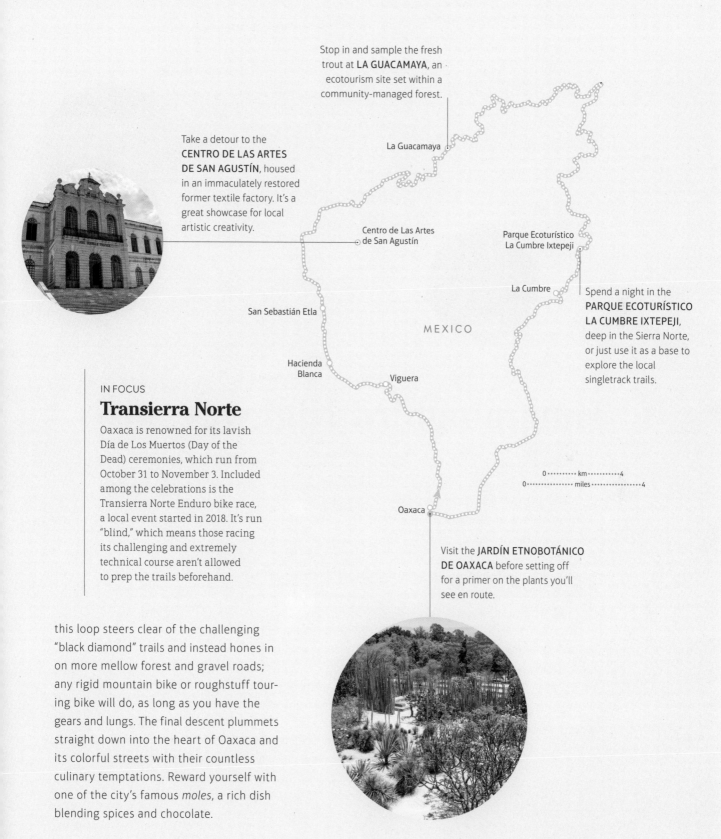

Stop in and sample the fresh trout at **LA GUACAMAYA**, an ecotourism site set within a community-managed forest.

La Guacamaya

Take a detour to the **CENTRO DE LAS ARTES DE SAN AGUSTÍN**, housed in an immaculately restored former textile factory. It's a great showcase for local artistic creativity.

Centro de Las Artes de San Agustín

Parque Ecoturístico La Cumbre Ixtepeji

San Sebastián Etla

La Cumbre

MEXICO

Spend a night in the **PARQUE ECOTURÍSTICO LA CUMBRE IXTEPEJI**, deep in the Sierra Norte, or just use it as a base to explore the local singletrack trails.

Hacienda Blanca

Viguera

0 ·········· km ·········· 4
0 ·········· miles ·········· 4

IN FOCUS

Transierra Norte

Oaxaca is renowned for its lavish Día de Los Muertos (Day of the Dead) ceremonies, which run from October 31 to November 3. Included among the celebrations is the Transierra Norte Enduro bike race, a local event started in 2018. It's run "blind," which means those racing its challenging and extremely technical course aren't allowed to prep the trails beforehand.

Oaxaca

Visit the **JARDÍN ETNOBOTÁNICO DE OAXACA** before setting off for a primer on the plants you'll see en route.

this loop steers clear of the challenging "black diamond" trails and instead hones in on more mellow forest and gravel roads; any rigid mountain bike or roughstuff touring bike will do, as long as you have the gears and lungs. The final descent plummets straight down into the heart of Oaxaca and its colorful streets with their countless culinary temptations. Reward yourself with one of the city's famous *moles*, a rich dish blending spices and chocolate.

63

Belmopan

At the **LAMANAI CHOCOLATE FACTORY**, see how they make traditional stone-ground chocolate on a Mayan grinding stone—and taste some samples.

Herman's Blue Hole National Park

Lamanai Chocolate Factory

Spend a night at the **TOUCAN RIDGE ECOLOGY AND EDUCATION SOCIETY**. The cute wooden cabins have views of the Maya Mountains and lush jungle.

Cool off with a dip at **HERMAN'S BLUE HOLE NATIONAL PARK**. The inland Blue Hole (not to be confused with the oceanic Great Blue Hole) is a sparkling natural pool formed by a collapsed sinkhole.

Toucan Ridge Ecology and Education Society

Dangriga

BELIZE

0 ·······km·······10
0 ·········miles·········10

22

Hummingbird Highway

BELMOPAN TO DANGRIGA, BELIZE

Cycling along the Hummingbird Highway is like cycling through a slice of paradise. Lined with lush orchards, towering mountains, and sinuous rivers, this humble thoroughfare is justly deserving of its reputation as Belize's most beautiful road.

53 MILES (86 KM) 1,414 FT (431 M) PAVED

In a country where cycling is the unofficial national sport, there's no better way to feel at home in Belize than when perched on a bike seat. And what better place to saddle up than the iconic Hummingbird Highway? Connecting the capital city of Belmopan to the Caribbean coast town of Dangriga, the road is named after the country's profusion of hummingbirds—if you're lucky, you'll spot some as you're pedaling along.

Don't let the word highway scare you. This is more of a quiet country road, lined by the simple delights of nature and small villages. Gently rolling hills make it easy to settle into a rhythm, so there's plenty of time to sit back and enjoy the scenery: sweet-smelling citrus plantations, meandering rivers, the looming peaks of the Maya Mountains, and tangled jungle foliage.

As you coast down the final section into Dangriga, some of the best beaches in Belize will appear on the horizon—they're the perfect finale to the highway's end.

ELEVATION PROFILE

1,500 ft (457 m)

0

0   53 miles (86 km)

23

Lake Nicaragua

SAN JUAN DEL SUR TO OJO DE AGUA,
OMETEPE ISLAND, NICARAGUA

*Welcome to the land of fire and nice: a country shaped by volcanic
and political unrest, Nicaragua is now one of the friendliest cycling
destinations in Central America, rich in wildlife and scenic beauty.*

46 MILES (75 KM) · 1,945 FT (593 M) · PAVED / DIRT / GRAVEL

Dominated by a string of grumbling volcanoes and with
decidedly uneven road quality, Central America's largest
country might seem daunting to cyclists. In fact, it's a treat
where on even the roughest of routes you'll be cheered on
by exuberant kids and raucous howler monkeys.

Enjoy a snapshot of its wonders with this scenic slice
of the southwest. Starting at the surf-smoothed beaches of
San Juan del Sur, you'll steer north past rustic farmsteads
and fruit plantations to the port town of San Jorge, on Lake
Nicaragua. A ferry crossing takes you to the twin volcanoes
of Ometepe Island, where the ride ends with a pedal
between its peaks and a soak in the natural springs at Ojo
de Agua. As the Nicos proclaim, *deacachimba*—awesome!

REFUEL
Feast on Fish

Typical Nico cuisine is based around
rice and beans, but around Lake
Nicaragua, you'll also be treated to
freshwater fish. Scour menus for
guapote (rainbow bass)—a hefty
fish that's especially tasty cooked
asado (grilled)—usually served
with rice, salad, and fried plantain.
It's best washed down with a
chilled *refresco* (fruit-juice drink).

ELEVATION PROFILE

1,500 ft
(457 m)

0

0   46 miles (75 km)

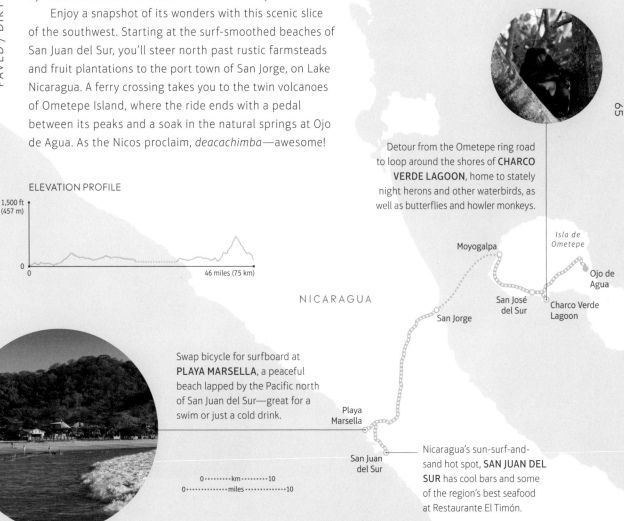

65

Detour from the Ometepe ring road
to loop around the shores of **CHARCO
VERDE LAGOON**, home to stately
night herons and other waterbirds, as
well as butterflies and howler monkeys.

NICARAGUA

*Isla de
Ometepe*

Moyogalpa

San José
del Sur

Ojo de
Agua

Charco Verde
Lagoon

San Jorge

Swap bicycle for surfboard at
PLAYA MARSELLA, a peaceful
beach lapped by the Pacific north
of San Juan del Sur—great for a
swim or just a cold drink.

Playa
Marsella

San Juan
del Sur

0 ········· km ········· 10
0 ········· miles ········· 10

Nicaragua's sun-surf-and-
sand hot spot, **SAN JUAN DEL
SUR** has cool bars and some
of the region's best seafood
at Restaurante El Timón.

CENTRAL AND SOUTH AMERICA

24

Costa Rica Highland Fling

LOS ÁNGELES DE TILARÁN TO
MUELLE SAN CARLOS, COSTA RICA

Ride above sparkling Lake Arenal on an adventure across Costa Rica's verdant highlands, passing through lush rain forest guarded by smoking volcanoes.

83 MILES (133 KM) / 7,293 FT (2,223 M) / PAVED / DIRT / GRAVEL

"Pura vida!" ("Pure life!")—you'll soon be familiar with this typical Tico greeting as you pedal across Costa Rica. It's a perfect encapsulation of what this pocket gem delivers in spades: clean air, boundless energy, and a panoply of spectacular wildlife. More than a quarter of the country's land area is protected, ensuring its birds and beasts thrive among their many and varied habitats. You'll spy plenty of these animals on a series of meandering bike stages through the northern highlands around Arenal Volcano and its namesake lake just to the west.

For the best views, follow the good, albeit undulating, road that traces the lake's northern shore. Pick up the trail at the western end, with Tenorio Volcano at your back, and prepare for climbs: the route doesn't stick to the water's edge but rises and falls as it skirts the adjacent hills, regularly dipping into clumps of rain forest. In this humid tropical environment, temperatures quickly soar when the sun emerges, so take frequent breaks in the shade of the canopy. On such stops, you might spy columns of leafcutter ants, vivid blue morpho butterflies and gaudy

There are some great cafés along the road near **NUEVO ARENAL**, where you can watch gorgeous birds at feeders—look for the Montezuma oropendola, with a yellow tail, blue cheeks, pink wattle, and orange bill.

Rio Piedras

Nuevo Arenal

Lake Arenal

Los Ángeles de Tilarán

ELEVATION PROFILE

3,000 ft (914 m)

0

0   83 miles (133 km)

The cloud-topped Arenal Volcano, softly illuminated at sunset

Take a break from the bike in **LA FORTUNA** and head to the nearby national parks for some hiking or zip-lining—or simply relax in one of the hot-spring complexes above town.

The river banks at **MUELLE SAN CARLOS** are home to clusters of hefty iguanas that lounge lazily on tree branches and bridge cables alongside the river.

La Fortuna

○
Arenal
Volcano

COSTA RICA

Muelle San Carlos

0 ·········· km ·········· 5
0 ·········· miles ·········· 5

San Isidro

Javillos

Browse the fruit stalls that line the roads around **JAVILLOS**, picking up supplies of fresh mangos, pineapples, and papayas.

keel-billed toucans. Watch out, too, for gangs of roguish coatis—long-nosed raccoons that hop out from the undergrowth to accost cyclists for snacks.

Reaching the eastern end of the lake, you'll cross the dam that created this handsome reservoir; it makes a prime viewing point for admiring Arenal Volcano ahead (cloud cover permitting). Just beyond this peak lies the lively town of La Fortuna, where there's a chance to enjoy some R&R before you embark on the final leg to Muelle San Carlos. The lush countryside undergoes a distinct change in character from here, with haphazard rain forest replaced by a more orderly assortment of sugar-cane, banana, and pineapple plantations. But there's still one last wildlife sighting in store—waiting to welcome you into Muelle San Carlos are huge iguanas on the banks of the river.

REFUEL
Get Fruity

Typical Tican fare is pretty basic: rice, beans, and maybe some fried plantain and meat or fish. Fruit, though, is dizzying in its diversity: as well as lip-smacking melons, mango, and papaya, try red *pitaya* (dragon fruit), like figgy sweet potato; sugary custard apple; and purple-fleshed, floral *caimito* (star apple) for starters.

The middle section, from Chivirico to Pilón, is about as far off the beaten track as you can cycle without requiring a helicopter.

Climb the steps to the sunflowery Celia Sanchez memorial—dedicated to a local revolutionary—in **MANZANILLO**, then enjoy oyster cocktails, rum, and music in the central square.

Stop for snacks and supplies at **LA MULA**, a ramshackle but friendly municipal campsite and resort. Maybe take a quick dip in the warm Caribbean waters while you're there.

Watch out for feisty crabs crossing the road in huge numbers at **CALETÓN BLANCO**.

Manzanillo

Campechuela

Media Luna

C U B A

Caletón
Blanco

Chivirico

Santiago de Cuba

Uvero

La Plata

La Mula

Playa de
Mar Verde

Pilón

Brace yourself for the short, steep hills of **LA PLATA**. They're tough on the legs but offer plenty of opportunities to stop and enjoy the vivid coastal scenery on the way to Pilón.

Hit the road at dawn, while most tourists are still asleep, to see **SANTIAGO DE CUBA**'s energetic morning life and snag breakfast coffee and buns from a local kiosk.

0 ·········· km ·········· 30
0 ················· miles ················· 30

ELEVATION PROFILE

1,500 ft
(457 m)

0

0   172 miles (278 km)

25

Cuba's Coast Road

SANTIAGO DE CUBA TO MANZANILLO, CUBA

A world away from Cuba's resorts is this forgotten old highway along the south coast, where bicycles rule the road. Ride between towering cliffs and glittering sea, through isolated, welcoming communities.

172 MILES (278 KM)

7,175 FT (2,187 M)

PAVED / GRAVEL

Cycling in Cuba is like nowhere else. Even on main roads, there's little traffic—you might be sharing a "highway" with only a horse and cart. Towns and villages, forced into self-sufficiency by decades of economic isolation, are like Cuba's ubiquitous 1950s cars: basic and battered, but defiant and surviving with style.

This route is bookended by Santiago de Cuba and Manzanillo, vibrant cities alive with music and art. In between is small-town and tiny-village Cuba, where visitors are rare, accommodations informal, and bicycles practically the only mode of transport. Locals here are extremely welcoming to cyclists and will be happy to help you find something to eat and somewhere to stay.

Most of the way is intact and smooth, except for a few short, dramatic stretches of improvised dirt road. The middle section, from Chivirico to Pilón, is about as far off the beaten track as you can cycle without requiring a helicopter. Here, the coast road is impassable to almost all vehicles, following hurricane damage in 2012. But it's easily cyclable, and for around 100 miles (160 km), you'll share the highway with locals perched on a range of much-patched and oft-repaired bikes. There are no shops or stalls in the remote central section, but elsewhere roadside kiosks provide plenty of chances to refuel. Enjoy fresh sugar-cane juice, fruit shakes, and snacks—even cigars and rum, if you want to fully embrace the local lifestyle. After the brief tropical twilight turns hot day into warm evening, family-run *paladares* (restaurants in private houses) offer home comforts for aching muscles and empty stomachs. Expect heaped plates of chicken, beans, rice, and fresh fruit, and perhaps also lobster if you're lucky. You may be cycling beyond the back of beyond, but nowhere has ever felt so civilized.

ANOTHER WAY
Tropical Trundles

If it's short, scenic circular rides you're after, base yourself in Viñales, west of Havana. Explore the lush landscape of tropical plantations, caves, lakes, and villages on largely flat country lanes that wind between pretty sugarloaf hills called *mogotes*.

Top Tip

Streams are plentiful,
so save weight by
carrying just a few
bottles and the means
to purify water.

Cycling through
Cotopaxi National Park,
with the famous volcano
in the background

26

Trans Ecuador Mountain Bike Route

TULCÁN TO CUENCA, ECUADOR

Running the length of the Avenue of the Volcanoes, the Trans Ecuador Mountain Bike Route follows in the footsteps of the explorer and naturalist Alexander von Humboldt, crossing national parks and market towns alike, on an epic journey through the country's Andean highlands.

657 MILES (1,060 KM)

93,210 FT (28,410 M)

PAVED / DIRT

In the early 1800s, the Prussian explorer and naturalist Alexander von Humboldt coined the phrase the "Avenue of the Volcanoes" while traveling through Ecuador. He was referring to the 47 volcanoes that run down the country's Andean spine and his journey was part of a pioneering odyssey—one that put the South American continent on the map for generations of travelers to come. This same cratered avenue—and Humboldt's inspired expedition—underpins the Trans Ecuador Mountain Bike Route over 200 years later.

There are, in fact, two versions of the Trans Ecuador Mountain Bike Route (or the TEMBR, as the ride is also known). This description follows the dirt-road version, the mellower younger sibling to the original—and more technically difficult—singletrack option.

ELEVATION PROFILE

16,500 ft
(5,029 m)

0

0   657 miles (1,060 km)

CENTRAL AND SOUTH AMERICA

Don't for a minute think that you're in for an easy ride though—in a country as mountainous as Ecuador, "mellow" is very much a relative word. The weather can be tempestuous, the climbs are hard fought, and surfaces range from cobblestones to dirt tracks to rural paved roads. But thankfully, and unlike its hike-a-bike obsessed sibling, this dirt-road version is almost completely ridable—aside from the odd push and shove, of course.

In choosing to cross the country in this decidedly unconventional way, the TEMBR is a showcase for Ecuador's natural grandeur and its cultural intrigue—be it by experiencing the technicolored hubbub of its market towns, riding past the country's conical showstoppers, like Volcán Cotopaxi and Volcán Chimborazo, or biking across off-piste paramo. This high-altitude, humid tundra is unique to Ecuador, Colombia, and Venezuela—thanks to their

Exploring a landscape of unusual *frailejón* plants in the El Angel Ecological Reserve

IN FOCUS
Alexander von Humboldt

Alexander von Humboldt (1769–1859) was a world-renowned naturalist who, along with the French botanist Aimé Bonpland, explored South America from 1799 to 1804. They climbed many of Ecuador's volcanoes, including Chimborazo. Drawing from these travels, Humboldt is credited with being the first person to recognize human impact on climate change and for being a "founding father" of environmentalism.

proximity to the equator—and is synonymous with the Ecuadorian highlands.

The full length of the dirt-road TEMBR stretches for 733 miles (1,180 km), from the city of Tulcán, at the Colombian border in the north, to Vilcabamba, close to the border with Peru in the south. But this slightly shorter route, covering the first 657 miles (1,060 km) between Tulcán and the colonial city of Cuenca, is of the most interest to adventurous bicycle tourers. It's here that Humboldt's Avenue of the Volcanoes is to be found.

Before you head off, though, a note on weather—because it's as much a part of Ecuador as the riding itself, and it's sure to make the TEMBR a character-forming endeavor. June to mid-September is the dry season in the Ecuadorian Andes, but even so, be prepared for extended bouts of rain throughout the year. There is, after all, a reason why this petite parcel of land is so very lush and green.

Meander through the otherworldly **EL ANGEL ECOLOGICAL RESERVE**. Leave your bike with the guards at the refuge, then follow the short self-guided hike for views of the *frailejón*.

Tulcán

El Angel Ecological Reserve

Head to **OTAVALO**'s Plaza de Ponchos to experience Ecuador's biggest handicraft market in full swing. It runs every day, though it's at its biggest on Saturday.

Otavalo

Camp at the **COTOPAXI LODGE**, found within the eponymous national park. Its telescope is great for watching climbers tackle the summit of Ecuador's most photogenic volcano.

Cotopaxi Lodge

Pause at the low-key tourist hub around **LAGUNA DE QUILOTOA**, from where you can tackle the four-hour hike around the crater's rocky rim.

Laguna de Quilotoa

Zumbahua

ECUADOR

73

Salinas de Guaranda

Refugio Carrel

Detour to Refugio Carrel to spend a night at the foot of Ecuador's highest volcano, **CHIMBORAZO**. You can camp or indulge in a cozy bed and a hot meal in the refuge itself.

Plan your itinerary around **GUAMOTE**'s excellent Thursday-morning market—a great spot for local delicacies and fresh produce.

Guamote

Cuenca

Top Tip

The sun can be strong at high altitude, even in cloudy conditions, so be sure to bring plenty of sunscreen.

Admire the architecture in **CUENCA**—the city's historic center has been designated a UNESCO World Heritage Site.

PERU

0 ⋯⋯ km ⋯⋯ 50
0 ⋯⋯ miles ⋯⋯ 50

A group of graceful vicuñas grazing near the towering volcano of Chimborazo

Strapping your bags to your bike, you'll set off from highland Tulcán. Following in the footsteps of von Humboldt, you meander through misty groves of otherworldly foliage as you skirt the El Angel Ecological Reserve. Here, tens of thousands of *frailejón*—a genus of perennial sub-shrubs—cover every square yard of the hillsides, growing among tussock grasses at elevations above 9,843 ft (3,000 m). As tall as people and sporting velvet-leaved hairstyles, these characterful plants catch moisture in the air and feed it into the earth.

Continuing south, there's a protracted descent into the Inter Andean Valley—aka the Avenue of the Volcanoes—which brings respite from mountain hardships in the form of a stopover in Otavalo. Famous for being the country's textile hub, it's a great showcase for Quechuan handicrafts and its Saturday market is not to be missed. Just don't get too comfortable, because it's followed quickly by a gamut of challenging conditions—including a network of cobbled and sometimes grassy back roads—as you gain elevation once more in search of the

perfectly conical Cotopaxi. Towering high above the tree line, Ecuador's most iconic volcano is set within a national park that's speckled with miniature and delicate flora.

This sense of duality epitomizes both Ecuador and this route, and is further revealed as you trade Cotopaxi's quiet and captivating wilderness for signs of human habitation. The fertile highlands around the emerald-hued crater lake of Quilotoa reveal yet another new landscape, where steep-sided hills are home to shepherds, sheep, and llamas, as well as patchwork quilts of quinoa and potato fields.

Beyond the rustic market town of Zumbahua, a roller coaster of a highland route leads onward, with one particularly steep and never-ending series of climbs after the village of Angamarca. Rugged dirt roads reveal themselves in the swirling mist, rising and falling across the land like an ocean tide, as the TEMBR's last volcano is approached. Luckily for your heavy legs, the path to Volcán Chimborazo brings a welcome perk in the form of Salinas de Guaranda. This small settlement is home to a thriving grassroots tourism and local business infrastructure—including its own chocolate factory.

Tasty treats consumed, no visit to Ecuador would be complete without taking in the full grandeur of Chimborazo, around

Rugged dirt roads reveal themselves in the swirling mist, rising and falling across the land like an ocean tide

which vicuñas, the lithe siblings to llamas, like to graze. The country's highest peak, it also—thanks to a bulge in Earth's curvature—marks both the closest point to the sun and the farthest point from the center of Earth. As you climb your way up to Refugio Carrel at the foot of the volcano, spare a thought for von Humboldt, who ascended Chimborazo laden with recording equipment back in 1802. (And like the Prussian, you can also pause to inspect Ingapirca, the 16th-century Incan ruins that come shortly afterward.)

Now, the end is finally in sight, via one last push on rolling paved roads that culminate in a bike path leading straight into the heart of Cuenca. With its colonial architecture and its strong artistic and musical vibe, this resplendent city is the perfect finale to the TEMBR experience.

ANOTHER WAY
Los Tres Volcanes

Check out Los Tres Volcanes for a five-day, 258-mile (415-km) bikepacking route that connects Ecuador's most quintessential volcanoes: picture-postcard Cotopaxi, the impressive crater lake of Quilotoa, and lofty Chimborazo, albeit over a shorter distance and with more focus on singletrack, hike-a-bikes and open paramo. Find logistical details at *bikepacking.com*.

Because that's what the TEMBR is— it's an experience. Revealing Ecuador's enchanting Andes in their most varied and authentic form, it's a challenging yet magnificent endeavor that von Humboldt himself would surely applaud.

Rolling through the remote and deserted wilderness of Cotopaxi National Park

Pull over for an energy-boosting hit of *aguapanela con queso* (a soup of sugarcane and soft cheese) at the **ROADSIDE CAFÉ** 41 miles (66 km) into the climb.

Mariquita

Roadside café

Delgaditas

Fresno

Look back in triumph at the climb you've just conquered from the top of **ALTO DE LETRAS**.

Alto de Letras

COLOMBIA

For most riders, it takes roughly two hours to reach the bustling hillside town of **FRESNO**, making it the perfect spot for a roadside refuel of *arepas* and coffee.

0 ·····km····· 10
0 ·····miles····· 10

27

Alto de Letras

MARIQUITA TO ALTO DE LETRAS, COLOMBIA

There are only a handful of road climbs on Earth that rise over 9,850 ft (3,000 m) in a single stretch. Letras is one of them, climbing 50 miles (81 km) from the Colombian jungle up into the sky.

Top Tip
Don't underestimate the altitude here; always allow plenty of time to acclimatize before setting out.

76

50 MILES (81 KM)

13,163 FT (4,012 M)

PAVED

It feels, in the final miles of the world's longest road climb, like you could reach up and touch the ceiling of the world. Clouds snag on ridges, pulling softly apart, like curtains at the world's greatest show. They obscure and then unveil vistas that drop thousands of feet down to valleys of dense jungle and plateaus of coffee plantations.

Rising from the small crossroads town of Mariquita, the road to Letras passes in time with your pedal strokes from oppressive lowland heat to the crisp, unmistakable chill of high altitude. Light trucks stacked with bananas slither past, men hanging off welded railings. The scent of sizzling grills wafts across the road from open-air restaurants, pulling on senses already overwhelmed by the staggering beauty of rural Colombia. The good news is that you'll have plenty of time to take it all in. The whole ride is uphill, after all.

ELEVATION PROFILE

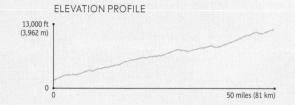

13,000 ft (3,962 m)

0

0

50 miles (81 km)

The road to Letras, weaving past verdant fields and coffee trees

28
Death Road

LA CUMBRE TO YOLOSA, BOLIVIA

This thrilling route—also known as the North Yungas Road—zigzags down from a mountain pass near La Paz all the way to the forested Bolivian Yungas, offering riders an astonishing 11,811-ft (3,600-m) descent in a matter of hours.

This is the kind of thing that bucket lists were made for. It might not be technically difficult or physically demanding, but whizzing down this looping, sheer-sided road—fingers never far from your brakes—is an experience you'll remember forever. If you set off early in the morning, by lunch you'll have descended as much height as if you had ridden from the summit of Everest down to Base Camp.

Starting from the mountain pass of La Cumbre, the top section of the route is a paved road that winds past herds of fluffy alpacas and llamas. But don't be fooled—this luxurious surface soon gives way to a rough track, carved out of the mountainside with a vertical cliff face to the right and a huge, unprotected drop on the left. With a white-knuckle grip on the handlebars, you'll fly from high up in the mountains—adrenaline rushing through you—down, down, down to the low cloud forest of the Bolivian Yungas. On the way, you'll cross streams, zoom under waterfalls, and spy spectacular rain-forest viewpoints. Now, if you fancy a real challenge, turn around and ride back up.

Visit **LA SENDA VERDE**, a sanctuary in Yolosa for wild animals rescued from cruelty, habitat destruction, and illegal trafficking.

ELEVATION PROFILE

16,500 ft (5,029 m)

0

0 — 38 miles (62 km)

Yolosa

BOLIVIA

Postcard Corner

Start of Death Road

Marvel at the cloud forest from **POSTCARD CORNER** before riding under the tumbling San Juan waterfalls.

LA CUMBRE offers panoramic views of the Andean Altiplano's grandeur.

La Cumbre

0 ·········· km ·········· 10
0 ·········· miles ·········· 10

Top Tip

Fit the largest volume tires your frame can take and run them at low pressure for a more comfortable ride.

29

Lagunas Route

UYUNI, BOLIVIA, TO SAN PEDRO DE ATACAMA, CHILE

The Lagunas Route has drawn hardy bicyclists to the Bolivian Altiplano for years, with its promise of high-altitude lakes, flocks of flamingos, and mesmerizing rock formations—plus the chance to conquer one of the world's toughest trails.

290 MILES (467 KM)   11,312 FT (3,448 M)   PAVED / DIRT

Make no mistake about it: the Lagunas Route is an incredibly tough ride. For starters, you can expect to contend with the vagaries of high-altitude riding—at 13,123 ft (4,000 m), breathing is often labored, even if you're moving slowly. Strong winds blast restlessly across the open plateaus, with temperatures dropping as low as −4°F (−20°C) in winter—the best time to do this ride—requiring you to bring a warm sleeping bag and bundle up in every one of your layers at night, like a Russian doll. And then there's the terrain itself. Extended sections of the Lagunas Route can be sandy, and most travelers will likely huff and push their bulky rigs for sizable chunks of the ride. On other parts of the track, you'll have to navigate around busy fleets of backpacker-filled jeeps and the extremely corrugated surface they leave in their wake. Throughout, there's a distinct lack of fresh food, so get used to llama jerky and packaged crackers as your trail snacks.

All in all, this ride isn't for the faint-hearted—so why do it? Well, first, because it's the ultimate cycling challenge through Bolivia's back country—survive this and you can survive pretty much anything. But it's more than that: while the Bolivian Altiplano is a land of extremes, it's also a place of transcendental beauty. Here, volcanoes tower high and minerals saturate mountains, lending the panoramas a unique, Mars-like hue. Bizarre, wind-hewn rock formations loom on the horizon, and the beds of Bolivia's famous *salar* (salt flats) scrunch under your tires. A

ELEVATION PROFILE

16,500 ft (5,029 m)

6,500 ft (1,981 m)

0   290 miles (467 km)

Pausing for a rest amid the arid expanse of the Bolivian Altiplano

At Rio Grande, take a brief detour to visit the **SALAR DE UYUNI**, the world's largest salt flat. It's a bleached white canvas of cactus-ruled islands and lavender-tinted sunrises.

Uyuni

Enjoy a good meal before leaving **UYUNI**— it'll be the last chance for fresh food until you finish the ride.

Rio Grande

ANOTHER WAY

Take the Long Road

To avoid the jeep tourists, take the longer, alternative route that runs between Uyuni, San Vicente, San Pedro de Lipez, San Antonio de Lipez, and Quetena Chico. It also offers the chance to ride up to an old sulfur mine at an oxygen-depleted 18,953 ft (5,777 m).

Laguna Hedionda

BOLIVIA

Admire the bewitching **LAGUNA COLORADA** in the Eduardo Avaroa Andean Fauna National Reserve, tinted red with algae pigmentation.

Arbol de Piedra

Laguna Colorada

Be amazed by the wind-hewn **DESIERTO DE DALÍ**, whose bizarre rock formations look like a surrealist painting.

CHILE

Desierto de Dalí

Laguna Verde

San Pedro de Atacama

0 ········km········50
0 ········miles········50

smattering of striking, colorful lakes— after which this route is named—dot the landscape, populated by bowlegged pink flamingos picking their way through pungent sulfur deposits. And then, when you think you've seen it all, the bleached winter light instills a further sense of otherworldliness—before gradually fading into black in the evening, to reveal a night sky filled with more stars than you ever imagined possible.

Spilling out between the bases of two volcanoes, **LAGUNA VERDE** is just as its name suggests—a gorgeous expanse of emerald-colored water.

30

Peru's Great Divide

HUARAZ TO HUANCAVELICA, PERU

Striking deep into Peru's remote Central Cordillera, by way of a network of old mining roads and dirt tracks, Peru's Great Divide showcases some of the most scenic riding in South America.

558 MILES (898 KM)

75,130 FT (22,900 M)

PAVED / DIRT

80

Enjoy a walk around the tree-lined main square in the city of **HUARAZ**, spectacularly located at the foot of the snowcapped Cordillera Blanca range.

○ Huaraz

Conococha

Cajatambo

Pull in at the mining town of **OJON**. There might not be much going on here, but it's a good place to stock up on supplies and try a big bowl of chicken claw soup.

Ojon

PERU

Given the continent's diversity—from the jungles of the Amazon to the windswept shores of the Pacific Coast—there's no shortage of adventurous options for cyclists in South America. But it's to the high mountains of the Andes that most bicycle tourers are drawn, despite the promise of nearly endless climbs and the vagaries of riding at altitude. Peru's Great Divide zones in on a little-traveled range that runs south from the fabled high peaks of the Cordillera Blanca, popular with hikers and climbers, into the pass-riddled heart of the remote Central Cordillera.

The route was dreamed up in 2013 by the Pikes, an intrepid couple from the UK. Since then, it's steadily grown in popularity among bicycle tourers the world over and

REFUEL
Underground Ovens

Your starting point, Huaraz, is a great spot to sample regional Andean cuisine—and fuel up for the ride ahead. Head to the Sunday food market in Jose Olaya Street to try *pachamanca*—an assortment of meats baked underground using hot stones, wrapped in banana or corn leaves.

is now a classic. For good reason: when it comes to dirt roads, jagged mountains, snowy glaciers, sweeping vistas, and sublime camping, it's hard to imagine much better.

While the full Peru Great Divide runs for 870 miles (1,400 km), this section—stretching between the city of Huaraz and the remote settlement of Huancavelica—is undoubtedly its highlight. Not that this abbreviated version is a short ride by any means. Allowing time for acclimatization and a few rest days, you'll still need close to a month to do it justice.

ELEVATION PROFILE

16,500 ft
(5,029 m)

0

0   558 miles (898 km)

Bike touring through the rugged
landscapes of the Peruvian Andes

When it comes
to dirt roads, jagged
mountains, snowy
glaciers, sweeping
vistas, and sublime
camping, it's hard to
imagine much better.

Admire the sparkling waters of **LAGOS
ANTACOTA AND LAGOS MARCAPOMACOCHA**
as you cycle along the thin sliver of ground
that separates these two lakes.

Lagos Antacota
and Lagos
Marcapomacocha

Take time off the saddle to
explore the idyllic **RESERVA
PAISAJISTICA NOR YAUYOS-
COCHAS**, home to a series of
tiered, aquamarine lakes and
waterfalls along the Rio Cañete.

Yuracmayo

Reserva
Paisajistica Nor
Yauyos-Cochas

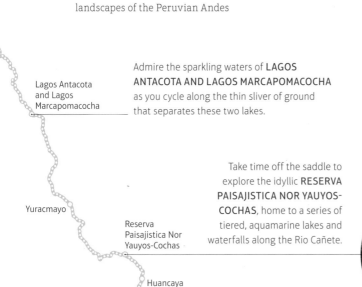

Huancaya

Viñas

Rest up at the end of your ride in the low-
key town of **HUANCAVELICA**—it's famed
among cyclists for the quality of its cakes.

Huancavelica

0 ·············km ·············50
0 ·············miles ·············50

Settle into the switchbacks
on the way to **VIÑAS**, keeping
an eye out for alpacas at the
side of the road.

CENTRAL AND SOUTH AMERICA

Top Tip

Basic accommodations are available at some of the villages en route, but you'll need camping gear for the more remote sections.

Leaving the comforts of Huaraz behind, you join the Great Divide's network of jeep tracks to embark on a real roller coaster of a ride, straddling the mountainous boundary that divides the watersheds of the Pacific to the east and the jungly sprawl of the Amazon and the Atlantic to the west. You'll bounce along rough, unmaintained roads from one settlement to the next, gathering basic supplies as you ride south through the mountains. Along the way, larger settlements promise bowls of hot soup, gristly meat and all, or mounds of rice and fried eggs—the Peruvian mountain staple. It's a high mountain ride that's shared with few others, besides herds of wiry llamas, fluffy alpacas, and the occasional dilapidated bus that might pass by, usually accompanied by a serenade of its horn.

A world away from the Peru of Machu Picchu and mass tourism, it's these unpaved roads—painstakingly chiseled into the sheerest and most stark of mountain sides—that are the real lifeblood of the country. Like the varied mineralogy that lends this range its distinct color palette, they course through a land that's isolated beyond imagination. Passing turquoise lakes and golden pampas, these dirt ribbons connect the most minuscule of *pueblocito* (villages), often no more than a collection of stone houses, a well-kept plaza, and a weathered church.

Let's get technical and talk numbers for a moment, as this isn't your typical bike tour. Four weeks to ride 558 miles (898 km)? If that doesn't sound too bad, just bear in mind that you'll need to conquer 75,130 ft (22,900 m) of elevation gain along the way—and don't forget this is at high altitude, with all your gear, on variable road surfaces. An approximate daily distance of 31 miles (50 km)—which works out to a rough average of 4,101 ft (1,250 m) of climbing per each of the 18 riding days—should allow you enough time to enjoy the majesty of the mountains and really challenge yourself. A rigid mountain bike or roughstuff touring bike is best, given the road conditions, but the key thing is to pack light and to time your ride for the dry season (May to September), or you'll have to factor mud and heavy rain into the mix.

You'll have to work for your dinner on this ride, but rest assured: Peru's Great Divide is a mountain pass medley that will reward you with some of the very best views in the Andes. What's more, you'll have them largely to yourself.

MAKE IT LONGER

Conquering Punta Olímpica

If you have a few extra days to spare and your lungs are ready and willing, it's well worth tackling Punta Olímpica (16,043 ft/4,890 m) and Portachuelo de Llanganuco (15,341 ft/4,676 m) while you're in Huaraz. Not only do these two passes make a worthy shakedown ride to test your setup, but they offer a fantastic overview of Peru's Cordillera Blanca—among the most beautiful mountain ranges in the Andes.

31

Ausangate Bikepacking Loop

PITUMARCA, PERU (LOOP)

This tough bikepacking loop encircles Mount Ausangate, the headline attraction of the Cordillera Vilcanota, rewarding riders with some of the most dramatic, up-close mountain vistas in the Peruvian Andes.

78 MILES (125 KM)

9,580 FT (2,920 M)

DIRT

If there's a name synonymous with Peru, it's Machu Picchu. And yet, the often overlooked but no less majestic Ausangate mountain could surely give it a run for its money. Sitting high above the clouds at a lofty 20,906 ft (6,372 m), this soaring peak was believed by the Incans to be one of the holiest *apus* (mountain spirits) in the land.

At its simplest, this 78-mile (125-km) ride neatly loops all the way around Ausangate, using the small settlement of Pitumarca as an entry and exit point. But don't let the diminutive distance lull you into a false sense of security. There's a 16,404-ft- (5,000-m-) high pass and extended "hike-a-bikes" to contend with, where your bike will need to be shouldered or pushed. The rewards? The sweetest, most scenic singletrack you've likely ridden, weaving past sparkling lakes and dramatic glaciers, with pristine camping spots from which to appreciate the stellar mountain views.

Riding through snow on the section of trail leading into Chillca

84

ELEVATION PROFILE

16,500 ft (5,029 m)

10,000 ft (3,048 m)

0   78 miles (125 km)

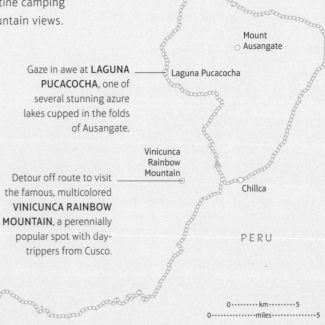

Set up camp for the night in **UPIS**, surrounded on all sides by snow-covered mountains. There's even a hot spring nearby, too.

Upis

Mount Ausangate

Gaze in awe at **LAGUNA PUCACOCHA**, one of several stunning azure lakes cupped in the folds of Ausangate.

Laguna Pucacocha

Vinicunca Rainbow Mountain

Chillca

Detour off route to visit the famous, multicolored **VINICUNCA RAINBOW MOUNTAIN**, a perennially popular spot with day-trippers from Cusco.

PERU

Stock up on supplies in **PITUMARCA**, before embarking on an early-morning start to Ausangate itself, following a gradual dirt-road climb.

Pitumarca

0 ········· km ······· 5
0 ········· miles ········· 5

Enjoy the sweeping vistas at **MIRADOR DEL PIL PIL**, a viewpoint overlooking the calm azure waters of Lake Lácar.

Lago Lácar

San Martín de los Andes

Mirador del Pil Pil

ARGENTINA

CHILE

Lago Hermoso

Lago Villarino

Lago Falkner

Lago Escondido

Head off the RN-40 at the northern end of Lago Traful and hike down a signposted track to **CASCADAS ÑIVINCO**, a group of five gorgeous waterfalls.

Cascadas Ñivinco

Stop off at the enchanting **LAGO ESCONDIDO** (Hidden Lake), perhaps the most beautiful of the seven *lagos* on the route.

Lago Espejo Grande

0 ·········· km ·········· 15
0 ·········· miles ·········· 15

Lago Correntoso

Villa La Angostura

Lago Nahuel Huapi

Before setting off from **VILLA LA ANGOSTURA**, get into the spirit of the route by taking a boat tour on Lago Nahuel Huapi.

32

Ruta de Los Siete Lagos

VILLA LA ANGOSTURA TO SAN MARTÍN DE LOS ANDES, ARGENTINA

Explore the best of northwestern Patagonia on a relaxed, easy-to-navigate ride, which rolls through a landscape of glacial lakes, emerald-green forested hills, and ragged Andean peaks.

70 MILES (112 KM)
5,840 FT (1,780 M)
PAVED

Taking you through Patagonia's idyllic Lake District region, the Ruta de los Siete Lagos (Route of the Seven Lakes) is famed as one of Argentina's most spectacular drives. But it's a journey that's even better by bike—this is scenery that demands to be pored over, and only on two wheels can you give it the time and attention it deserves.

Largely flat, the route follows part of the RN-40, Argentina's longest road. Winding through two national parks—Nahuel Huapi and Lanín—you'll be surrounded by breathtaking Andean vistas, complete with snowy peaks, crystal-clear rivers, and pristine beaches. It's an easy-going ride, and there are plenty of opportunities to hop off your bike and immerse yourself in the picture-perfect scenery, from a cooling dip in one of the mirrorlike lakes to a hike through rain forest chiming with birdsong. Taking it slow has never been more appealing.

ELEVATION PROFILE

5,000 ft (1,524 m)

0

0

70 miles (112 km)

Top Tip
Carry ample spares and supplies, as the only bike repair shops on the highway are in Coyhaique.

33

Carretera Austral

PUERTO MONTT TO VILLA O'HIGGINS, CHILE

Gear up for one of South America's most challenging—and rewarding—rides. Tracing the route of the Andes, the "Southern Highway" takes you through the dramatic, rugged, and sparsely populated landscapes of Chilean Patagonia.

750 MILES (1,208 KM)
60,475 FT (18,433 M)
PAVED / GRAVEL / DIRT

Built to connect remote frontier communities in Chilean Patagonia, the Carretera Austral (Southern Highway) should not be taken lightly—this is a journey into the heart of one of the world's last remaining wildernesses. Long sections of the road remain unpaved and are dotted with deep potholes; there are even rock- and landslides to contend with. There are numerous difficult ascents and descents, including tricky switchback turns and thigh-achingly high passes. And, even during summer (roughly December to March), the weather here is highly changeable—expect rain, fierce headwinds, and cold temperatures.

Yes, the going will be tough, but the hardships are more than worth it. Along the way you'll encounter smoldering volcanoes and iceberg-filled fjords, tranquil lakes and churning whitewater rapids, and swathes of dense rain forest and open steppe sprinkled with grazing guanacos (wild relatives of the llama).

Best ridden from north to south, the Carretera Austral (also known as Ruta 7) starts in the port city of Puerto Montt and finishes in tiny Villa O'Higgins, close to the Argentinian border. En route it meanders for 750 miles (1,208 km), incorporating several ferry crossings and passing through scores of remote communities and majestic national parks. Some cyclists power straight through from start to finish. Yet the ride is far more enjoyable if you allow plenty of time for pit stops and diversions.

Heading along a gravel section of the Carretera Austral, up through a narrow, tree-lined valley

Puerto Montt

Stop off to explore the hiking trails at the beautiful **PARQUE NACIONAL PUMALÍN**, home to temperate rain forests, snow-covered mountains, rumbling volcanoes, pristine lakes, and thundering waterfalls.

Take a detour to the picturesque town of **FUTALEUFÚ**, where you can swap your bike for a raft and tackle the world-class whitewater rapids on its namesake river.

Parque Nacional Pumalín

Chaiten

Puerto Cardenas

Futaleufú

Ventisquero Colgante

Soak your aching bones in one of the hot springs dotted around **PUYUHUAPI**, a charming village that sits on the edge of a stunning fjord surrounded by forested hills.

Puyuhuapi

Hop off the bike and hike to **VENTISQUERO COLGANTE** in the Parque Nacional Queulat. This magnificent white-blue glacier is jammed between two stark rock faces high above a turquoise lake.

Coyhaique

CHILE

ARGENTINA

87

Villa Cerro Castillo

Lago General Carrera

Marvel at the rippling aquamarine waters of **LAGO GENERAL CARRERA**, extending across the border into Argentina to form the second-largest lake in South America.

Cochrane

Caleta Yungay

Villa O'Higgins

Dismount at the tiny hamlet of **CALETA YUNGAY** and take the ferry across Mitchell Fjord to Villa O'Higgins, the southernmost stop on the highway.

0 ·········· km ·········· 100
0 ·········· miles ·········· 100

ELEVATION PROFILE

4,000 ft
(1,219 m)

0

0   750 miles (1,208 km)

CENTRAL AND SOUTH AMERICA

REFUEL
Casa Tropera

By the time you reach the welcoming regional capital Coyhaique, you'll have earned a treat. Head over to the Casa Tropera microbrewery *(tropera.cl)* for a refreshing and much-deserved *cerveza*—Tropera's range includes lagers, blond beers, IPAs, and porters— accompanied by a hearty burger, sandwich, or sharing platter to carb-load for the ride ahead.

As you pedal south from Puerto Montt, initially hugging the shimmering coastline, Chile slowly breaks up into a tangle of islands, peninsulas, and channels. The terrain grows steadily wilder, towns and villages become ever more sparse, and the paved surface is largely replaced by gravel and dirt (a combination known locally as *ripio*), much of it in a bone-shaking washboard pattern—you'll need all the suspension you've got to tackle it.

Pedaling along rough roads lined with dense foliage, you'll soon reach Pumalín, one of Chile's newest national parks. This is a great place to stretch your legs off the bike, with trails through moss-scented forests of towering alerce trees, some more than 3,000 years old—plus bracingly cold rivers, lakes, and waterfalls, where you can refresh your tired limbs.

As you continue south, rounding the placid, trout-filled waters of Lake Yelcho— shaded by snowy peaks and tree-covered hills—you'll gradually find your rhythm, gaining confidence on the *ripio* and steeling yourself against the inclement weather. Farther along, the highway weaves between mountains of emerald-green forest as it traces the route of two serpentine rivers—first the Frio and then the Palena—tinged with hues of electric blue and turquoise. A little farther south, legs definitely aching now, you'll reach Puyuhuapi, a mist-shrouded village on the shoreline of a gorgeous fjord. Take time out here to visit one of the hot springs, ideal for any cyclists feeling a little saddlesore, and call into the nearby Parque Nacional Queulat, home to a famous "hanging glacier" seemingly suspended from a cliff face.

Farther on, between the city of Coyhaique and the hamlet of Villa Cerro Castillo, you'll reach the highest point on

Walking in the Parque Nacional Pumalín, a worthwhile stop-off on the Carretera Austral

The Yelcho Bridge, crossing over the eponymous river that feeds into Lake Yelcho

the ride, a 3,537-ft (1,078-m) pass. It's a steep and draining ascent, but the sense of achievement at the summit is immense—and, even better, is swiftly followed by the adrenaline rush of the descent. From there, the highway loops through largely uninhabited wilderness until you reach the vast Lago General Carréra, which has a warm microclimate and small settlements dotted along its edges. As you skirt the plains of the Reserva Nacional Tamango, home to rare huemul deer, you may glimpse the recently rewilded Parque Nacional Patagonia in the distance—but don't get too distracted, as you'll need to concentrate for the tricky stretch of *ripio* that follows.

Eventually, exhausted but elated, you'll reach the end of the road. Flanked by tall peaks, the peaceful village of Villa O'Higgins is an appropriately far-flung place to finish this remote ride down the Carretera Austral.

MAKE IT LONGER
El Chaltén

From Villa O'Higgins, adventurous cyclists can continue across the border into Argentina. A tough but rewarding one-day ride— via off-road tracks and two ferry crossings—takes you to the trekking center of El Chaltén, gateway to the spectacular Parque Nacional Los Glaciares.

CENTRAL AND SOUTH AMERICA

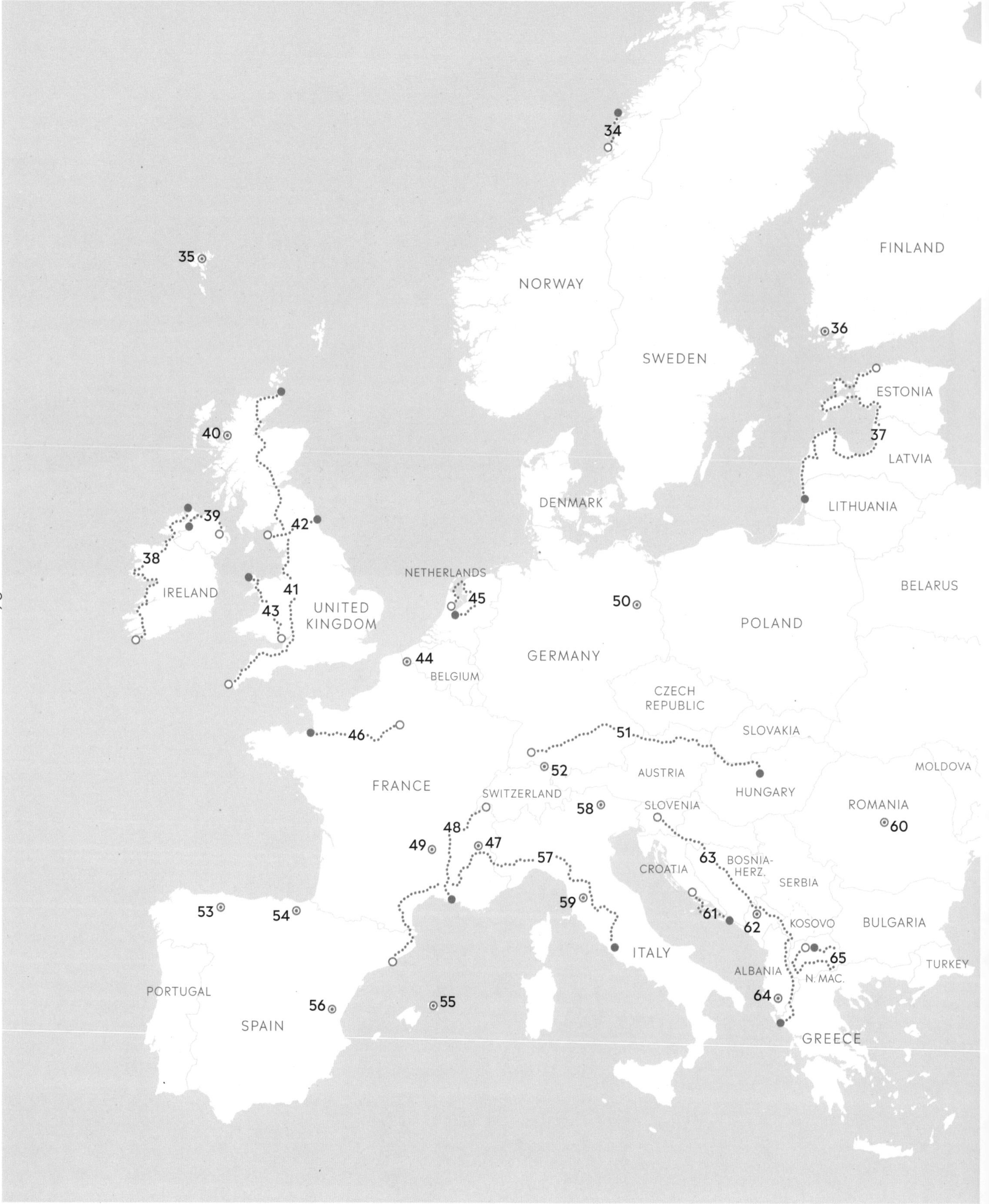

FINLAND

NORWAY

SWEDEN

34

35

36

ESTONIA

37

LATVIA

LITHUANIA

BELARUS

40

42

39

38

IRELAND

41

43

UNITED
KINGDOM

NETHERLANDS

45

44

BELGIUM

GERMANY

POLAND

50

DENMARK

CZECH
REPUBLIC

SLOVAKIA

51

MOLDOVA

46

FRANCE

52

AUSTRIA

HUNGARY

ROMANIA

58

SLOVENIA

60

SWITZERLAND

48

49

47

57

63

CROATIA

BOSNIA-
HERZ.

SERBIA

53

54

59

61

62

KOSOVO

BULGARIA

PORTUGAL

SPAIN

56

55

ALBANIA

64

65

N. MAC.

TURKEY

ITALY

GREECE

UKRAINE

EUROPE

34

Helgeland Coast

BRØNNØYSUND TO SANDNESSJØEN, NORWAY

Explore a little-visited corner of Scandinavia on this tour of Helgeland, a remote island chain in northern Norway. Here, the fairy-tale landscapes are every bit as appealing as the local cycling facilities.

126 MILES (204 KM) · 4,396 FT (1,340 M) · PAVED / GRAVEL

Helgeland is home to more islands than people; over 6,500 of these rugged isles rise majestically out of the dark-blue sea. While cycling here, the islands and their mountain peaks are a constant, comforting presence. They form shapes that look as if they've been lifted from a storybook, so it's no surprise that local legends about them abound. There's Dønnamannen, the range that looks like a giant who's lying down to look at the stars; Torghatten, a mountain with a big hole in its center, which formed when the King of Sømnafjellene threw his hat to block a deadly arrow; and Seven Sisters, the troll daughters who snuck out when their father fell asleep but were turned into stone. These mythic forms are so pronounced that they'll help you orientate exactly where you are on the archipelago as you pedal along.

Hugging the windswept coastline for most of the way, the route tracks across three small islands: Vega, Herøy, and Dønna. Happily, these closely clustered isles are serviced by an efficient ferry system that, along with providing picturesque views, makes the logistics of cycle touring Helgeland's coastline a breeze. Many of the accommodations are helpfully geared toward cyclists—look out for official "Syklist Velkommen" signs, which indicate secure bike parking, late-night food, and packed-lunch options, plus facilities to dry and wash clothes.

The ride itself is reasonably relaxed, following paved and gravel roads on which cars are generally infrequent. That said, the route is fairly undulating in parts—locals call the gradient "Norwegian flat," with a wink—though there are (thankfully) no epic mountain climbs. Expect to see traditional wooden houses, renovated

REFUEL

Vegalefsa Voom

Power your ride like a local by gorging on *lefse*, a tasty Norwegian pastry that's a bit like a pancake and is a great source of energy. The local version, *vegalefsa*, is filled with butter, sugar, and cinnamon and sold at the Sandmo Farm Bakery (*sandmogard.no*) on Vega.

Looking out over the archipelago from Vega

fishing huts, and cute cabins in hues of mustard, brick red, and gray everywhere you look—the only problem is, they're so photogenic that you'll constantly want to stop and take pictures. Ditto the golden-sand beaches, deserted other than the odd string of seaweed or immaculately maintained wooden fishing boat.

Helgeland is just below the Arctic Circle, which makes for beautiful light but extreme and variable weather conditions. Summers are usually kind, but you should be prepared for showers and pack water-proof clothing. This definitely isn't a route you should take on in winter. Then, the islands are best left to the locals, who hunker down while the snow blankets their fairy-tale landscapes.

Spend the night at **ELFIS SJØSTUER**, which means "sea camp," on the island of Herøy. The waterfront setting is breathtaking.

Park your bike beside the old wharf and head into **HEIDI'S CHOCOLATE FACTORY** in Dønna for a tour and tasting.

Heidi's Chocolate Factory

Dønna

● Sandnessjøen

Herøy

Elfis Sjøstuer

Visit the **VEGA WORLD HERITAGE CENTRE** to learn all about the relationship between the locals and eider ducks, and how—partly due to this—the island was awarded UNESCO status.

Tjøtta

Vega World
Heritage Centre

Vega Havhotell

Gladstad

Vega

NORWAY

0 ·········· km ·········· 20
0 ·········· miles ·········· 20

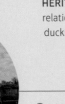

Treat yourself to a delicious meal cooked by one of Norway's most famous chefs, Jon Aga, at the grass-roofed **VEGA HAVHOTELL**.

Brønnøysund

ELEVATION PROFILE

650 ft
(198 m)

0

0   126 miles (204 km)

While cycling here, the islands and their mountain peaks are a constant, comforting presence.

Save some energy for a guided hike up to the islands' spectacular northernmost extremity—the vertiginous cliff at **CAPE ENNIBERG**, raucous with seabirds.

Detour along the peaceful Saksunardalur valley to the lonely hamlet of **SAKSUN**, perched above a lagoon fed by ribbonlike waterfalls.

Roam the narrow backstreets and tar-blackened wood cabins of Tinganes, the medieval old quarter of **TÓRSHAVN**.

FAROE ISLANDS

Cape Enniberg
Viðareiði
Hvannasund
Eiði
Gjógv
Saksun
Leirvik
Sørvágur
Miðvágur
Toftir
Tórshavn
Kirkjubøur

0 ······· km ······· 20
0 ······· miles ······· 20

Visit the Viking settlement at **KIRKJUBØUR**—its 900-year-old farmhouse is one of the oldest inhabited timber houses in the world.

35

Five-Island Faroes Epic

SØRVÁGUR, VÁGAR, FAROE ISLANDS (LOOP)

Explore the extremities of these wild North Atlantic isles on a challenging circuit past ancient Viking villages, sparkling fjords, and sheer, seabird-thronged cliffs.

218 MILES (351 KM)

18,475 FT (5,631 M)

PAVED

One thing you can predict about your Faroese odyssey: it'll be unpredictable. Not for nothing was this craggy archipelago dubbed "the Land of Maybe"—you can expect four seasons in one day here, with sun, showers, buffeting winds, and even snow in quick succession. But that epithet also captures the wonder of this cycling circuit, where you can pick and choose stops according to the weather and your mood.

The route starts on Vágar, leading you across the Faroes' five principal islands via undersea tunnels (these can be long and dark, so are best traveled on the local bike-friendly buses). Distances stretch on roads that hairpin around fractal coastlines and sheer peaks, with each bend revealing a fresh surprise. You'll pass thundering cascades, rainbow-hued fishing villages, and surf-smashed sea stacks and see tempting detours to Viking-era settlements, ancient grass-roofed churches, and cliffs lined with legions of birds. Sure, the hills en route are a challenge—but conquer those and you'll enjoy a cycling experience worthy of its own epic saga.

ELEVATION PROFILE

3,000 ft (914 m)

0

0

218 miles (351 km)

36

Turku Archipelago

TURKU, FINLAND (LOOP)

Go island-hopping across one of the world's most beautiful archipelagos. You'll discover the laid-back rhythm of Finnish life on this leisurely loop, which was made for relaxed touring.

149 MILES (240 KM) — 3,888 FT (1,185 M) — PAVED / GRAVEL

Known as Turun Saaristo in Finnish and Åbo Skargård in Swedish—the first language of many in this region—the Turku Archipelago is made up of 20,000 islands scattered off the coast of Finland. The landscape here is imbued with a natural sense of calm and, unless you're racing to catch the next ferry, there's little reason to hurry.

Setting off from the lively city of Turku, the route winds alongside rocky bays, past traditional wooden houses, and through rustling forest. Time seems to slow with each pedal stroke, giving you the chance to bask in the archipelago's beauty. There are plenty of chances to stop along the way: pause to admire the ship models that are a feature of many churches and gaze at the decorative Midsummer Poles found in every village. Take time, too, for exploratory detours down quiet side roads or forest paths, or simply perch on sun-warmed granite and look out over the inky-blue, island-speckled sea.

Top Tip
The full circuit is only feasible in summer (roughly June–August), as some ferries are seasonal.

Spend a day in **NAANTALI**, one of the best-preserved wooden towns in Finland. Its quaint harbor is a particularly pleasant spot to wander around.

Relax and enjoy the scenery on the **MOSSALA TO INIÖ FERRY**, the longest crossing on the route. Look out for birds, such as common and Arctic terns.

FINLAND

Taivassalo
Naantali
Turku
Pargas
Nagu
Korppoo

Spend the night in picturesque **KORPPOO**, home to a pretty harbor, a striking stone church, and two intriguing local history museums.

0 ···· km ···· 20
0 ···· miles ···· 20

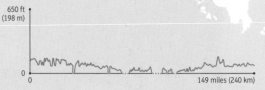

ELEVATION PROFILE

650 ft (198 m)

0

0   149 miles (240 km)

95

EUROPE

The colorful old town of Tallinn, the capital of Estonia

955 MILES (1,537 KM)

13,370 FT (4,075 M)

PAVED / GRAVEL

37

Baltic Sea Cycle

TALLINN, ESTONIA, TO NIDA, LITHUANIA

This is a route for lovers of nature and solitude. You'll discover the spiritual heart of the Baltics here, touring past gently scenic villages, woods, and seasides.

The three Baltic States—Estonia, Latvia, and Lithuania—make up one of Europe's least explored but most distinctive corners. They're not quite European, not quite Scandinavian, and not quite Russian, with wide natural spaces that come from having a combined population less than that of Madrid. This route takes you from the Estonian capital of Tallinn to the Lithuanian port city of Klaipėda along a section of the EV10—part of the Eurovelo network of cycle routes, running 5,282 miles (8,500 km) around the Baltic Sea.

It's a coastal ride, but don't expect one long promenade. Much of the route is actually inland, with the sea evident only as a salty tang in the air. Aside from the capitals and a few large towns, these are mainly lands of pine woods, low-key farms, big skies, and flat horizons.

ELEVATION PROFILE

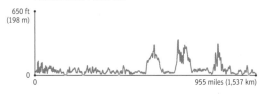

650 ft (198 m)

0

0   955 miles (1,537 km)

The second-largest island in Estonia, **HIIUMAA** is recognized by UNESCO for its sustainable and eco-friendly lifestyle.

Compare past and present **TALLINN** with a walk around the medieval old town and a cycle through the dynamic modern city along waterside bike paths.

Tallinn

ESTONIA

Haapsalu

Hiiumaa

Muhu

Saaremaa

Pärnu

Kuressaare

Marvel at the unexpected sight of nine meteorite craters at **SAAREMAA**, created around 3,500 years ago.

Explore the colorful Baroque churches and tree-lined streets of the lively beach resort of **PÄRNU**.

Salacgrīva

Ventspils

LATVIA

Jūrmala

Experience life as an inmate in **KAROSTA PRISON**, a bizarre museum-adventure that re-creates the Baltics' turbulent Soviet past.

Kuldīga

Tukums

Rīga

Karosta

Liepāja

Admire the Art Nouveau architecture and walk the splendidly restored pedestrian streets of **RĪGA**.

LITHUANIA

Ride to the end of the long L-shaped wooden pier in **PALANGA** for a bracing out-to-sea feel, then warm yourself in one of the resort's bars, cafés, or bistros.

Palanga

Klaipėda

Curonian Spit

Nida

0 ········· km ········· 50

0 ········· miles ········· 50

Distances here are short: it's never far to the next historic town square or village, and there's always a good wild camping spot around the corner. You'll have most of the route to yourself, and the only sounds will be breeze, birdsong, maybe the tide—and the hum of tires on back-road pavement or the gentle crunch of forest road. Meals will be Baltic-style, with simple but tasty dishes of porridge, yogurt, black bread, stews, smoked fish, foraged berries, and mushrooms, perhaps washed down with a Lithuanian craft beer or Rīga Black Balsam liqueur. And, like the laid-back locals, you'll find a gentle calm in contemplating the serenity of your surroundings.

The first half is in Estonia—the most developed and Western European of the three countries, with the best signage and surfaces. It can feel like nearby Finland, with its smooth cycle paths, unpaved but

Changing States

The Baltic States were part of the Russian Empire for centuries until they gained independence in 1918. However, they were soon reoccupied and annexed by the Soviet Union (though Nazi Germany briefly had control during World War II). After the Berlin Wall fell in 1989, the states fought for independence again, finally achieving it in 1991. All three states joined the EU (and NATO) in 2004.

well-kept forest tracks, e-savvy villages, and an outdoor culture that actively encourages wild camping (and saunas). The similarities aren't all that surprising: the Estonian language resembles Finnish, and cultural links are strong.

Starting in Tallinn, you head west to the picturesque town of Haapsalu for the ferry across to the islands of Hiiumaa, Saaremaa, and Muhu. For many riders doing the EV10, the islands are a major highlight of the trip, so there's no reason to rush. Old-world thatched cottages, windmills, and the odd castle look out over the endless gray-blue sea, and brightly painted boats bob up and down by the jetty. The only other people exploring the nature reserves are likely to be fellow bike tourists, and the only people in a hurry are Estonian road cyclists, out training on the smooth, empty roads.

Back on the mainland via another ferry, whispering forest tracks and softly murmuring paved country lanes take you to the seaside town of Pärnu, which may feel like a noisy metropolis after the hush of the islands. But the urban hum doesn't last for long—tranquility is soon restored as you head south to the Latvian border.

Pausing outside the Koguva Kula village museum on Muhu island, Estonia

Land of Milk

The Baltic tradition of dairy farming means milk products are common and deliciously high quality. Breakfasts in particular will feature some or all of milk, curd, cottage cheese, sour cream, kefir (fermented milk), and yogurt, in addition to berries, jams, and fresh bread. For many riders, drinking yogurt is a staple (and cheap) keep-you-going energy source.

As you enter Latvia, things subtly change. The landscapes feel similar to—and yet distinct from—those you traveled through in Estonia: as unassuming and quiet, but with swathes of pastureland punctuated by wooden houses and brick cottages. In fine spring or summer weather, the rural meadows will be bright with flowers.

The EV10 route is less clear here. Signage is more haphazard, surfaces not quite so consistent, and facilities more modest. Camping won't be as easy as in Estonia. But the Baltics are far enough north that summer days are long and June and July nights never really get dark, so there'll be plenty of time—even in late evening—to find the ideal campsite away from the road (and the bogs).

To avoid sandy seaside tracks and busy main roads, the route cuts inland after Salacgrīva, a pleasant lighthouse town of boxy wooden houses. Signposts give up just outside Rīga, but it's obvious which way to go, and you'll soon be in its grand historic center—full of trendy hostels, bars, and restaurants—and probably walking the bike in preference to rattling over the cobblestones.

Just west of Rīga is the elegant spa resort of Jūrmala, where the trail runs alongside the beach. After a stretch of suburban highway, normal EV10 service is resumed, with long, straight, quiet paved roads through shady woods as you cross inland. On this section you'll pass through Tukums, a pleasant town with old buildings in pastel shades, attractive squares, and

Above Following the route along the beautiful sandy beach at Jūrmala

Below Sidewalk cafés in Dome Square, at the heart of Rīga's old town

fairy-tale castles and churches, as well as Kuldīga, Latvia's "Venice of the North." There are no gondolas here, but you'll find plenty of snug bars and cafés where you can fuel up on rustic stews and soups.

Russia's influence over the Baltics has loomed large for centuries, and there's a sharp reminder of this as you ride through Karosta, a former military base. While the rural Baltics in May are delightful, old garrison towns like this one can be grim in a wet November. Today, Karosta is a suburb of the more cheery cultural resort of Liepāja. It's known locally as the "city of wind" and, once over another frictionless border into Lithuania, it's clear why, as you follow the shoreline gusts and sandy paths to the seaside town of Palanga.

Shortly beyond is the historic city of Klaipėda, which signals that your Baltic journey is coming to an end. But the ride's not over just yet—Klaipėda is the gateway for the Curonian Spit, one of Europe's more unusual biking experiences. This narrow filament of sand is held together by pine trees and extends 31 miles (50 km) out to sea, touching the border with Kaliningrad, a detached piece of Russia. At times it's only a few yards wide, with water to the horizon on both sides—it feels like cycling on a road across the ocean. What more fitting way to end this long, coastal ride than surrounded by sea?

MAKE IT LONGER

Iron Curtain Trail

The EV10 forms part of the even longer Eurovelo route EV13, or Iron Curtain Trail, which runs 6,183 miles (9,950 km) from the Barents Sea to the Black Sea, along the former border between Western and Eastern Europe. It's a mighty cross-continental trip that will take you through a staggering 16 countries.

A group of cyclists pedalling past dark-green pine trees on the Curonian Spit in Lithuania

38

MizMal

MIZEN HEAD TO MALIN HEAD, IRELAND

Both a cycle for sore eyes and sore thighs, this classic along Ireland's entire western fringe is a journey into the nation's Gaelic culture amid some of the wildest landscapes in Europe.

591 MILES (952 KM)

31,778 FT (9,686 M)

PAVED

Linger long enough in a local pub and you'll be sure to experience the famed Gaelic *craic*

Cycling the length of a country is a feat of endeavor and achievement. At times you will find this ride formidably rugged and there will be moments when your calves scream "enough!" But these moments pass faster than the Atlantic Coast's fleeting liquid sunshine, because beyond every bend awaits yet more of Ireland's dramatic scenery.

Your motivations to forge ever onward will be many: rainbows arcing across the skyline; the surging Atlantic pulverizing brooding cliffs; distant outlines of stoic castles, once symbolic of oppression during the troubled era of British rule over Ireland. And then there's the inevitable heartfelt welcome you'll receive in the small traditional villages you pass through along the way. Linger long enough in a local pub and you'll be sure to experience the famed Gaelic *craic*, accompanied by tasty fresh seafood, fine beer and whiskey, and the melodious sounds of a fiddle or penny whistle.

The route itself is the brainchild of Northern Irishman Paul Kennedy, who, after taking some friends cycling along Ireland's magnificently moody Atlantic Coast, dared to dream. Nobody else was running tours along the entire length of Ireland, so he quit his job in IT and formed Wild Atlantic Cycling to guide bike tours along this route. Paul even registered the name MizMal—a portmanteau of the southernmost and northernmost points of Ireland, Mizen Head and Malin Head—as a trademark.

Riding along a rural section of traffic-free trail near Westport in County Mayo

ELEVATION PROFILE

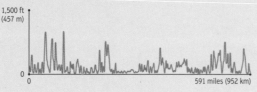

1,500 ft
(457 m)

0

0   591 miles (952 km)

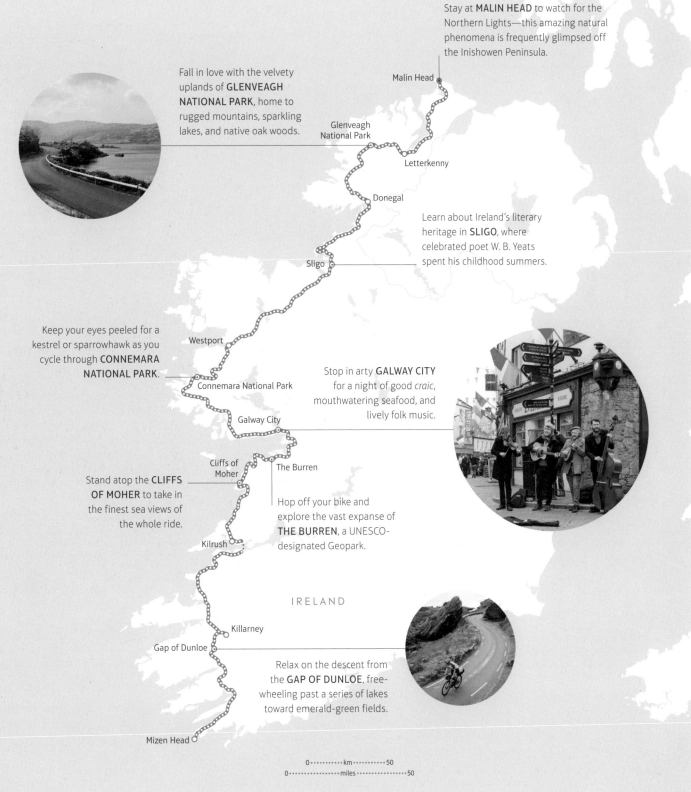

Stay at **MALIN HEAD** to watch for the Northern Lights—this amazing natural phenomena is frequently glimpsed off the Inishowen Peninsula.

Malin Head

Fall in love with the velvety uplands of **GLENVEAGH NATIONAL PARK**, home to rugged mountains, sparkling lakes, and native oak woods.

Glenveagh National Park

Letterkenny

Donegal

Learn about Ireland's literary heritage in **SLIGO**, where celebrated poet W. B. Yeats spent his childhood summers.

Sligo

Westport

Keep your eyes peeled for a kestrel or sparrowhawk as you cycle through **CONNEMARA NATIONAL PARK**.

Connemara National Park

Stop in arty **GALWAY CITY** for a night of good *craic*, mouthwatering seafood, and lively folk music.

Galway City

Cliffs of Moher

The Burren

Stand atop the **CLIFFS OF MOHER** to take in the finest sea views of the whole ride.

Hop off your bike and explore the vast expanse of **THE BURREN**, a UNESCO-designated Geopark.

Kilrush

IRELAND

Killarney

Gap of Dunloe

Relax on the descent from the **GAP OF DUNLOE**, free-wheeling past a series of lakes toward emerald-green fields.

Mizen Head

0 ·········· km ·········· 50
0 ·········· miles ·········· 50

The ride starts as it continues, with a steep pedal around the gnarly cliffs of Mizen Head and into Kerry's verdant mountains. There'll be a few cars in summer on the minor roads, exploring the touring route of the Wild Atlantic Way, but you'll never feel harried here.

Kerry is famous for its cows, but less so for the secretive Black Valley, a wild and remote landscape of sculpted tawny hills and tumbling streams. A pulsating, twisting descent into this pinched heather-filled valley ends with a bang: a hard-going but exhilarating slog up the majestic Gap of Dunloe. This narrow mountain pass takes you past a picturesque stone bridge known as the Wishing Bridge, where you might want to pause to request some magical assistance for your tired legs.

Beyond Ireland's longest river, the Shannon, the route heads into counties Clare and Galway, coming within sight of the steely Atlantic Ocean. Perhaps you'll see a basking shark lolling in the shallows of the daunting cliffs, none of which casts a greater shadow over the ocean than the immense Cliffs of Moher. It may be hard to believe, but beyond Moher, the scenery just keeps getting better. Farther up the coast lies a surreal loop around a natural limestone pavement cracked in a checkerboard pattern; known as the Burren, it was formed 350 million years ago, in long-gone lime-rich seas.

There's a chance to chill a bit thereafter amid the Bogs of Connemara: flat peatlands where the soft grasses toast reddish-orange in summer. You'll then skim past the haunting Classiebawn Castle in Sligo, where Earl Mountbatten was assassinated by the IRA in 1979, before passing by Drumcliffe Church, where you can pay homage to W. B. Yeats, interred in the cemetery. While Yeats can lay claim to

REFUEL
Seafood Chowder

Harmonizing the best of western Ireland's ocean produce and the need for replacement carbohydrates, a welcoming bowl of chowder can be had in pubs and restaurants along the length of the MizMal. It'll typically feature cod, smoked haddock, shrimp, and mussels, with the added oomph of potatoes and lashings of cream. Of course, it's great washed down with a pint of—well, no need to tell you what.

the title of Ireland's greatest poet, it was his contemporary Oscar Wilde who perhaps best summed up this coast when he described it as "a savage beauty."

By the time you've drained your last drop of Guinness or Jameson's whiskey and your legs have recharged, gird yourself for one final craggy ascent on the dramatic Inishowen Peninsula. The end comes with a venomous kick to Malin Head lighthouse, marking the culmination of your ride. All that lies ahead of you now is the intense satisfaction of your achievement and sweeping views over the Atlantic Ocean.

Opposite The towering Cliffs of Moher on the Atlantic Coast

Below A lakeside stretch of the MizMal through Connemara National Park

Spend some time exploring the famous **GIANT'S CAUSEWAY**, a vast terrace of hexagonal stone columns that resemble a giant's rough garden patio.

Make a short detour to the wobbly, vertiginous **CARRICK-A-REDE ROPE BRIDGE**, which vaults from a mainland clifftop to an island opposite.

IRELAND

NORTHERN IRELAND

Giant's Causeway

Ballycastle

Coleraine

Derry

Cushendall

Glenarm

Larne

Belfast

DERRY's 17th-century city walls are among the most complete and unchanged in Europe—walk their length for fine views of the old town.

0 ·········· km ········· 25
0 ·········· miles ········ 25

Take a pre-ride tour of the political murals in **BELFAST** for an insight into Northern Ireland's troubled history.

39

Antrim Coast

BELFAST TO DERRY, UK

Wheel around the northeast seaboard of Northern Ireland along a spectacular coastal road. You'll hug the shore under Antrim's hills, with Scotland looking almost close enough to touch.

145 MILES (233 KM)

7,205 FT (2,196 M)

PAVED

Although it begins in the heart of Belfast, this ride is mostly a rural waterside journey. Riverside cycle paths lead you out of the city, but it's not until Larne that you rejoin the coast. And what a road you emerge onto—long and flat, snaking around the shore, with steep cliffs on one side and sparkling sea and Scottish mountains on the other. It's not all easy riding, though. Stiff hill climbs on narrow back lanes give your legs a workout—and provide lofty views—before you swoop down to historic villages such as Glenarm or Cushendall for a well-earned rest in a cozy village pub. A brief dip into Ireland (via ferry) brings a scenic segment alongside splendid Loch Foyle, with the final leg taking you back over the border and into Derry. Mark your arrival at Northern Ireland's second city with a ride across the landmark Peace Bridge, before pedaling off to explore its urban charms.

ELEVATION PROFILE

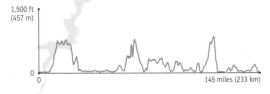

1,500 ft
(457 m)

0

0   145 miles (233 km)

40
Applecross Peninsula

ACHNASHEEN, UK (LOOP)

Brace your legs. This undulating tour around the rugged Applecross Peninsula will test both your resolve and your thighs—but it'll also reward you with some of Scotland's most stunning coastal scenery.

Bealach na Ba, twisting through the rugged Scottish Highlands

90 MILES (145 KM)

6,100 FT (1,860 M)

PAVED

Beginning in the diminutive village of Achnasheen, at the center of the northern Highlands, this circular ride gets off to a deceptively easy start. The gentle road to Lochcarron winds through green valleys and alongside sparkling lakes before delivering you to the bottom of the infamous Bealach na Ba. This 5-mile (8-km) road ascends 2,054 ft (626 m), taxing both body and mind with hairpin bends of up to 20 percent. The pain you'll feel is more than worth it though—from the top you'll be treated to spectacular views over the brooding Isle of Skye and the idyllic Outer Hebrides. And if this panorama doesn't take your breath away, then the steep descent back to sea level certainly will.

On reaching Applecross village, you might think the hard part is over—but you'd be wrong. The route then follows a gruelling coastal road that demands a further 3,250 ft (990 m) of climbing, before oscillating along the mountain-lined Glen Torridon. By the time you get back to Achnasheen, you'll definitely have earned a dram or two.

ELEVATION PROFILE

3,000 ft (914 m)

0

0   90 miles (145 km)

Take a break from the bike at the coastal village of **SHIELDAIG**, offering stunning views over Loch Shieldaig, as well as a friendly pub and award-winning café.

Pop into the Walled Garden in **APPLECROSS**. This small market garden is nestled in the Applecross Estate and serves delicious food from its converted glasshouse café.

The top of **BEALACH NA BA** offers expansive views over the Western Isles—though there's a strong possibility that you'll find the pass's summit completely encased in cloud.

Kinlochewe

Achnasheen

Torridon

Shieldaig

SCOTLAND

Applecross

Bealach na Ba

Lochcarron

0 ·········· km ·········· 10
0 ·········· miles ·········· 10

41

Britain End to End

LAND'S END TO JOHN O'GROATS, UK

The ultimate British cycle ride, the End to End is a fascinating cross section of the island's scenery, history, and culture—and a challenging rite of passage that will make you a member of the nation's cycling elite.

1,099 MILES (1,769 KM)

48,150 FT (14,676 M)

PAVED

Ask any self-respecting British cyclist, and they've either done the End to End, or they're hoping to. This bucket-list favorite is like a degree in touring, with its own qualification abbreviations to put after your name: E2E (End to End); LEJOG (Land's End–John o'Groats); JOGLE (John o'Groats–Land's End).

Without a doubt, it's a physical challenge—tough on the lungs and the thighs, and leaving you crawling upstairs on all fours by the time you finish. But it's also about life-affirming memories. Trim villages with tiny churches and pond-side tearooms; restless cities pulsing with sports, music, and commerce. Sociable evenings in traditional market-square pubs; wild-camping solitude by far-flung lakesides. Grand monuments recalling major historical events; quirky museums about pencils or lawnmowers. A sunny picnic by an ancient packhorse bridge; the shivering chocolate-bar refuel as you wait out a downpour in a bus shelter.

Riding along a clifftop country lane on the north Devon coast

There's no standard route for this ride, but whichever way you go, you'll get a top-to-bottom (or bottom-to-top) study of all sides of Britain—and of yourself. There are plenty of organized tour options to choose from, which come with the benefit of accommodations (and luggage transfers) being provided for you, but if you prefer more freedom, you can plan your own journey. The only givens for the ride are the start and end points. Some people finish in a week—pounding main roads at more than 100 miles (160 km) a day—but the more time you take, the more rewarding it'll be.

ELEVATION PROFILE

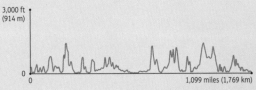

3,000 ft
(914 m)

0

0   1,099 miles (1,769 km)

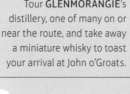

John o'Groats

Tour **GLENMORANGIE**'s distillery, one of many on or near the route, and take away a miniature whisky to toast your arrival at John o'Groats.

Top Tip

Bike space is limited on trains to Penzance (near Land's End) and back from Thurso (near John o'Groats). Book well in advance.

Glenmorangie Distillery

Inverness

SCOTLAND

Perth

Edinburgh

Clatter along the cobbled Royal Mile to **EDINBURGH**'s castle, followed by a walk up Arthur's Seat for mountaintop views in the city center.

Carlisle

Lancaster

Liverpool

Savor regional specialities in **LUDLOW**, one of England's best foodie towns—and also one of its prettiest, with a medieval castle and streets lined with half-timbered buildings.

ENGLAND

Ludlow

Hereford

WALES

Bristol

Cheddar Gorge

Barnstaple

Newquay

Land's End

St Michael's Mount

Wait for the tide to go out before crossing the cobbled road to **ST. MICHAEL'S MOUNT**, a rocky island housing a medieval church and castle.

ANOTHER WAY

Wilderness Challenge

LEJOG off-road is an off-the-scale challenge that offers extreme landscapes and rugged hills, well away from urban Britain. There's no standard route; the few hardy bikepackers who have completed it combine off-road bike trails such as the Pennine Bridleway and West Highland Way with bridle paths and country lanes.

Ride up the dramatic **CHEDDAR GORGE**, home to prehistoric caves that have provided people with shelter here for over 40,000 years.

0 ·········· km ·········· 100
0 ·········· miles ·········· 100

REFUEL
Scottish Staple

Scotland's classic dinner of haggis, neeps, and tatties (spiced offal or a vegetarian/vegan alternative, mashed turnips, and mashed potatoes) is a delicious must-try, and a staple of pretty much all pub and café menus north of the border. In a hurry? Get an order of haggis and fries from a local fish-and-chip shop instead.

Stopping for supplies in Exford, a rural village in Somerset

This ride combines several National Cycle Network routes to showcase a range of cities, towns, and villages, as well as a selection of remarkable sights, natural and man-made. It kicks off on the wild, windy cliffs of Land's End, where a simple white signpost marks the start of your tour. The prevailing tailwind here will be welcome: the first two days are the toughest of the trip. Cornwall and Devon are decidedly hilly, with gradients of up to 30 percent—there's no shame in getting off to push.

Constantly changing views will more than make up for it, though—as will the copious meat pies and cream teas. Here, as throughout Britain, café and restaurant menus are often chic and locally sourced, while fresh picnics can be easily assembled from artisan bakeries and street markets—and perhaps even the odd honesty-box farm stall.

The terrain levels out as you enter Somerset, which comes as a relief to weary legs. Soothe your aching body parts by treating yourself to a pint of local cider from one of England's many thriving craft breweries. Don't worry if it's cloudy—like the weather, that's entirely normal.

From here, Middle England passes in a pleasant blur of tiny lanes, country pubs, winding roads, and gentle farmland. One old market cross or flower-covered cottage may be hard to distinguish from the next when you look through your pictures.

As you head farther north, things get grittier and more dramatic. Cottage roofs turn from thatch to slate; village houses fade from honey-colored to gray; and cafés and pubs begin to feel more like a traveler's refuge. Narrow lanes pick their way through austere hills and moors, and for hours at a time you'll have only sheep as your riding companions.

You head up into the Highlands through ever-bigger and ever-barer mountain landscapes. Villages and towns get steadily farther apart, with settlements almost outnumbered by whisky distilleries

Crossing into Scotland takes you through the beautiful, unsung Borders region, where the traditional shops and streets—and lack of phone signal—make it feel like you've stepped back into the 1960s. After Edinburgh and the old Forth Bridge (open to bikes but not cars), you head up into the Highlands through ever-bigger and ever-barer mountain landscapes. Villages and towns get steadily farther apart, with settlements almost outnumbered by whisky distilleries (often convenient places to visit, especially to dodge a rain shower).

Wilderness takes over in the far north, but climbs will be fewer and more gradual—though often longer—than you might expect. At last, the sea appears on the horizon and you arrive with euphoria, or perhaps simply relief, at the John o'Groats signpost that mirrors the one at Land's End. Say cheese: your final selfie here is your cycling graduation photo.

Cycling through spring sleet in the Scottish Highlands

ANOTHER WAY
Go Off-Road

Want to ride where few C2Cers venture? Then take the off-road Old Coach option from Keswick. This lung-busting, rubble-strewn climb feels like hell, but you'll be in heaven after cresting the initial gradient. Enjoy staggering views toward the iconic Lakeland peak of Blencathra, along a now easy off-road upland plateau ride.

42
Sea to Sea

WHITEHAVEN TO TYNEMOUTH, UK

This is the must-do ride in northern England. Running between two charming seaside towns, the iconic Sea to Sea takes you on a journey through the region's rich history, from bucolic to post-industrial, passing by spectacular vistas on the way.

140 MILES (225 KM) · 16,535 FT (5,040 M) · PAVED / GRAVEL

There are actually several variations of the Sea to Sea (or C2C), but they all share the same goal—to travel across the width of England, between the Irish and the North seas. This ride follows the classic route, starting on the west coast in the Georgian town of Whitehaven. Before you set off, there's an important ritual to carry out: tradition says you must begin the ride by dipping your back wheel in the Irish Sea.

Formalities over, a steady climb along a quiet railpath leads you into the Lake District, where a typically romantic landscape awaits: sheep-speckled fields and rolling mountains, dotted with centuries-old farmsteads and historic inns. Yet more climbs (are you sensing a theme here?) take you onto the "roof" of England—the North Pennines. Evidence of the area's

Rolling through the quintessential green countryside of the Lake District

industrial past is dotted across these lonely hills, including former mine workers' cottages, nestled idyllically in the folds of the rugged moors. But modern civilization soon beckons as you sweep through a sea of heather and emerge into energetic, post-industrial Newcastle. From here, it's an easy pedal to the seaside town of Tynemouth, where the ride is only complete once your front wheel has touched the North Sea.

ELEVATION PROFILE

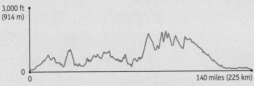

3,000 ft (914 m)

0

0   140 miles (225 km)

Pause at the tiny village of **ROOKHOPE**, where the remnants of Victorian mining structures lend the windswept moors a forlornly beautiful air.

Ponder the mysteries of the **CASTLERIGG STONE CIRCLE**, a 3,000-year-old monument, nestled in the heart of Lakeland's towering hills.

ENGLAND

Tynemouth

Newcastle

㊷

Rookhope

The C2C takes you right past **GATESHEAD MILLENNIUM BRIDGE**, the world's only tilting bridge. At night it becomes a glowing, high-tech light show.

Penrith

Whitehaven

Castlerigg
Stone Circle

Gaze at the **MENAI STRAITS** and imagine how farmers once swam their cattle through here before a bridge was built.

Holyhead

Menai Straits

Porthmadog

Harlech

WALES

Machynlleth

The descent into **HARLECH** provides one of the ride's most memorable views: Edward I's 13th-century castle towering over the coastal dunes from atop a rocky crag.

Rhayader

㊸

Brecon

Merthyr Tydfil

0 ········· km ········· 40
0 ········· miles ········· 40

Cardiff

43

Lon Las Cymru

CARDIFF TO HOLYHEAD, UK

Get ready to cycle the length of Wales on a demanding route that winds its way through some of the nation's most beautiful mountainous landscapes.

A showcase for the best of Welsh cycle touring, the Lon Las Cymru offers a little bit of everything that makes Wales special. It's got history: you'll pass countless crumbling castles and stop in traditional stone-built market towns. It's got adventure: you'll rattle down a former coach road clad with loose cobblestones and clatter across Wales's longest timber viaduct at Barmouth. And, of course, it's got plenty of climbs: between Cardiff and Holyhead your legs and lungs will be taken to task by the undulating hills of the Brecon Beacons, the wind-blasted Cambrian Mountains, and the lofty peaks of Snowdonia National Park. Just be sure to stock up on the local bara brith (a fruity bread)—it's a perfect hill-cyclists' snack.

257 MILES (413 KM)   15,236 FT (4,644 M)   PAVED / GRAVEL / DIRT

113

ELEVATION PROFILE

3,000 ft
(914 m)

0

0   257 miles (413 km)

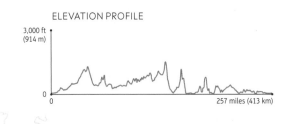

Immerse yourself in Welsh culture at St. Fagans National Museum of History in **CARDIFF**.

44

In Flanders Fields

YPRES, BELGIUM (LOOP)

Bicycles are a way of life in Belgium, and Ypres is no exception. Steeped in history from World War I, the town is flanked by some of the country's most scenic and challenging cycling.

55 MILES (88 KM)

2,675 FT (815 M)

PAVED

114

Tracing part of the iconic Gent–Wevelgem—In Flanders Fields race, an annual Spring Classic named after the war poem "In Flanders Fields" by Canadian soldier John McCrae, this testing ride weaves its way through the infamous hills of the French-Belgian border. With Ypres as its start and end point, the route incorporates some of the most grueling climbs in the region—and, indeed, the whole of Europe. In French Flanders, there's the Catsberg, or Mont des Cats. This 2.5-km (1.5-mile) climb averages 8 percent gradients and maxes out at a punishing 18 percent. On the Belgian side of the border stands the legendary Kemmelberg, West Flanders's highest point and the setting for the finale of the Gent–Wevelgem. At 512 ft (156 m), this snaking climb is paved with rectangular cobblestones, making an already difficult ascent even trickier to tackle.

But there's more to this ride than just a straightforward physical challenge. As the Gent–Wevelgem's name suggests, this is a route that's immersed in the history of World War I. Much of it passes through former battlefields, and you'll encounter numerous stark reminders of Flanders's conflict-strewn past as you pedal through the verdant countryside. Dozens of war cemeteries can be found along the route, and their somber lines of graves provide a sobering insight into the vast loss of life that occurred here over a century ago.

Moving memorials also stand in towns such as Dranouter, used by fighting units and field ambulances during World War I, and Mesen, the site of the Christmas Truce in 1914, where soldiers battling along the Western Front reportedly laid down their arms to play a football match. Even the Kemmelberg was the scene of a bloody battle in April 1918, and you can visit a monument at its summit that's dedicated to the French units who fought there.

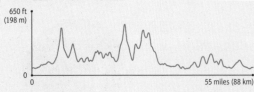

Boeschepe

Godewaerswelde

Catsberg

Rest at the top of the **CATSBERG** and visit the Mont des Cats Abbey, where you can refuel with some of its famous cheese.

ELEVATION PROFILE

650 ft
(198 m)

0

0   55 miles (88 km)

As you make your way back into Ypres, these thought-provoking historical records culminate with a cycle through the arched Menin Gate. This imposing war memorial marks the entry point to the town, and is the setting for a nightly service held to honor the war dead. For a fitting end to your tour, pay a visit to the nearby In Flanders Fields Museum. The monumental gray-stone building it's housed in was decimated during the conflict, and since being rebuilt now stands as a symbol of the town's—and region's—resilience.

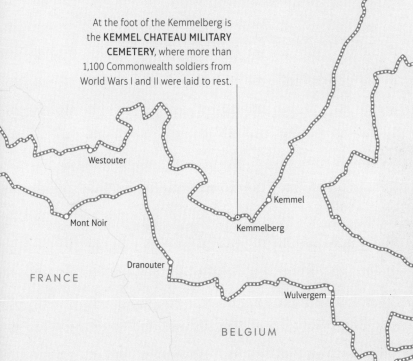

REFUEL
Belgian Beer

Just like bikes, beer is a way of life in Belgium. Combine the two with a mid-ride stopover at De Musette in Dranouter (*demusette.be*). This bike-friendly restaurant is the perfect place to quench your thirst with a smooth St. Bernardus beer and replenish your energy reserves with some mouthwatering Belgian *frites*.

The Menin Gate in **YPRES** is inscribed with the names of more than 54,000 British and Commonwealth soldiers who died in Belgium during World War I and have no known graves.

At the foot of the Kemmelberg is the **KEMMEL CHATEAU MILITARY CEMETERY**, where more than 1,100 Commonwealth soldiers from World Wars I and II were laid to rest.

Ypres

Zillebeke

Soak in the significance of the Christmas Truce at **MESEN**'s memorial, decorated with footballs from around the world.

Westouter

Kemmel

Mont Noir

Kemmelberg

Mesen

Dranouter

FRANCE

Wulvergem

BELGIUM

0 ·········· km ·········· 2
0 ·········· miles ·········· 2

45

Zuiderzeeroute

AMSTERDAM, NETHERLANDS (LOOP)

*From the canal-side pathways of historic Amsterdam, this waymarked route
explores the delightful towns of the "Golden Circle" around Lake IJssel, via
huge swathes of level countryside with an abundance of iconic windmills.*

250 MILES (403 KM)

1,600 FT (488 M)

PAVED

116

With dedicated cycle tracks and protected intersections, plus bicycle parking on every corner, the Netherlands is a haven for anyone who likes to travel on two wheels. For perfect proof of that fact, look no further than this relaxed, multiday ride. Signposted along its length and enjoying an absence of hills, this gentle route takes you through a quintessential Netherlands landscape.

The ride traces the outline of the IJssel, now a freshwater lake but once a large, shallow bay of the North Sea known as the Zuiderzee. Over the centuries, land has been reclaimed to create polders—low-lying areas protected by dykes—where you will rarely need to change gear. Heading north from Amsterdam, the trail follows the western shore of the lake through North Holland's rustic splendor, passing through a cornucopia of pleasant towns and villages. At Den Oever, you'll find the ingeniously engineered Afsluitdijk; this dam, completed in 1932, closed off the Zuiderzee from the North Sea. Riding across its causeway is a truly unique experience—for 20 miles (32 km) you have the wild North Sea to your left and the tame Lake IJssel to the right.

The local character changes a little across the water, as you enter the province of Fryslân, or Friesland, which has its own language (West Frisian) and is a great place to spy wildlife. Farmland birds such as skylarks and lapwings sing and dance overhead, and in winter you'll see enormous flocks of geese. There are also several thriving bases for watersports here, including Makkum—a good option for an aquatic rest day.

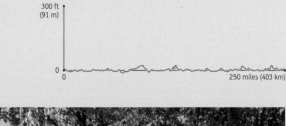

ELEVATION PROFILE

300 ft
(91 m)

0

0   250 miles (403 km)

The leafy path that
leads into the fortified
town of Naarden

As you leave behind Friesland and the shore of Lake IJssel, the route proceeds back to Amsterdam around the large polders that make up the province of Flevoland. Passing through old harbor towns that are no longer beside the sea, such as medieval Elburg and Spakenburg, you may see inhabitants still wearing the lace caps and high-shouldered floral *kraplaps* that make up the traditional Dutch costume. Savor these scenes of rural tranquility before you plunge back into the capital's urban bustle.

REFUEL
Everlasting Edam

In the charming town of Edam, visit the Kaaswaag weighing house to stock up on supplies of the eponymous cheese. Known for its smooth, sweet, and nutty flavour, Edam travels and ages well—at the peak of the Dutch Empire it was taken on voyages to all corners of the world.

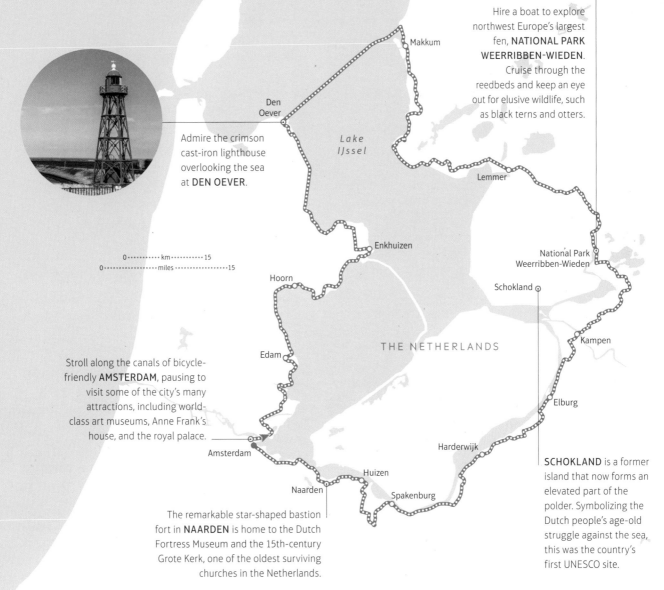

Hire a boat to explore northwest Europe's largest fen, **NATIONAL PARK WEERRIBBEN-WIEDEN.** Cruise through the reedbeds and keep an eye out for elusive wildlife, such as black terns and otters.

Admire the crimson cast-iron lighthouse overlooking the sea at **DEN OEVER.**

Makkum

Den Oever

Lake IJssel

Lemmer

Enkhuizen

National Park Weerribben-Wieden

Schokland

Hoorn

Kampen

0 ········· km ········· 15
0 ········ miles ········ 15

Edam

THE NETHERLANDS

Elburg

Stroll along the canals of bicycle-friendly **AMSTERDAM**, pausing to visit some of the city's many attractions, including world-class art museums, Anne Frank's house, and the royal palace.

Harderwijk

SCHOKLAND is a former island that now forms an elevated part of the polder. Symbolizing the Dutch people's age-old struggle against the sea, this was the country's first UNESCO site.

Amsterdam

Huizen

Naarden

Spakenburg

The remarkable star-shaped bastion fort in **NAARDEN** is home to the Dutch Fortress Museum and the 15th-century Grote Kerk, one of the oldest surviving churches in the Netherlands.

46

Veloscenic

PARIS TO MONT-SAINT-MICHEL, FRANCE

One of France's most popular long-distance cycle routes, the Veloscenic takes in four iconic UNESCO World Heritage Sites and immerses you in the rural delights of the picturesque French countryside.

283 MILES (455 KM) 8,908 FT (2,715 M) PAVED / GRAVEL

Uncover a rich legacy of both royal and religious splendor on this ride between two of France's great spiritual and visual icons: Notre-Dame Cathedral in Paris and Mont-Saint-Michel on the Normandy coast. Taking you on a cultured two-wheeled odyssey through ancient royal hunting forests and past sumptuous palaces, rural chateaux, and mighty cathedrals, this ride has plenty to savor.

Much of the journey is on dedicated cycle paths and quiet rural roads where motor vehicles are rare, so for large sections the ride is refreshingly traffic-free. And while there are short, sharp climbs in places, these are the exception to the gentler gradients that rule the rest of the route. This may not sound like it makes for particularly challenging riding conditions, but the Veloscenic's length and many passages through deepest

ELEVATION PROFILE

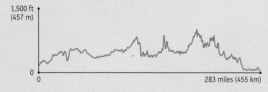

1,500 ft (457 m)

0

0   283 miles (455 km)

REFUEL
Menu du Jour

Make sure you hit Thiron-Gardais in the Perche at midday to sample the superb *menu du jour* at the Restaurant de la Forge (*a-la-forge.com*). You'll get top-drawer dishes at a lunchtime price – go for the daily changing haute-cuisine option or dig into that French fast-food staple, *steak haché* (steak burger and French fries).

Savour the last mile along the **MONT-ST-MICHEL GREENWAY**, as the towering spire of France's most famous monastery slowly rises into view.

Mont-St-Michel

Domfront

Bagnoles-de-l'Orne

Find a bench in the castle ruins of **CHÂTEAU DE DOMFRONT** and soak up the sweeping crag-top views, ideally with a bag of tasty treats from Le Fournil du Château Antoine et Muriel bakery on the high street.

rural Normandy are more than enough to inspire a feeling of adventure.

Anyway, there's no need for speed on this route—the abundance of historical sights invites plenty of stops, and the legendary delights of French cuisine mean that there's always a good excuse for a rest break. Cozy cafés and a bewildering variety of freshly baked boulangerie treats await in the many towns and villages you pass through, so you'll have endless options for any time of day. Worked up a real lunchtime appetite? Stop at a bistro and sample the *plat du jour*, a French institution of a meal whose ingredients vary daily. Pressing on? Pep up your pedaling with a quick *café au lait* at an outdoor café in a town square.

Pausing by a windmill amid the golden wheatfields of Normandy

Freshly baked boulangerie treats await in the many towns and villages you pass through

Home to deep valleys, leafy woods, and quaint villages, the delightful **CHEVREUSE REGIONAL NATURE PARK** is right on the capital's doorstep.

Beautiful **ALENÇON** offers a number of attractions, including the lace collection in the Musée des Beaux-Arts and the Martin family house where 19th-century nun St. Therese of Lisieux was born.

Versailles   Paris

Rambouillet

Chevreuse Regional Nature Park

Chartres

Alençon

FRANCE

Thiron-Gardais

Nogent-le-Rotrou

Illiers-Combray

The soaring north tower of **CHARTRES CATHEDRAL** offers bird's-eye views of town, countryside, and the cathedral itself—and as much vertigo as you can handle.

0 ·········· km ·········· 30
0 ·········· miles ·········· 30

An elaborate fountain in the ornate gardens of the Palace of Versailles

Once you have managed to tear yourself away from the towering presence of Notre-Dame, the ride's first World Heritage Site, you'll encounter a startling transformation as you pedal out of Paris. The bustling, colorful backstreets of the famously creative Left Bank give way to smooth cycle-path riding through busy suburbs, before you breeze across the infamously traffic-clogged Périphérique on a dedicated bike highway to join a corridor of manicured greenery. The pretty little Bièvres River acts as your guide to the grandiose gates of World Heritage Site number two, the spectacular Palace of Versailles. Built by the Sun King Louis XIV, this sumptuously decorated residence is surrounded by equally extravagant gardens; it's worth an overnight stay here to allow enough time to explore (not least because it will give you somewhere secure to store your luggage).

As you reboard your bike, relaxed royal splendor soon gives way to small, sharp climbs through the deep valleys of the

Chevreuse Regional Nature Park to arrive at Rambouillet. Look out for the classical- and hunting-themed statues as you pass through the 18th-century gardens of this former royal palace, before aiming your wheels toward Chartres and the soaring towers of its cathedral. This Gothic masterpiece marks your third World Heritage Site; take some time to go inside and trace the path of its mysterious labyrinth. Back on the road, you'll wander along waterside paths through the city's historic center, before rolling through emerald-green meadows and sun-yellowed cornfields to Illiers-Combray. Literature fans can immerse themselves in the abiding presence of philosopher-writer Marcel Proust, who used the village's intimate charms as a backdrop for his monumental work *À la Recherche du Temps Perdu*.

The French culture and history on offer become delightfully lower key as you cruise ever closer to the coast, along tree-lined railpaths and calm country roads. You might spy ancient manor houses in the bucolic wheatfields of the Perche, while

You might spy ancient manor houses in the bucolic wheatfields of the Perche.

the remoter, denser woodland of Normandy Maine hides natural treasures such as rare freshwater pearl mussels. In between lie welcome oases of French town life, including the imposing Château Saint-Jean at busy little Nogent-le-Rotrou and the elegant belle époque buildings of thermal spa town Bagnoles-de-l'Orne.

Nothing, though, prepares you for the breathtaking medieval monastery of Mont-Saint-Michel. As you pedal through golden wheatfields, Le Mont—your fourth and final World Heritage Site—pops tantalizingly in and out of view. If you want to really feel why it is regarded by the French

MAKE IT LONGER
Extended History

Why not continue cycling through France's history by heading along the signed route from Mont-Saint-Michel to Bayeux—home to the famous 230-ft- (70-m-) long tapestry depicting the Battle of Hastings? From there you can carry on to the D-Day beaches where Allied troops landed during World War II, forcing the end of German occupation.

as *la merveille* (the marvel), park your bike and come in the quiet of early morning on foot. As you calmly survey the vast sweep of bay from Le Mont's castlelike walls, you'll wonder if rides can ever get much better than the Veloscenic.

The picturesque approach to the island of Mont-Saint-Michel

Top Tip
Look out en route for Acceuil Vélo accommodations providers— they offer secure bike storage and repair facilities.

Revive your legs with a break from the bike in the ski resort of **ALPE D'HUEZ**. The restaurants here serve up fortifying Alpine cuisine, perfect for re-energizing for the rest of the ride ahead.

Alpe d'Huez

The pretty **ST. FERRÉOL D'HUEZ CHURCH**, crowned with a stone bell tower, is a great place to take a breather on the ascent to Huez village.

Huez

St Ferréol d'Huez Church

Bourg-d'Oisans

47

Col de Sarenne Circuit

BOURG D'OISANS, FRANCE (LOOP)

Pedal skyward along a trail of legends. The Tour de France's fearsome 21 bends are a supreme test of cycling endurance, while the gentle Col de Sarenne sends you soaring among serrated peaks.

35 MILES (57 KM)

6,565 FT (2,001 M)

PAVED / DIRT

The 21 bends, a brutal serpentine between Bourg d'Oisans and Alpe d'Huez, often decide the outcome of the Tour de France. With a fiendish 7.9 percent average incline, this notorious section of the famous cycling race is the ultimate test of strength. Tackling these muscle-stiffening switchbacks will give you a renewed appreciation for the superhuman endurance of Tour de France athletes, while the scenic Alpine circuit back to Bourg d'Oisans will provide a soothing balm for your thudding heart.

At the height of summer, up to 1,000 cyclists attempt the 21 bends each day, so it's worth setting out early. But pace yourself—depending on your fitness, it will probably take around two hours to tackle the ascent, and there's only a brief warm-up leaving the level terrain of Bourg d'Oisans, before you're forced to click into a lower gear. Each bend is marked with a sign, counting down from 21. There's

Approaching one of the 21 bends between Bourg d'Oisans and Alpe d'Huez

ELEVATION PROFILE

6,500 ft (1,981 m)

0

0   35 miles (57 km)

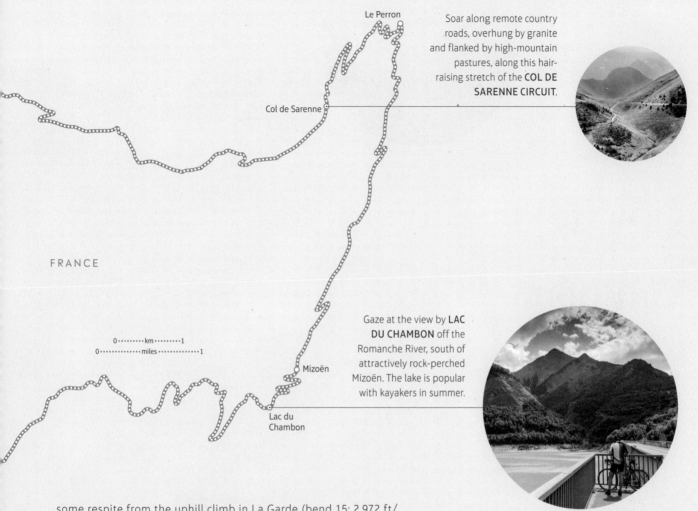

Le Perron

Soar along remote country roads, overhung by granite and flanked by high-mountain pastures, along this hair-raising stretch of the **COL DE SARENNE CIRCUIT**.

Col de Sarenne

FRANCE

Gaze at the view by **LAC DU CHAMBON** off the Romanche River, south of attractively rock-perched Mizoën. The lake is popular with kayakers in summer.

0 ·········· km ·········· 1
0 ··········· miles ··········· 1

Mizoën

Lac du
Chambon

some respite from the uphill climb in La Garde (bend 15; 2,972 ft/ 906 m)—it's an opportunity to pick up speed if you're really tough, or, more likely, rest your trembling legs for the slog between bends 12 and 9. Adrenaline will be coursing through your veins by Huez village; keep at a steady speed to maintain momentum up to the Alpine settlement of Alpe d'Huez (6,102 ft/1,860 m), where you can pause for a well-earned rest.

When your legs have stopped shaking from the ascent, cycle east to the dramatic Col de Sarenne. It's straight sailing along a high-altitude road, flanked by mountain vistas, until the breathtaking up-down zigzag around Le Perron. South of here, the tree-lined trail descends to Mizoën, where the road skirts Lac du Chambon, a 3,412-ft- (1,040-m-) altitude reservoir; it's a good spot to break for a snack as the incline increases farther along. Before arriving back at the bends, you'll soar along a spectacular stretch of road carved into sheer granite, alternating between tunnels and sweeping views of farmland backed by mountains. Spare a thought for the poor souls making their own ascent of the bends as you pass them on the final downhill—that's one challenge you can now proudly say you've completed.

IN FOCUS

Jacques Anquetil

The Tour de France has launched many riders into the limelight, and French cyclist Jacques Anquetil (1934–1987) became particularly well known for his grit during the race. This steely Frenchman was nicknamed "Monsieur Chrono" for his masterful timing, something he used to conquer the 21 bends repeatedly, becoming the first rider to win the Tour de France five times.

SWITZERLAND

Lake Geneva

St-Gingolph

Admire **GENEVA**'s Jet d'Eau, a fountain that shoots water 460 ft (140 m) into the air.

Geneva

FRANCE

Lyon

Valence

Visit one of **CHÂTEAUNEUF-DU-PAPE**'s world-famous wineries to learn about the process of winemaking and try a tasting.

Châteauneuf-du-Pape

Avignon

Arles

Camargue

Port-St-Louis-du-Rhône

0 ·········· km ·········· 75
0 ·········· miles ·········· 75

48
ViaRhôna

ST-GINGOLPH TO
PORT-ST-LOUIS-DU-RHÔNE, FRANCE

The River Rhône will be your constant companion on this meandering ride, leading you through world-renowned wineries and past splendid Roman architecture.

443 MILES (713 KM)

10,525 FT (3,208 M)

PAVED

On this riverside cycle you'll see the Rhône mature from fast-flowing truculent teenager in the Alps around Lake Geneva to a grand old dame, meandering toward her denouement in the Mediterranean. The journey starts with youthful energy in Haute-Savoie, passing through forested mountains and plunging gorges as you skirt around fortified medieval villages like Pérouges. But gastronomic Lyon brings a coming of age, with world-class cuisine and the cherished wines of Châteauneuf-du-Pape setting a new tone for the ride ahead.

Relax on one of the sandy beaches of **PORT-SAINT-LOUIS-DU-RHÔNE**.

Sunshine and cicada calls intensify as you arrive in the deep south of France. By now, the Rhône is in her prime, sweeping around the striking UNESCO-listed walled city of Avignon and guiding you toward Arles, with a Roman amphitheater to rival most in Italy. After pedaling across the pancake-flat Camargue, observed by its famous white horses, the Rhône delta appears. Pulling to a halt on the Mediterranean sands, it's time to bid adieu to this companionable river.

ELEVATION PROFILE

3,000 ft (914 m)

0

0   443 miles (713 km)

124

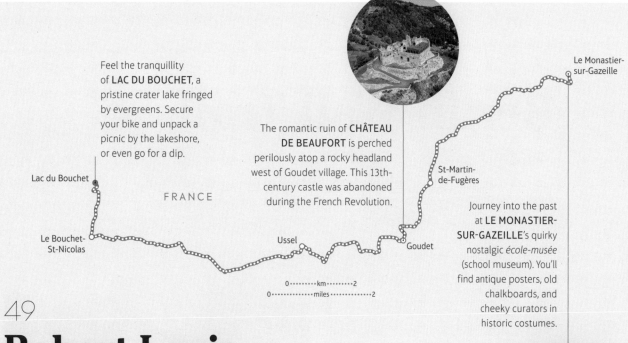

Feel the tranquillity of **LAC DU BOUCHET**, a pristine crater lake fringed by evergreens. Secure your bike and unpack a picnic by the lakeshore, or even go for a dip.

The romantic ruin of **CHÂTEAU DE BEAUFORT** is perched perilously atop a rocky headland west of Goudet village. This 13th-century castle was abandoned during the French Revolution.

Journey into the past at **LE MONASTIER-SUR-GAZEILLE**'s quirky nostalgic *école-musée* (school museum). You'll find antique posters, old chalkboards, and cheeky curators in historic costumes.

Lac du Bouchet

FRANCE

Le Bouchet-St-Nicolas

Ussel

Goudet

St-Martin-de-Fugères

Le Monastier-sur-Gazeille

0 ···· km ···· 2
0 ···· miles ···· 2

49

Robert Louis Stevenson Trail

LE MONASTIER-SUR-GAZEILLE TO LAC DU BOUCHET, FRANCE

Follow in the illustrious footsteps of Treasure Island *author Robert Louis Stevenson. This challenging cycle ride blazes a trail through France's rugged heart, navigating bucolic meadows, woodlands, and volcano-scarred terrain.*

16 MILES (26 KM)

2,448 FT (746 M)

PAVED / GRAVEL / DIRT

The Scottish author Robert Louis Stevenson trekked for 12 days across the rocky trails and remote villages of south-central France, chronicling his adventures in *Travels with a Donkey in the Cévennes* (1879). Today, you can swap four legs for two wheels and embark on this thrilling literary route by bike.

The full Stevenson Trail covers a scenic 169 miles (272 km) end to end, but this shorter spin begins in Le Monastier-sur-Gazeille and follows the GR 70 to a succession of charming villages. The rugged terrain, formed by ancient volcanoes, can make for a challenging ride. Tires kick up rust-colored dust and there are brake-clutching descents down rocky hills. At some ascents, you might want to hop off the saddle and walk. But rewarding your exertions are sweeping views of heaths and farmland, and stop-offs in villages where rustic Auvergnat cuisine reigns supreme. Meaty stews and *truffade*, a melted-cheese bake, are nourishing fuel for cyclists. Finish at Le Bouchet-Saint-Nicolas's stunning crater lake, a bucolic spot furred by pine trees—*magnifique*.

ELEVATION PROFILE

5,000 ft (1,524 m)

1,500 ft (457 m)

0

16 miles (26 km)

125

50

Berlin Wall Trail

BERLIN, GERMANY (LOOP)

Cycle an easy-going circuit from city center to tranquil countryside and back. Closely following the route of the old East–West barrier, the Berlin Wall Trail reveals both the somber history and flourishing contemporary culture of this compelling city.

103 MILES (166 KM)

2,375 FT (724 M)

PAVED

126

Cutting through Berlin are lines of bricks, found in, along, or across the roads, maybe disappearing into a building site or park. They mark the position of the Berlin Wall, that infamous symbol of the Cold War. Very little of it remains—it was torn down soon after the uprisings of 1989—but this well-signed, circular route along the wall's entire length remembers both the structure and the people who died trying to cross it. Monuments and plaques along the trail tell their poignant stories.

In practical terms, this is a leisure bike ride, almost all car-free and ideal for dawdling. Progress in the center won't be fast. The route zigzags unpredictably: one minute it's a busy shopping zone; the next, a quiet backstreet children's play area. Getting distracted is part of the fun—by street art, the aroma of a Middle Eastern grill, or the sight of an ice-cream parlor. And, since bikes are allowed on trains, and stations dot the route, you can be spontaneous about where you start or finish each day.

The route's southeast corner—industrial canals, flat farmland, dormitory suburbs—

Riding past a preserved section of the wall in the Rudow-Altglienicke Nature Reserve

isn't picture-postcard stuff. However, good paved surfaces, like (almost) everywhere en route, mean you soon get to Potsdam's grand monuments and lakeside parks. And around three-quarters of the circuit are surprisingly rural and tranquil, especially the western and northern quarters. You might mistake the paved paths alongside lakes, through woods, and over moorland for a railtrail—except for the odd sharp bend. This was the old patrol road, in the middle of a clearing that was the "death strip" between the inner and outer walls.

Despite tracing the infamous wall, the ride is never a gloomy experience. A reflective one at times, yes—but also a positive, uplifting, and enjoyable sample of 21st-century Berlin in all its forms.

ELEVATION PROFILE

650 ft
(198 m)

0

0   103 miles (166 km)

Clatter over the cobbled patrol roads once used by guards in **WALDGELÄNDE FROHNAU**. These isolated northern woods also house a rare surviving example of a rural watchtower.

IN FOCUS
A Wall Between Worlds

In 1961, the Communist regime of East Germany, worried about its citizens fleeing to the west, built a wall round West Germany's exclave in Berlin. As tensions grew, fugitives were shot on sight—around 200 were killed, though 5,000 escaped. In 1989, a revolt brought the wall down, symbolizing the downfall of Communism in Europe.

Take a detour to the pretty village of **LÜBARS**, nestled amid fields and meadows. Its tiny church and village green are particularly picturesque.

Start and finish at the imposing Wall Memorial on **BERNAUERSTRASSE**, where the biggest and most complete remains of the urban wall are found.

At the "East Side Gallery" along **MÜHLENSTRASSE**, murals and graffiti decorate one of the longest, and most-photographed, intact stretches of the wall.

Still-standing sections of the inner wall, weatherbeaten and covered in graffiti, can be found near **RUDOWER HÖHE**.

Take a break from the bike to spend a day exploring **POTSDAM**'s pretty palaces and period houses.

Waldgelände Frohnau

Hennigsdorf

Lübars

Rosenthal

Spandauer Forst

BERLIN

Bernauerstrasse

Brandenburg Gate

East Side Gallery

Gross Glienicker See

Kladow

Potsdam

Teltow

Rudower Höhe

Schönefeld

0 ········ km ········ 5
0 ············ miles ············ 5

Aerial view of the
Danube sweeping
through Passau, with
the Inn River behind

51

Danube Cycle Way

DONAUESCHINGEN, GERMANY,
TO BUDAPEST, HUNGARY

*Uncover the rich heritage of Central Europe as you
pedal alongside the blue waters of the River Danube.
Almost entirely hill-free, this relaxing ride offers a
wealth of eclectic museums, stunning architecture,
and delicious regional food to explore.*

754 MILES (1,213 KM) 5,807 FT (1,770 M) PAVED / GRAVEL

Accompanying the river from its Black Forest source in
Germany to the heart of Budapest in Hungary, the Danube
Cycle Way passes through an impressive four countries and
three capital cities, connecting a diverse array of people
and landscapes. The river's banks burst with history and
culture, so there's plenty of scope to tailor the ride to your
interests—the only difficulty will be fitting everything in.

Journeying downstream on largely traffic-free cycle
paths, this is a route that suits pretty much everyone,
including beginners. It's popular with cyclists from around
the world, so you'll always be able to find fellow riders to
chat with over drinks. The well-used path also has
excellent cycling facilities, including ferries and hotels that
are geared up for bikes, so if you're apprehensive about
heading off on your first cycling holiday, then the Danube
is a great place to get hooked.

ELEVATION PROFILE

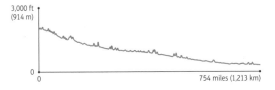

3,000 ft
(914 m)

0

0   754 miles (1,213 km)

Stop at **WALHALLA**, an incongruous building sitting above the Danube near Regensburg. Built for King Ludwig I in the 19th century, it contains busts of famous artists, scientists, and luminaries.

Make the popular detour to the Blautopf (Blue Lagoon) at **BLAUBEUREN**. Part of an underground cave system, the lime-rich water reflects the sun, turning it into an emerald-blue phenomenon.

GERMANY

Regensburg
Weltenburg
Straubing
Ingolstadt
Passau
Blaubeuren
Ulm
Inzigkofen
Donaueschingen

Wander through **PASSAU**'s cobbled streets to St. Stephen's Cathedral—its centerpiece is the world's largest church organ, with 17,774 pipes, 223 registers, and 4 chimes.

The ride starts with a suitably stately send-off next to the Danube Spring, or Donauquelle, in Germany's Black Forest town of Donaueschingen. Surrounded by graceful statues, this elegant sunken pool is merely a preliminary taster for the artistic treasures to come.

For now, though, the focus is more on natural beauty than the human-made kind. The Danube in its early stages is a sparkling shallow river, gurgling alongside you and even disappearing briefly underground through the porous limestone of the Danube Sinkhole. Pedal by pedal, you'll emulate its flow as it negotiates craggy cliffs, glides under woodland canopies, and crosses productive fields of corn and sunflowers. Listen for birdsong and look out near Inzigkofen for the dramatic Devil's Bridge, said by locals to have been built by Satan himself.

Within a few days you'll have settled into the rhythm of daily cycling, measuring your progress by the increasing width of the river. But as you breeze through historical towns with timber-framed houses, and peaceful farmland freckled with cheery red poppies, you'll find an increasing number of reasons to stray from your saddle. Ulm is the first major city you arrive at, and you could easily spend a full day here, exploring the cobbled streets in the medieval Fisherman's Quarter, visiting the unusual Museum of Bread Culture, and climbing to the top of the Minster for views of the Alps (weather permitting, of course).

Timber-framed buildings in Ulm's medieval Fisherman's Quarter

Take a ride on the giant Ferris wheel in **VIENNA**'s Prater amusement park. Film fans will recognize it from its starring role in *The Third Man*.

Take a small detour to visit the **DANUBIANA MEULENSTEEN** art museum. Romantically positioned on a spit of land, this low-lying building forms a harmonious part of the riverscape.

SLOVAKIA

Melk

Vienna   Bratislava

Donau-Auen
National Park

Danubiana Meulensteen

Visegrád

AUSTRIA

Soothe your well-worked muscles in **BUDAPEST**'s elegant Art Nouveau thermal baths. Szechenyi Bath is the most popular, and with 18 pools you could easily spend the day there.

Look over the Danube and the surrounding vineyards from the monastic terrace of **MELK ABBEY**. This immense complex appears to glow, thanks to its sunshine-yellow façade.

Budapest

HUNGARY

0 ·········· km ·········· 75
0 ················ miles ················ 75

131

But the temptations don't stop here: car lovers won't want to miss the Audi Mobile Museum in Ingolstadt, while a stop at Weltenburg Abbey—the world's oldest monastic brewery—is a must for beer fans.

The river soon reminds you it's the star of the show, though, and you get no greater sense of its might than on the bike-friendly ferry from Weltenburg to Kelheim, which passes through the craggy splendor of the breathtaking Danube Gorge. By the time you've passed through the captivating medieval city of Regensburg and arrived at Straubing, on a flat fertile plain, the river will be as familiar as an old friend. You'll be able to recognize subtle shifts in its character and energy as tributaries join and the underlying geography and weather change.

At Passau, the Danube becomes wider as it meets the Inn and Ilz Rivers. This confluence marks roughly your halfway point, and is an ideal place to enjoy a day off from pedaling. Let a boat take you on a river excursion, and admire the city's colorful Italianate buildings while being lulled by the gentle lapping of the water.

IN FOCUS

The River Danube

Europe's second-longest river (after the Volga), the Danube stretches for 1,770 miles (2,850 km), from the Black Forest to the Black Sea. It passes through no less than ten countries—Germany, Austria, Slovakia, Hungary, Croatia, Serbia, Romania, Bulgaria, Moldova, and Ukraine—and has been an important trade route for centuries, playing a key role in the region's history.

Left The Citadel at Visegrád, Hungary, overlooking the Danube Bend

Below The grand stairway of the Natural History Museum in Vienna, Austria

Steins of beer will be swapped for glasses of wine as you cycle through the lush vineyards of Austria's Wachau Valley

Right Riding over the New Bridge in Bratislava, Slovakia

As you cross the border into Austria, the river is now ringed by mountains and busy with shipping. You'll notice other changes, too: the creamy German cheesecakes on the menus at your café stops will be replaced with sweet apple strudel and rich *Sachertorte*. And steins of beer will be swapped for glasses of wine as you cycle through the lush vineyards of Austria's Wachau Valley—it's well worth stopping for a tour and a tasting.

Farther east lies the dazzling Austrian capital of Vienna, which will spoil you with its choice of world-class museums. Visit the Natural History Museum for a unique insight into the wonders of nature, or head to the stately Belvedere—a former palace—to see the world's biggest collection of paintings by Gustav Klimt. There's also the chance to delve into the waters of the Danube, by joining the locals at one of the bathing spots on Vienna's Alte Donau—a safe and attractive branch of the Danube that's now disconnected from the river.

By this stage you're getting close to the Slovakian border, but before leaving Austria you'll ride through the lush surroundings of Donau-Auen National Park. This area of wetland and leaf-dappled backwaters will bring you back in touch with the wild spirit of the river, as you breathe in its damp earthy fragrance while pedaling along. The Danube has been sustaining life in this area for millennia, and the Roman ruins of Carnuntum, in nearby Petronell, are a potent reminder of that fact.

Your time in Slovakia is short but sweet, with a brief whirl through the capital of Bratislava before you arrive at your third and final border crossing. It may be only a whistle-stop tour, but it still brings some memorable cycling moments: as you ride alongside the Danube banks, you'll glimpse the futuristic form of Bratislava's stylish New Bridge, known by locals as the "UFO Bridge" for its distinctive, flying saucer–shaped observation deck.

From here, the Danube flows confidently into Hungary, seemingly aware of its own importance as the route reaches its grand finale. The river gets steadily broader, sweeping through flat fields before winding into the Danube Bend, a supremely photogenic curve of the river overlooked by a chaotic pile of castles at Visegrád. This is the river's final turn before the home stretch into the magnificent Hungarian capital of Budapest. Packed with elegant architecture, relaxing thermal baths, and quirky ruin pubs, the city is overflowing with countless cultural attractions. But for now, rest your weary legs and celebrate your arrival with a plate of *Dobos torte*— layers of sponge and chocolate, topped with delicious brittle caramel—and raise your fork in thanks to the Danube, your constant and reliable companion.

MAKE IT LONGER

Danube Cycle Way: Part Two

The Danube Cycle Way originally ended in Budapest, as traveling farther east wasn't straightforward when the route was established. Today, however, if you're hooked, you can follow the river all the way to the Black Sea, an additional 1,067 miles (1,717 km). This is a quieter, more adventurous ride, needing up-to-date maps and guides to help with wayfinding.

52
Bodensee-Radweg

KONSTANZ, GERMANY (LOOP)

Weave in and out of Germany, Switzerland, and Austria on a circular tour of Europe's largest freshwater lake. You'll have the majestic Alps as your backdrop at every turn of the handlebars.

159 MILES (256 KM) · 3,650 FT (1,112 M) · PAVED / GRAVEL

Circumnavigating the Bodensee (Lake Constance), this mostly flat, waterside route offers the perfect introduction to cycling in Central Europe. Expect jaw-dropping scenery daily—the turquoise lake, snowcapped Alps, and picture-perfect towns and villages will have you reaching for your camera at almost every pedal stroke.

The Bodensee is formed by the mighty Rhine, which marks the start, middle, and end of the ride—don't miss a quick detour to the enormous dykes outside Bregenz to get an idea of the size of this giant water-way. Along the lakeshore you'll pass woods, fields, sandy beaches, and leafy vineyards, while riding effortlessly along perfectly signposted and squeaky-clean cycle tracks. The only hint of a border crossing comes with the odd flag or an extortionately priced cup of coffee (the latter is always a sign that you've arrived in Switzerland). But wherever you are on the route, you can be sure that the brilliant-blue lake and towering Alps will be lying in wait on the horizon.

Picturesque **MEERSBURG** dates from the Middle Ages. Take a tour of the castle, the oldest inhabited fortress in Germany.

ELEVATION PROFILE

3,000 ft (914 m)

0

0   159 miles (256 km)

LINDAU's old town sits on an island packed with colorful Renaissance buildings. Don't miss the port, which houses the only light-house in Bavaria and a 20-ft- (6-m-) tall lion.

Admire the Baroque skyline and the Kunsthaus "glass cube" in **BREGENZ**, before enjoying coffee and cake in the town's Kornmarkt.

GERMANY

Überlingen

Radolfzell

Meersburg

Friedrichshafen

Konstanz

Bodensee

SWITZERLAND

Romanshorn

Lindau

0 ···· km ···· 10
0 ···· miles ···· 10

Rorschach

Bregenz

AUSTRIA

Alto de l'Angliru

OVIEDO, SPAIN (LOOP)

Prepare to feel the burn. This ride takes in the Vuelta a España's hardest climb, "El Angliru"—7.5 miles (12 km) of lung-straining steepness—as well as stunning views of the rugged Picos de Europa mountains.

45 MILES (72 KM)

6,900 FT (2,103 M)

PAVED

Warm up your legs as you pedal downhill out of the historic city of Oviedo on the N-630. Following the banks of the River Caudal, you'll catch glimpses of the towering Picos de Europa for the first time. Steel yourself for the ascent ahead as you approach L'Ará, the little village at the Angliru's foot. At a murderously steep average gradient of 10 percent, it's hard just to keep the pedals moving on the climb—you'll wonder how the professionals manage to race up such a monster. The best strategy? Put your bike in its easiest gear and spin your way to the top. And remember: what goes up must come freewheeling back down.

From the Angliru's base, retrace your steps to the town of Soto de la Ribera, before turning west to meet the Fuso de La Reina. The perfect antidote for tired legs, this car-free bike path winds its way through rolling hills back to Oviedo.

Before you set off, fuel up with generously sized portions of Asturian tapas in the historic city of **OVIEDO**.

135

ELEVATION PROFILE

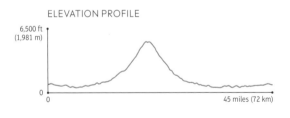

6,500 ft
(1,981 m)

0

0   45 miles (72 km)

Cruise back to Oviedo along the secluded **FUSO DE LA REINA BIKE PATH**, following an old railway line through the hills.

Oviedo

Fuso de la Reina

Soto de la Ribera

SPAIN

L'Ará

Angliru

0 ·········· km ·········· 5
0 ·········· miles ·········· 5

On your way back down from the top of the Angliru, pause at the viewpoint found above the final set of switchbacks to enjoy views over the craggy **PICOS DE EUROPA**.

54
Across the Sierra de Aralar

ANDOAIN TO BEASAIN, SPAIN

Easily accessed by low-traffic bike paths from the historic, coastal city of San Sebastián, Aralar Natural Park makes a perfect family bikepacking getaway through the heart of the Basque Country.

49 MILES (78 KM)
5,600 FT (1,707 M)
PAVED / GRAVEL / DIRT

This traverse of the diminutive Sierra de Aralar makes a great adventure for all ages. First, it's close to San Sebastián—a beautiful and bike-friendly city with nearby beaches. Second, it includes a wonderful prelude to the park itself. The *via verde* (greenway) that you join at Andoain (a quick train ride from the city) promises all manner of sights and experiences, including refreshing mountain springs, historic bridges, and several spooky tunnels to ride through.

Last, but by no means least, there's Aralar park itself. Here, you can look forward to druid stones, caves, underground rivers, gullies, and fluted rock pinnacles, perfect for off-the-bike scrambles and picnic stops. Largely following low-traffic dirt roads, the terrain is mostly manageable, other than a few short, rougher sections where pushing may be required, depending on ages involved.

The descent out of the mountains offers one final thrill (though take care, as it's steep) before the ride ends at the town of Beasain. Take public transportation back to San Sebastián, where a relaxing family day on the beach awaits as a reward.

136

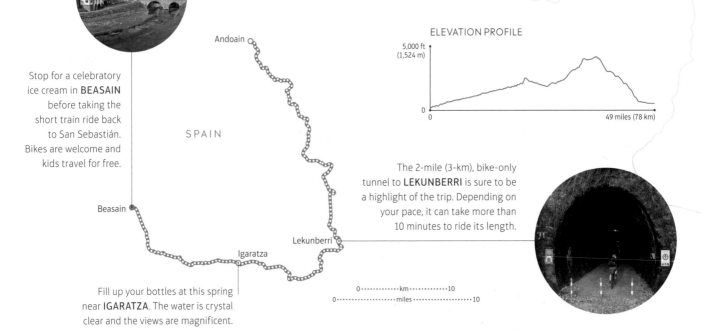

Stop for a celebratory ice cream in **BEASAIN** before taking the short train ride back to San Sebastián. Bikes are welcome and kids travel for free.

Andoain

SPAIN

Beasain

Igaratza

Lekunberri

Fill up your bottles at this spring near **IGARATZA**. The water is crystal clear and the views are magnificent.

The 2-mile (3-km), bike-only tunnel to **LEKUNBERRI** is sure to be a highlight of the trip. Depending on your pace, it can take more than 10 minutes to ride its length.

ELEVATION PROFILE

5,000 ft (1,524 m)

0

0   49 miles (78 km)

0 ···········km···········10
0 ···········miles···········10

South of **PUNTA NATI**, follow a rocky section of the Cami through an eerie limestone landscape, edged by cave-pierced sea cliffs and dotted with animal shelters that resemble ancient burial cairns.

Punta Nati
Cala Morell
Platja de Fornells
Ciutadella
MENORCA
S'Albufera d'Es Grau Natural Park
Cala en Turqueta
Cala Macarella
Cala en Bosch
Cala Llucalari
Cala en Porter
Maó
Punta Prima

0 ········· km ········· 10
0 ········· miles ········· 10

Get two coves for the price of one at **CALA MACARELLA** and **CALA MACARELLETA**. These white-sand beaches are framed by silvery cliffs.

Visit the freshwater lagoon at the heart of **S'ALBUFERA D'ES GRAU NATURAL PARK**; look out for coots and ospreys. Nearby Es Grau has a beach bar where you can watch the famous Menorcan horses exercising in the shallows.

55

Cami de Cavalls

MAÓ, MENORCA, SPAIN (LOOP)

Circumnavigating the island of Menorca, this largely off-road route is wonderfully diverse. Take it slow to fully appreciate its varied scenery and ever-changing trails.

114 MILES (184 KM)

7,497 FT (2,285 M)

PAVED / GRAVEL / DIRT

"Follow the coast" sounds simple, but things just keep changing on this looping route around Menorca's coastline; you can be riding through fragrant pine forest one minute, negotiating clifftop singletrack above the blue Mediterranean the next. The trail itself keeps you on your toes—sweeping smooth paths can morph at any moment into a rocky descent. It's not hardcore, but basic mountain biking skills are essential for enjoyment here.

The north coast has wilder scenery and tougher riding overall, but the south is no anticlimax. The stretch between the sandy coves of Cala en Turqueta and Cala Galdana is rich in teasing descents and testing climbs, but never too gnarly. A little later, Cala Llucalari's secretive cove ushers in a delightful inland digression, where orchids line shady paths and farm tracks wind through orange groves. If variety is the spice of life, then the Cami de Cavalls is a highly seasoned feast.

Riding past one of the ancient livestock shelters that speckle the rocky landscape south of Punta Nati

ELEVATION PROFILE

650 ft (198 m)

0

0   114 miles (184 km)

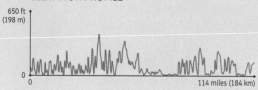

56

Ojos Negros Via Verde

TORRES TORRES TO TERUEL, SPAIN

Following a disused railway line, the Ojos Negros Via Verde climbs steadily through off-the-beaten-track inland Spain, from lush Valencian orange groves to the World Heritage Site of Teruel.

80 MILES (129 KM) 4,910 FT (1,497 M) PAVED / GRAVEL

138

Starting near Torres Torres, among brightly colored and aromatic orange trees, it's hard to believe that this ride has industrial origins. The route dates back to 1907, when high fees on the local railway prompted mine owners in the town of Ojos Negros to build their own parallel track for

ELEVATION PROFILE

5,000 ft
(1,524 m)

0

0   80 miles (129 km)

The skyline of Jérica, dominated by the town's distinctive Mudéjar tower

transporting iron ore to the Mediterranean. The ill-fated line only lasted a few decades before increased production meant it was no longer up to the job. Happily, however, it has since secured a new lease on life as a *via verde* (greenway).

Today, it's the gentle clicking of gear changes, rather than clanking engines, that will be your accompaniment on this mostly uphill ride. Settle into a steady rhythm as you pedal through olive and almond trees, enjoying the slow burn of the easy-going gradient—it was designed for small engines, so you won't encounter any get-off-and-walk climbs. The well-made track is lined with flowering bushes that lightly brush your legs, releasing fragrant scents as you pedal past. Monumental viaducts and deserted stations provide plenty of photo opportunities, as do the panoramas of attractive hilltop towns and soaring mountains found at welcome picnic sites. Occasionally, the view disappears entirely as you plunge into dark tunnels.

Refresh yourself with a break at Navajas, where cool springs gurgle and a spectacular 98-ft (30-m) single-drop waterfall plunges into the gorge—local legend tells the tragic tale of a couple

The decorative wooden ceiling in **TERUEL'S CATHEDRAL** is the Mudéjar equivalent of the Sistine Chapel.

Teruel

Puerto Escandón

0 ·········· km ·········· 20
0 ·········· miles ·········· 20

Admire the elegant arches of the impressive viaduct found close to the village of **ALBENTOSA**.

Albentosa

SPAIN

Jérica

Navajas

Park up your bike at **JÉRICA** to visit its iconic Mudéjar tower, which rises high above the town's ocher-roofed houses.

You'll uncover the stunning Salto de la Novia waterfall close to the village of **NAVAJAS**. Take a dip in the blue-green pool found at its base.

Torres
Torres

who drowned here while taking part in a traditional marriage leap. Farther on, dismount from your bike to meander through the narrow streets of Jérica, with its unusual octagonal Mudéjar tower. Take some time to relax in the sunshine here, looking over the river, crag martins soaring overhead, or head down to the bathing pools with your swimwear.

The scenery changes as you climb even higher, becoming a remote arid land dotted with green juniper bushes and picturesque abandoned stone farmhouses. Your highest point, the Puerto Escandón, is now in sight, and the seductive pull of dazzling Teruel—packed with outstanding

IN FOCUS
Mudéjar Architecture

Characterized by intricate geometric patterns of terra-cotta bricks and glazed tiles, Mudéjar architecture was an elegant fusion of Islamic art and European-Christian styles that flourished from the 12th to 17th centuries. Examples of it can be found along the ride, including the Mudéjar towers in Jérica and Teruel.

Mudéjar buildings—feels ever stronger. As you freewheel down to the breathtaking city, you're almost at the end of the line. The turbines on the hillside hint that strong winds are common here; let's hope yours is a tailwind.

EUROPE

Cycling the famous
Col Agnel, with spec-
tacular views over the
surrounding mountains

57

In the Footsteps of Hannibal

BARCELONA, SPAIN, TO ROME, ITALY

Swap pachyderms for pedals as you ride to Rome in the footsteps of Hannibal, one of history's greatest military commanders. Setting out from Barcelona and crossing three mountain ranges, this challenging route is best enjoyed in the slow lane.

1,538 MILES (2,475 KM)   144,325 FT (43,990 M)   PAVED

140

When Hannibal Barca set off from the Iberian Peninsula in 218 BCE with his army of 60,000 men and 37 elephants, little did he know that his unprecedented march on Rome would become the inspiration behind an epic cycling route. Two millennia on, you can channel your inner Carthaginian with a ride that spirits you across three countries and some of Europe's most stunning scenery. From the rural Catalonian countryside and pine-covered Pyrenees to the sleepy hilltop towns and chiming church bells of Italy, this is a journey far greater than A to B. Blending unknown lanes and some of the most iconic climbs in cycling, the ride is perfect for pedaling gastronomes, oenophiles, and anyone with an interest in history, culture, and the road less traveled.

    The Hannibal Ride is the brainchild of Sam Wood, an Australian archaeologist and founder of both Ride & Seek and Bike Odyssey, touring companies specializing in

IN FOCUS
Who was Hannibal?

Hannibal Barca commanded Carthage's main forces against the Roman Republic during the Second Punic War. Seeking revenge after his father was killed in battle, he famously led his army over the Alps with 37 elephants after setting out from modern-day Spain in 218 BCE. He won several large battles, but never sacked Rome and was forced to return to North Africa.

pedal-powered adventures in the footsteps of historical figures. After creating the BBC documentary *On Hannibal's Trail*, Wood devised this challenging route taking in some of the main flashpoints of the general's bold foray through the Roman Empire—including, of course, his famous crossing of the Alps.

    The ride can be done as part of a tour or self-supported. Whichever you choose, you'll stay in family-run gîtes, sprawling villas, and charming *agriturismi*. You'll devour hearty breakfasts every morning and then dine out each night on fresh produce, toasting your daily achievements with the local tipple.

ELEVATION PROFILE

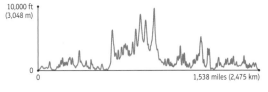

10,000 ft
(3,048 m)

0

0   1,538 miles (2,475 km)

Top Tip
Ride in autumn when the days are still long, the temperatures cooler and the roads far quieter.

Reward yourself with a 19-mile (30-km) descent after entering Italy from France via the **COL AGNEL**, the third-highest paved road in the Alps.

Alpe d'Huez

Col de l'Izoard

Col Agnel

Fossano

FRANCE

Tick another famous climb off the bucket list as you negotiate the 21 hairpin bends of **ALPE D'HUEZ** that are often featured in the Tour de France.

The magnificent **PONT DU GARD**, the highest and best-preserved Roman aqueduct of its kind, overlooks the peaceful Gardon River here.

Mont Ventoux

Pont du Gard

Avignon

Forget that Hannibal never went up it; no serious cyclist can come so close to **MONT VENTOUX** without scaling its notorious slopes.

Carcassonne

142

Peyrepertuse

Take a break from the saddle with a short but sharp hike to the mystical ruins of the majestic Cathar castle at **PEYREPERTUSE** as the sun sets over the French Pyrenees.

Empuriés

Girona

SPAIN

Barcelona

Setting off from Barcelona, your first Hannibalistic port of call is the ancient city of Empuriés on the Costa Brava, where the Carthaginian army gathered before entering Gaul via the rugged foothills of the Pyrenees. You'll then cross southern France, discovering a patchwork of regions each with its own distinct character and delicacies. As the beautiful vineyards of Languedoc merge into the fragrant lavender fields of Provence, you'll soon lose track of the days—days which will include an assortment of Roman ruins, Cathar castles, medieval bridges, and tranquil town squares, as well as many a buttery croissant.

Passing through the countries featured in pro cycling's biggest races—the Tour de France, Giro d'Italia, and Vuelta a España—you'll occasionally follow in the tire tracks of the sport's big stars. In fact, after emulating Hannibal's crossing of the Rhône near Avignon, there's the option for a detour to scale the legendary Mont Ventoux—one of the Tour's most grueling climbs and a taxing prelude to the ascents on the horizon.

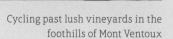

Cycling past lush vineyards in the foothills of Mont Ventoux

Enjoy an aperitif at the **CASTELLO DI RIVALTA** overlooking the River Trebbia, where Hannibal enjoyed his first victory against the Romans. A commemorative elephant statue stands nearby.

Castello di Rivalta

Gavi

After your Alpine exertions, there's no better spot than the fortress town of **GAVI** in the rolling hills of Piedmont; sample the famous Gavi di Gavi white wine here.

Savour the twisting descent of the **PASSO DELLE RADICI** in the Apennines safe in the knowledge that the last big uphill test of the route is over.

Passo delle Radici

Florence

0 ········· km ········· 50
0 ········· miles ········· 50

Siena

Lake Trasimene

The ruins of the aptly named **SANGUINETO**, on the banks of Lake Trasimene, were the site of the bloodiest encounter of the Second Punic War.

Rome

While the exact route of Hannibal's Alpine march isn't known, evidence suggests it may have been via the majestic Col Agnel, where a plaque today commemorates his feat. With the more illustrious peaks of the Galibier and Izoard already in the legs—not to mention the famous 21 bends of Alpe d'Huez—you'll tackle the gentle lower slopes of the Agnel with a spring in your step before pushing on to its imposing summit. From here, the highest border crossing in Europe, you can gaze over multiple horizons toward Italy before starting the final phase of your ride to Rome.

Bidding adieu to the Alps will not spell the end of the climbing. Some of the steepest slopes and punchiest peaks appear along the Apennine backbone of Italy as you dart (or plod) between the stunning hilltop towns of Piedmont, Emilia-Romagna, Tuscany, and Umbria—unforgiving land that proved a match for the pachyderms of Carthage. On this last leg, you'll take in the location of Hannibal's victorious ambush on the banks of the Trebbia River as well as the bloody massacre of the Roman army at Lake Trasimene.

Your journey ends with a real sense of achievement as you pedal into the heart of Rome along the winding Tiber—an elephantine feat Hannibal himself never accomplished.

REFUEL
Pasta Extravaganza

If carbs are a cyclist's best friend, then Italy, with its pizza and pasta, is the holy land. And when in Rome, do as the Romans do with a decadent bowl of *cacio e pepe*. Usually made with a thick spaghetti called *tonnarelli*, the ingredients of this traditional dish may be simple—black pepper and grated Pecorino—but the result is divine.

58

Sella Ronda

CORVARA, ITALY (LOOP)

Taking in four mountain passes, the taxing Sella Ronda certainly packs a punch—both in ascent and beauty. The Dolomites form the dramatic backdrop, with granite peaks jutting out of emerald hills.

32 MILES (52 KM)

5,390 FT (1,642 M)

PAVED

Make like the legendary Fausto Coppi or modern master Vincenzo Nibali—both world-famous Italian cycling champions—and tackle the Sella Ronda. This challenging loop is made up of a quartet of legendary passes—the Campolongo, the Pordoi, the Gardena, and the Sella—three of which rise above 6,562 ft (2,000 m). The ride may be physically demanding—all of the climbs have been regularly featured in the Giro d'Italia—but it also has an otherworldly quality to it. Here, the luscious green pasturelands create a wonderful contrast to the harsh, jagged outlines of the mountain peaks that tower above.

While you can start your battle against the Sella Ronda's four fearsome peaks from any point on the loop, it's best to begin in Corvara. Cycling counterclockwise from this Alpine town means that you save the easiest ascent—the Campolongo—for last.

Passo Gardena, winding beneath the peaks of the mighty Dolomites

The climbing begins right from the get-go with the Passo Gardena. It's a real test of your legs, but this twisting, tree-lined road leading up to saw-toothed peaks is one of the most beautiful you'll ever ride. It's also an excellent idea to get the longest climb of the day out of the way early.

Next, battle up the leg-cramping Sella, the steepest of the four. Luckily it's also the shortest. Go easy on the descent—it's the most technically challenging of the passes, with some tortuous hairpins. Plus, going slower will let you fully enjoy the

ELEVATION PROFILE

8,200 ft
(2,499 m)

3,000 ft
(914 m)

0   32 miles (52 km)

IN FOCUS
Fausto Coppi

Coppi was nicknamed Il Campionissimo, "the champion of champions," because he was such an all-conquering force in postwar bike racing. He established his reputation in the Dolomites, particularly on the Sella Ronda's Passo Pordoi, which he was the first rider to summit in five separate editions of the Giro d'Italia.

Pause for a moment at the **RIFUGIO FRARA** at the summit of the Gardena. It's the perfect spot to fuel up for the next climb with an energizing espresso.

Restaurants in **CORVARA** serve up *Tiroler gröstl* (a deliciously rich combination of bacon, potatoes, eggs, and onions).

Colfosco

Passo Gardena

Corvara

ITALY

Passo Campolongo

Passo Sella

Arabba

The south-facing viewing platform atop the **PASSO SELLA** is an excellent spot to snap a photo of the area's spectacular granite peaks.

Passo Pordoi

0 ·········· km ·········· 2
0 ·········· miles ·········· 2

Pay your respects to Fausto Coppi at the memorial to him at the summit of the **PASSO PORDOI**, the highest point on the Sella Ronda loop.

incredible views of forested valleys rising up toward monumental chunks of granite. Third comes the mighty Pordoi, the highest point on the ride, with a joyously long descent amid more spectacular scenery to Arabba, where the road climbs up for the final time.

The Campolongo is not as fearsome as its bigger brothers, but it nevertheless serves up both sweeping switchbacks and stunning views of soaring granite peaks. Drink in the last blissful moments of the Sella Ronda loop, before dropping back into Corvara in time for a well-earned Aperol.

Making the steady climb up to the summit of the Passo Pordoi

Immerse yourself in Renaissance art at the world-famous Uffizi in **FLORENCE**.

Sit down for a well-deserved gelato in the main square of imposing **MONTERIGGIONI**. This 13th-century town atop a quads-testing hillock is known for its impressive walled fortifications, which include 14 towers.

0 ···· km ···· 20
0 ···· miles ···· 20

ITALY

Florence

San Gimignano

Monteriggioni

Siena

Val d'Orcia

Altesino

Pienza

Bagno Vignoni

Enjoy a tasting at **ALTESINO**, one of the greatest names in Tuscan wines. It is particularly renowned for its Brunellos.

Treat sore legs to a "hyper-thermal" spa in enchanting **BAGNO VIGNONI**, famous for its natural mineral-rich hot springs. At 126°F (52°C), they're the hottest in Tuscany.

59

A Taste of Renaissance Tuscany

FLORENCE TO PIENZA, ITALY

Cycling through Tuscany is like riding into a Renaissance painting: cypress trees stand sentinel over squads of grapevines, while fields blanketed in wild flowers stretch toward sun-kissed hilltop villages.

146

123 MILES (198 KM)

12,854 FT (3,918 M)

PAVED / GRAVEL / DIRT

This ride starts as it continues, with a captivating view over Florence from Piazzale Michelangelo. From there, it's pretty much classic Tuscan landscapes all the way, as you pedal to Pienza along the Via Francigena—once an important pilgrimage route to Rome, and now a cycling and hiking trail.

Postcard-perfect Tuscany comes into view through Val d'Orcia, with its green hills and stately cypress trees. But it's not all a rolling romance. There are plenty of sustained climbs to medieval villages, the most famous of which is San Gimignano, known as "the town of fine towers." Yes, it's hilly, but there's no better way to work off a justified overindulgence in local delicacies like truffle pappardelle and melt-in-your-mouth pork lardo.

At the end of each day, tired riders are greeted at the many bike-friendly *agriturismos* (farmhouses), B&Bs, and boutique hotels with a warm "*benvenuto*" (welcome). Kick off your clay-crusted bike shoes and treat yourself to a celebratory glass of Chianti as you sit back and soak up the beauty of your surroundings.

ELEVATION PROFILE

3,000 ft (914 m)

0

0   123 miles (198 km)

60

Fortified Villages of Saxon Transylvania

SIGHISOARA TO VISCRI, ROMANIA

You'll feel like you've pedaled back in time on this ride, as you roll through beech forests, endless wildflower meadows, and pretty Saxon villages that could be straight out of the pages of a fairy tale.

29 MILES (47 KM)
3,337 FT (1,017 M)
PAVED / GRAVEL / DIRT

You're likely to see more horse-drawn carts than cars on this wonderfully varied route between Sighisoara, Transylvania's jewel in the crown, and the UNESCO village of Viscri. The ride starts on pavement, but that quickly gives way to gravel, and then dirt in the beech and oak forests that follow the high contours of the countryside—they're home to Europe's largest population of brown bears, and a few wolves, too.

Wildflower meadows of bright yellows and pinks usher you into the village of Mesendorf, which makes a great stop for a local lunch. As you climb back up into the hills afterward, keep an eye out for a sheepfold—there, if you're lucky, hospitable shepherds might treat you to a dessert of fresh cheese. It's largely downhill from this point, so sit back and enjoy the descent through yet more idyllic meadows to Viscri. As you celebrate your arrival with a beer on the high street, watch the communal herd of cattle return from their day on the pastures, peeling off into their owners' gates in a daily ritual that's been going on for 800 years.

147

Wander the pretty cobbled streets of **SIGHISOARA**. The city is famed as the birthplace of Vlad the Impaler, the inspiration for Bram Stoker's Count Dracula.

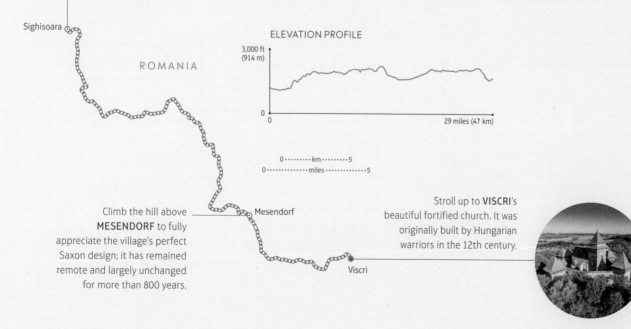

Sighisoara

ROMANIA

ELEVATION PROFILE

3,000 ft
(914 m)

0

0   29 miles (47 km)

0 ········· km ········· 5
0 ········· miles ········· 5

Climb the hill above **MESENDORF** to fully appreciate the village's perfect Saxon design; it has remained remote and largely unchanged for more than 800 years.

Mesendorf

Viscri

Stroll up to **VISCRI**'s beautiful fortified church. It was originally built by Hungarian warriors in the 12th century.

Looking over the Adriatic Sea and Pakleni islands from the hilltop above Hvar Town

61

Island-Hopping through Croatia

SPLIT TO STON, CROATIA

This island ride isn't one to rush. Cycle from Split to Ston via a chain of hilly limestone islands tracing an arc across the cobalt-blue and turquoise Croatian seas.

165 MILES (265 KM) | 10,597 FT (3,230 M) | PAVED

Quiet, gently winding roads lead you around some of Croatia's most idyllic isles on this laid-back route. The riding is a breeze, thanks to courteous drivers, super-smooth pavement, and well-engineered gradients. While there are a handful of long, hot uphills to reach each island's dry interior—with few roadside holm oaks or native pine trees to offer shade—you can take them as slow as you'd like. And remember: you'll soon be rolling downhill to one golden pebble beach or another, where you can cool off with a refreshing dip in crystal-clear waters.

Each island has its own distinct charms. Brač is famed for its pale-white limestone—spy it in walls, in roadside crags, and piled in fields, and even learn how it's carved at Pučišća. Hvar, meanwhile, is blanketed by purple lines of pungent lavender (early summer) and silvery-gray, postage stamp–size olive groves, while verdant rows of vines flow across Korčula and the Pelješac peninsula. Whichever island you're on, the best way to end each day is with a refreshing beer at a coastal *konoba* (tavern), watching the sun set over the sparkling Adriatic Sea.

148

Brave the evening waves for a refreshing swim, or just relax into fine golden pebbles on **ZLATNI RAT**, a 1,640-ft- (500-m-) long V-shaped spit.

Ascend innumerable steps to reach **HVAR**'s medieval fortress, which offers views over the offshore Pakleni islands.

CROATIA

As evening arrives in **KORČULA**, head to one of the restaurants lining the town's pretty harbor for a traditional dinner with spectacular sunset views.

ELEVATION PROFILE

3,000 ft (914 m)

0

0   165 miles (265 km)

Durmitor National Park

PLUZINE TO ŽABLJAK, MONTENEGRO

Winding its way through some of Europe's most awe-inspiring mountain scenery, this challenging route showcases the dramatic limestone peaks and windswept meadows of the off-the-beaten-track country of Montenegro.

30 MILES (48 KM) 5,207 FT (1,587 M) PAVED

Montenegro's geological wonders are never far away on this ride. Shortly after leaving the tiny waterside town of Pluzine, you'll get up close and personal with the Piva Gorge, as you take the bridge across its blue lake and ascend through a series of tunnels blasted out of the cliffs. Eventually the lofty views of the gorge give way to deciduous woodland and alpine meadows. The foliage becomes sparser as the road winds higher, and the gray linestone of the Durmitor massif starts to emerge from beneath the greenery. The road tops out at nearly 6,562 ft (2,000 m),

and you'll find yourself wanting to stop regularly, as much to catch your breath as to watch the light play across Durmitor's rippling limestone peaks. There follows a twisting descent, past shepherds' huts and the occasional roaming cattle, to Žabljak. This tiny resort town is the perfect place to take in even more incredible mountain scenery—this time with your feet up.

> There follows a twisting descent, past shepherds' huts and the occasional roaming cattle, to Žabljak.

As you pass the 3-mile (5-km) mark, pull in to admire the deep-blue waters of the **PIVA GORGE** from on high.

End your ride in the high-altitude city of **ŽABLJAK**; it makes a great base from which to explore the park further.

Piva Gorge · Pluzine · Durmitor National Park · Bobotov Kuk · Žabljak

MONTENEGRO

Around 12 miles (20 km) into the ride are incredible views of the **DURMITOR NATIONAL PARK** and a rather mysterious roadside basketball hoop.

Gaze up at the craggy summit of **BOBOTOV KUK**, popular with hikers, and then admire the surrounding lush green high pastures, home to thousands of sheep.

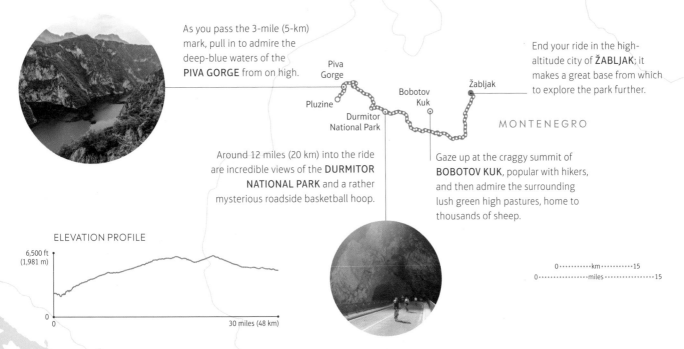

ELEVATION PROFILE

6,500 ft (1,981 m)

0

0   30 miles (48 km)

0 ·········km········· 15
0 ·········miles········· 15

Top Tip

Fill your bottles with natural spring water from the stone "taps" you'll see on the mountain roads.

Riding between the
peaks of the Dinaric
Alps in Montenegro

63

Dinaric Alps

LJUBLJANA, SLOVENIA,
TO IGOUMENITSA, GREECE

*This is one for riders who love big climbs. Crossing the
rugged Dinaric Alps, this demanding route offers up
some truly thigh-testing ascents, plus incredible alpine
landscapes and warm Balkan hospitality on the way.*

926 MILES (1,491 KM)
67,530 FT (20,583 M)
PAVED

Dividing the sparkling Adriatic Sea from the vast plains of
Eastern Europe, the Dinaric Alps are a chain of mountains
that stretch all the way from Slovenia in the north to Greece
in the south. On this challenging route you'll ride along their
length, powering through eight countries in total: Slovenia
and Greece bookend the route, with the western Balkans—
Croatia, Bosnia and Herzegovina, Montenegro, Kosovo,
Albania, and North Macedonia—sandwiched in between.

The sheer physical effort involved to ride an entire
mountain range is immense—expect more than your fair
share of leg-trembling climbs along winding roads. But the
breathtaking views and rapid descents make it more than
worth it. Plus, this area is little-visited by tourists, let alone
cyclists, meaning that you'll get a more than warm welcome
in the small mountain villages and towns you'll pass through.

The route lends itself to almost any type of touring
style—from traditional panniers with camping equipment
to fully supported options with restaurants and accommodations—so it's easy to make the adventure entirely yours.

ELEVATION PROFILE

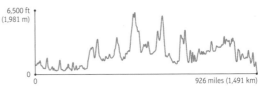

6,500 ft
(1,981 m)

0

0   926 miles (1,491 km)

Before you set off, take a spin around the leafy, car-free center of **LJUBLJANA**, Slovenia's pretty capital city.

SLOVENIA

Ljubljana

CROATIA

Beautiful Burek

In just about every bakery in every town in the Balkans, you will find an abundance of *burek*. Phyllo pastries filled with minced meat, potato, cheese, or spinach, they are laden in calories to power you up the next climb.

Banja Luka

BOSNIA AND HERZEGOVINA

Detour to **SARAJEVO** and spend a day exploring its mazelike Old Bazaar and fueling up on *cevapi* (grilled meat).

Sarajevo

Multicultural **PRIZREN** is known for its spectacular Ottoman and Byzantine architecture.

Durmitor National Park

Breathe the fresh alpine air in the magical **DURMITOR NATIONAL PARK**. The Prevoj Sedlo pass is the literal high point of your ride.

MONTENEGRO

KOSOVO

Prizren

152

A multitude of small fish restaurants line the shore of **LAKE OHRID**, making it the perfect place to stop for a freshly caught lunch.

NORTH MACEDONIA

Lake Ohrid

ALBANIA

GREECE

Igoumenitsa

0 ·········· km ·········· 100
0 ·········· miles ·········· 100

Celebrate the completion of your journey in **IGOUMENITSA**, with ouzo and authentic cuisine in a traditional Greek taverna.

This alpine route can be done in either direction, but pedaling north to south allows for a slightly more gradual start, both in altitude and temperature. With this in mind, begin your ride in Ljubljana, the cycle-friendly capital of Slovenia. This charming city, found at the crossroads of Eastern and Western Europe, is home to a vast network of dedicated bike paths—evidence of the country's exploding appetite for cycling infrastructure.

From the Slovenian capital, you'll follow marked bike routes as you pedal through a rolling countryside of cultivated hills and small vineyards, slowly but surely gaining height as you enter the lush green foothills of the Dinaric Alps. Treat this first, gently undulating section of the ride as a warm-up to the challenging climbs ahead. Your tires will roll effortlessly along smooth pavement as you pass by small villages clustered around ancient stone churches, glowing warm in the golden Slovenian sunshine. Be sure to fuel your legs for the ascents ahead at the sweet-smelling bakeries and cafés you'll pass en route; you're likely meet to friendly locals at these spots, who will be curious about your journey.

Slovenia is such a joy to cycle across that the eventual arrival of the Croatian border may be a bittersweet occasion—but worry not, Croatia will win your heart

as quickly as its neighbor did. Ancient fortresses dot the hills by the border and small churches stand proudly on grassy hilltops. More vineyards flow across the landscape, the emerald-green rows of neatly lined crops rolling over the endless hills; take time to hop off your bike here and sample a well-deserved glass of wine.

As you pedal farther into the mountain range, the climbs get longer and you gain more altitude. Soon the border with Bosnia and Herzegovina—marked by old stone fortresses on opposite river banks—materializes. Rolling over the frontier, the white peaks of the central Dinaric Alps start to take shape in the land in front of you—from here on the views of emerald-clad mountains improve by the hour. Busier roads appear as you skirt the edge of the country's cultured capital, Sarajevo—its quaint old town is a great place to explore if you fancy a day out of the saddle. Leaving the bustling city behind, in no time at all you'll return to the tranquility of the mountains on quiet old roads. From here, prepare your legs: the climbing starts to really get steep as you reach the heart of the Dinaric range and propel yourself toward the border of mountainous Montenegro.

A quiet cobbled street
in the Slovenian capital
of Ljubljana

ANOTHER WAY

Head Off-Road

The Dinaric Alps can also be completed on a grueling mountain bike adventure, linking hiking trails and gravel roads. Like the road version, you can ride fully supported, staying in villages, or choose to carry your own camping gear for a truly immersive wilderness experience.

Montenegro greets you with serpentine, turquoise rivers that snake between jagged vertiginous peaks. Go ahead and click over to your biggest climbing gear: the grades here can only be described as grinding, but the views are dramatic. Impossibly steep mountains plunge into ferocious river gorges, while the road winds precariously along the mountainsides, every twist and turn offering up a spectacular new vista. Possibly deterred by the gradients, few cyclists make it to this small country—a loss for others but all the better for you.

While catching your breath in the quiet villages found in between ascents, expect to encounter outstanding Balkan hospitality and welcoming locals. In fact, you may find yourself the only visitor in the places you stop to replenish. The Montenegrin villages you pass through feel quiet at first, where old stone houses with cherished gardens line wide paved streets, but if you find

your way to the local bar or café, you'll discover the heart of the village and be warmly beckoned in for coffee—or perhaps something stronger.

A highlight here is riding the scenic route through Durmitor National Park in western Montenegro, a UNESCO World Heritage Site. Grandiose peaks are flanked by rolling green hillside, bejeweled with wildflowers and home to abundant wildlife. The road through this park winds and grinds upward through a series of tunnels before delivering you to the alpine pass of Prevoj Sedlo, the highest altitude on your journey. Expect to reach the top with burning thighs and bursting lungs—you're going to be thankful for that fresh mountain air.

Yet another ascent, one of the route's longest, will wind you via lush alpine forests up to the remote border with Kosovo, sat atop a grand mountain pass. From here, a long and rapid descent will deliver you into one of the friendliest nations on Earth.

Looking out over the Dinaric Alps near the Kosovo–Albania border

Even fewer visitors grace this country than the regions you've already passed through, so you can expect an especially warm welcome. Drivers will slow down to greet you and you'll be quizzed about your trip anywhere you may be taking a break. But while the welcome may be warm, the weather often isn't. Even in the height of summer, the peaks here are likely to still hold snow and the afternoon thunderstorms are a force to be reckoned with.

From Kosovo it's—you've guessed it—yet another big climb to the Albanian border. This country's rocky mountains resemble those of its neighbor Montenegro and its forests are filled with life—you might spot a few squirrels or hear bird cries echoing off the mountains. As you're closer to the Adriatic Sea, the climate is warm and dry, especially in the height of summer;

you'll appreciate the abundance of roadside mountain springs to dunk your head under. Soon it's time for a break from Albania with a dip into North Macedonia, where you'll leave the tallest peaks behind and gradually begin to descend out of the Dinaric Alps. The clock doesn't move too fast here and, nearing the end of your tour, neither should you. Take time for a swim in the glittering waters of Lake Ohrid and enjoy a long lunch in local fish restaurants.

Crossing back into Albania and then on into Greece, the mountains flatten out into gentler hills and the climbs become smaller. Passing by traditional Greek villages, seemingly unchanged by time, you'll make for the seaside city of Igoumenitsa. Reward your tired limbs with a reviving soak in the sparkling Adriatic Sea and then devour some renowned Greek cuisine—*yamas*!

Taking a break at
the side of the road
in Albania

EUROPE

64

Historic Southern Albania

QAFE THANË TO VLORË, ALBANIA

Take a deep dive into the unique culture and tumultuous history of a long-isolated Balkan land, where Roman, Byzantine, Ottoman, and Communist heritage jostle in hilltop citadels and ancient bazaars.

306 MILES (492 KM) ⊖

21,650 FT (6,599 M) ⊘

PAVED ⊖

Gone are the days when Albania's reputation was as uneven as its potholed highways. Today, cyclists are welcomed with open arms—and open roads, mostly smoothly paved ribbons. On this testing eight-day loop around its southern reaches, encounter a succession of historic highlights and sample its cultural diversity: you'll detect hints of Turkish, Italian, and other influences in cuisine, architecture, and attitudes.

Begin your odyssey at Qafe Thanë, near Lake Ohrid. A level scoot along the shoreline of this vast body of water takes you toward the border with North Macedonia. Hop over it to discover the first of several UNESCO World Heritage Sites—the lakeside monastery of St. Naum.

The greatest hits come thick and fast over succeeding days as you challenge quads and calves on a ride south toward the Gramoz Mountains and the Greek border. Meandering stages traverse shady woods, lofty meadows, and rocky gorges,

The stunning coastline of the "Albanian riviera", on the edge of the Adriatic Sea

interspersed with reminders of the civilizations that have claimed Albania over the millennia. Korçë has its Ottoman-era bazaar, while Gjirokastër is dominated by the intimidating hilltop bastion rebuilt by Ali Pasha Tepelenë, the infamous "Lion of Ioannina." And the remains of Greek, Roman, Venetian, and Ottoman occupation survive at Butrint. Throughout, you'll enjoy opportunities to sooth limbs in hot springs and fuel up on hearty Albanian fare—beef and lamb, flaky pastry *byrek*, fish, and seafood.

The most attractive leg of the route is the final stretch north. Riding alongside sun-glinted sea, you'll pass the popular

ELEVATION PROFILE

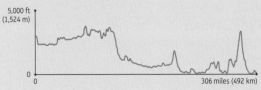

5,000 ft (1,524 m)

0

0   306 miles (492 km)

Accursed Mountains

Even less visited than the south, the country's northern reaches offer dramatic cycling. Pedal through the sheer, forbidding Albanian Alps, dubbed the "Accursed Mountains," from alluring Lake Shkodra to the timeless farming settlements and verdant valleys of Thethi and Valbona Valley National Parks.

Admire the Byzantine stone church and lush gardens of the **MONASTERY OF ST. NAUM** beside Lake Ohrid.

Cultural capital **KORÇË** is home to a five-centuries-old Ottoman-era bazaar. Explore its stone-built *khans* (traditional caravan-serais) and street-side cafés.

Watch for golden eagles, roe deer, wild boar, and even wolves in the dense forest surrounding **LLOGARA PASS**, a testing 3,281-ft (1,000-m) climb. Then enjoy an exhilarating descent toward the azure Adriatic.

Qafe Thanë

Lake Ohrid

NORTH MACEDONIA

St Naum

Pogradec

Korçë

Vlorë

ALBANIA

Orikum

GREECE

Llogara Pass

Himarë

Leskovik

Gjirokastër

Explore two and a half millennia of history at **BUTRINT**, wandering among a Greek acropolis and theater, Roman bathhouse, Byzantine basilica, and Venetian tower overlooking a lagoon.

Sarandë

Butrint

Hop off your bike to roam the precipitous "City of a Thousand Steps," **GJIROKASTËR**, dominated by its ancient castle.

0 ·········· km ·········· 20
0 ·········· miles ·········· 20

157

beaches of the so-called "Albanian Riviera" around Sarandë and Himarë. But this section is also the toughest, peaking with a hefty haul up the Llogara Pass—3,281 ft (1,000 m) of climbing, rewarded with a hurtle downhill through dense forest toward the finish line at the alluring resort of Vlorë. Here, overlooking the shimmering Ionian Sea, toast the end of your ride with a crisp Korçë beer or raki firewater.

On the edge of **LAKE MAVROVO** lies the partly submerged St. Nicholas Church. Nearby you'll find your first *spomenik*, a broad fresco of soldiers.

Gostivar

Mavrovo
National Park

Kichevo

Struga

Lake Ohrid

Stop off in **STRUGA**, on the shore of Lake Ohrid, to spy the ethereal white *spomenik* found in the town center.

65

Spomenik Spotting

SKOPJE, NORTH MACEDONIA (LOOP)

Explore the wildernesses of an often-overlooked European nation and discover its collection of otherworldly, Communist-era monuments. Built under Tito's Yugoslav dictatorship, each of these spomeniks *is utterly unique, combining brutalist concrete with space-age inspiration.*

464 MILES (747 KM)

30,200 FT (9,205 M)

PAVED / GRAVEL

North Macedonia is one of the youngest countries in Europe. Formerly part of Yugoslavia, it gained independence in the 1990s. Now, one of the last vestiges of the Communist era is the series of huge, sci-fi-like war memorials known as *spomeniks* erected during the reign of dictator Josip Broz Tito. North Macedonia is home to about 25 of them, and this route will take you to 12 of the most remarkable. They are in varying states of disrepair—some *spomeniks* are valued city-center landmarks, others stand on remote hillsides outside villages of no more than 15 homes—but the thing that unifies them all is their unearthly beauty. The hunt for these monuments winds through some spectacular landscapes: pedal between high mountain gorges and over scorched flatlands, deep into pine forests and to the shore of the gigantic inland Lake Ohrid. As you explore deeper, you'll discover a country that seems to defy definition.

ELEVATION PROFILE

6,500 ft
(1,981 m)

0

0

464 miles (747 km)

Begin your journey at the feet of Alexander the Great. A massive statue of him stands in the center of **SKOPJE**.

Top Tip

Spomeniks are war memorials and should always be treated respectfully, even those in a severe state of disrepair.

Kochani

Mitrašinci

Skopje

Veles

NORTH MACEDONIA

Above the town of **KAVADARTSI** lies a striking concrete "fortress" *spomenik*. It's reminiscent of the treehouses of Peter Pan, but with an eerie dystopian twist.

Berovo

Camp for the night in the woods above **BEROVO**, where there are a number of roadside picnic spots, perfect for cooking dinner and washing your clothes in the stream nearby.

Kruševo

Prilep

Kavadartsi

The *spomenik* in **PRILEP** is made up of a number of outsized "chessmen" figures, a powerful tribute to those from the city who fought in World War II.

Gevgelija

Climb the hill above **GEVGELIJA** to check out the strange "egg whisk" *spomenik* made from sheet metal, before rolling into town for a hearty lunch.

The skeletal remains of the Monument to Freedom at Gevgelija.

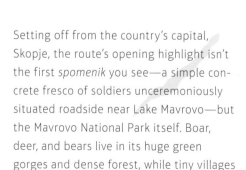

Setting off from the country's capital, Skopje, the route's opening highlight isn't the first *spomenik* you see—a simple concrete fresco of soldiers unceremoniously situated roadside near Lake Mavrovo—but the Mavrovo National Park itself. Boar, deer, and bears live in its huge green gorges and dense forest, while tiny villages tumble down its hillsides.

Left The Ilinden memorial at Kruševo, also known as the Makedonium

Traffic begins to pick up as you near Lake Ohrid—most of North Macedonia's tourism industry is situated around the shores of this vast lake, making it a fairly hectic place to be. Luckily, there are some of the country's very few bike lanes on the outskirts of lakeside Struga, which help to keep you somewhat protected from the trucks that hurtle by. You'll find another *spomenik* in the town center here, a tall,

twisting concrete obelisk in brilliant white, standing within its own park.

Leaving busy Lake Ohrid behind and turning your wheels northeast into the interior, things become more peaceful and wilder—and you, the cyclist, will become more of a curiosity. The highest point of the whole ride is at Krusevo, home to a gigantic *spomenik* that has been converted into a museum. The structure has a wide ramp leading up to it, while the center is a massive concrete globe with modular protrusions. It's often compared to a UFO that has—just moments ago—touched down on Earth's surface and unfurled its landing gear.

North Macedonia can be a furnace, so it's important to stay hydrated as you cross the plains in the center of the country. Keep an eye out for branches of Makpetrol, a domestic chain of gas

IN FOCUS
Recent History

North Macedonia became independent in 1991 after the break-up of Yugoslavia. Josip Broz Tito had ruled Communist Yugoslavia as a dictator from 1943 until his death—he initiated the great *spomenik*-building project. Formerly known as just Macedonia, the "North" was added in 2019 to bring to an end a long-running dispute with the country's southern neighbor, Greece.

stations full of icy refreshments and full-blast air conditioning. Most roadside stores sell bottled water, too.

Following the Vardar River, you'll reach Gevgelija and from there begin the return toward Skopje. In the eastern edges of the country you'll find secluded mountain villages nestled among the pine trees—a peaceful and cool escape from the heat of the flatlands. And just before Mitrašinci you'll encounter one of the east's few *spomeniks*, an upturned concrete claw that seems to be reaching up to the sky. It's nestled in a deserted forest atop a nearby hill, making it a tempting spot to camp.

It's not unusual in this part of the country to see shepherds tending their flocks, wooden crooks in hand, or find the road blocked by a herd of cows. You'll also glimpse some of the country's most run-down architecture in this region. Huge factory buildings, now empty shells, litter the landscape throughout the route, but are particularly frequent here.

North Macedonia might be tiny, but it has tremendous hidden depths. While many visitors merely skim the surface of this compelling country, by seeking out the *spomeniks*—lingering symbols of another era and a forgotten national identity—you'll discover another side of North Macedonia that few ever get to see.

Center Climbing from the flatlands around Strumica on the way to Berovo

Right The Monument to Brotherhood and Unity near Mitrasinci

North Macedonia might be tiny, but it has tremendous hidden depths.

162

MOROCCO

ALGERIA

WESTERN SAHARA

MAURITANIA

MALI

SENEGAL

GAMBIA

BURKINA FASO

GUINEA-BISSAU

GUINEA

BENIN

71

TOGO

SIERRA LEONE

CÔTE D'IVOIRE

GHANA

LIBERIA

69

AFRICA AND THE MIDDLE EAST

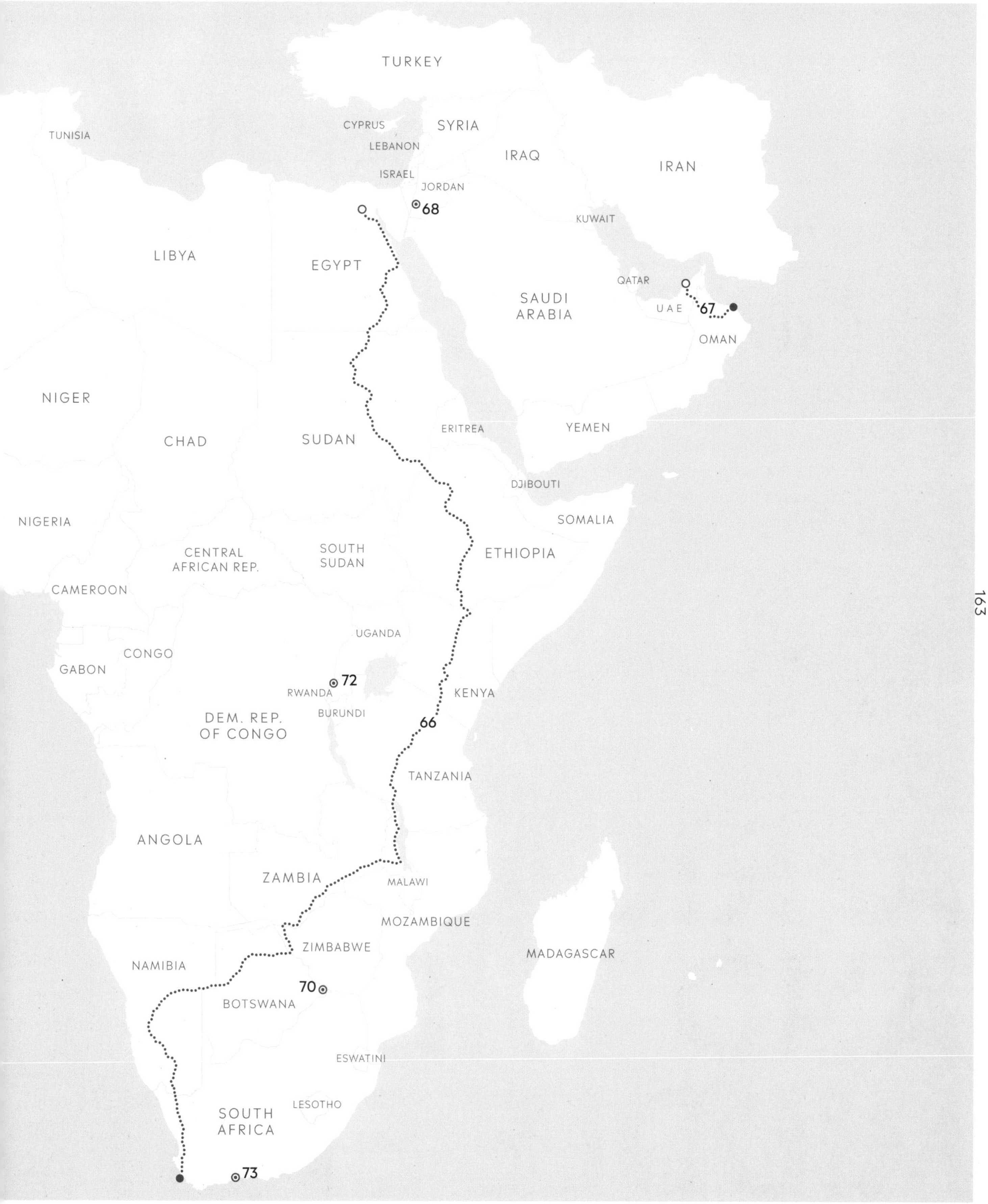
TURKEY
CYPRUS
SYRIA
TUNISIA
LEBANON
IRAQ
IRAN
ISRAEL
JORDAN
68
KUWAIT
LIBYA
EGYPT
QATAR
SAUDI ARABIA
UAE
67
OMAN
NIGER
CHAD
SUDAN
ERITREA
YEMEN
DJIBOUTI
NIGERIA
SOMALIA
CENTRAL AFRICAN REP.
SOUTH SUDAN
ETHIOPIA
CAMEROON
UGANDA
CONGO
GABON
72
RWANDA
KENYA
BURUNDI
DEM. REP. OF CONGO
66
TANZANIA
ANGOLA
ZAMBIA
MALAWI
MOZAMBIQUE
ZIMBABWE
MADAGASCAR
NAMIBIA
70
BOTSWANA
ESWATINI
LESOTHO
SOUTH AFRICA
73

Riders and support vehicles setting off from Cairo's pyramids on the Tour d'Afrique

66

Tour d'Afrique

CAIRO, EGYPT, TO
CAPE TOWN, SOUTH AFRICA

Tracing a route from the pyramids of Cairo to Cape Town's Table Mountain, the Tour d'Afrique has become a rite of passage for adventurous cyclists. This legendary trek promises a lifetime's worth of unforgettable experiences.

7,226 MILES (11,630 KM)

170,440 FT (51,950 M)

PAVED / GRAVEL / DIRT

Traversing the entire African continent from north to south, this extensive tour crosses through ten countries over four months. Each nation offers its own unique landscapes and languages, cultures and currencies, yet the tour's ten puzzle pieces fit together snugly to create a seamless adventure through the heart of Africa.

The Tour d'Afrique was the brainchild of Henry Gold, founder of cycling tour company TDA Global Cycling. He wanted to produce inexpensive, rugged mountain bikes in Africa, for Africans, as a solution to local transportation needs. Part of his launch strategy for the project was to organize a cycling tour that spanned the continent. The bicycle manufacturing didn't take off, but the inaugural Tour d'Afrique established a Guinness World Record for the fastest human-powered crossing of Africa and forever ensured the ride's revered status as the ultimate two-wheeled challenge.

ELEVATION PROFILE

10,000 ft
(3,048 m)

0

0   7,226 miles (11,630 km)

164

Top Tip
Wondering what kind of bike to bring? What kind of tires? Visit *tdaglobalcycling.com* for all the answers.

AFRICA AND THE MIDDLE EAST

REFUEL

Coke Stops

The Tour d'Afrique is famous for its Coke stops. These reviving rest stops in local villages allow dusty riders to rehydrate with a cold cola, orange Fanta, or apple-flavored Stim. Just as importantly, they provide a welcome opportunity to rub elbows with the locals and get a glimpse of everyday life in Africa.

The Tour d'Afrique is designed to cover an average of 78 miles (125 km) a day, but, of course, there's no such thing as average on this route. Every day of this ambitious ride is unique, because the journey encompasses all that Africa has to offer: endless wind-blown deserts, lush tropical vegetation, and frenzied city markets. During the 7,226-mile (11,630-km) expedition, you'll ride through the vast, arid expanse of the Sahara and the verdant forests of Tanzania, but you'll also wheel through the chaos and clamor of bustling urban centers like Addis Ababa, Nairobi, and Cape Town.

Along the way, you'll meet children offering high-fives from the side of the road, fellow cyclists with impossibly laden bicycles, and hard-working market traders selling a cornucopia of fresh fruit and textiles. You'll see a zoo's worth of wildlife, from the small (millipedes, chameleons, and scorpions) to the enormous (giraffes, hippos, and elephants). And you're likely to experience everything Mother Nature has in her arsenal, including sandstorms, rainstorms, headwinds, and heatwaves.

The Tour d'Afrique is an annual event run by TDA Global Cycling, but it's possible to ride the route self-supported if you're feeling brave. There's no doubt, however, that participating in the official tour brings some perks. TDA's two trucks do all the heavy lifting, so if you choose this option, then the only things you need to carry on each day's ride are snacks, water, and a few tools. Fresh meals are prepared for you daily by dedicated staff, who also set up the evening camp where you'll share the day's events with your fellow adventurers.

If you ride the route of the Tour d'Afrique self-supported, you'll need a trustworthy steel or aluminum bike, as well as dependable, lightweight camping and cooking gear. Being handy with a wrench is definitely an asset, although you'll find friendly, resourceful bicycle mechanics in every country you pass through. Food and supplies are inexpensive, especially in rural towns, but showers and clean toilets are few and far between. Staying hydrated is the key to staying healthy, so be sure to carry enough fresh water in bottles or a hydration pack.

A group of Tour d'Afrique cyclists chatting at a campsite in Kenya

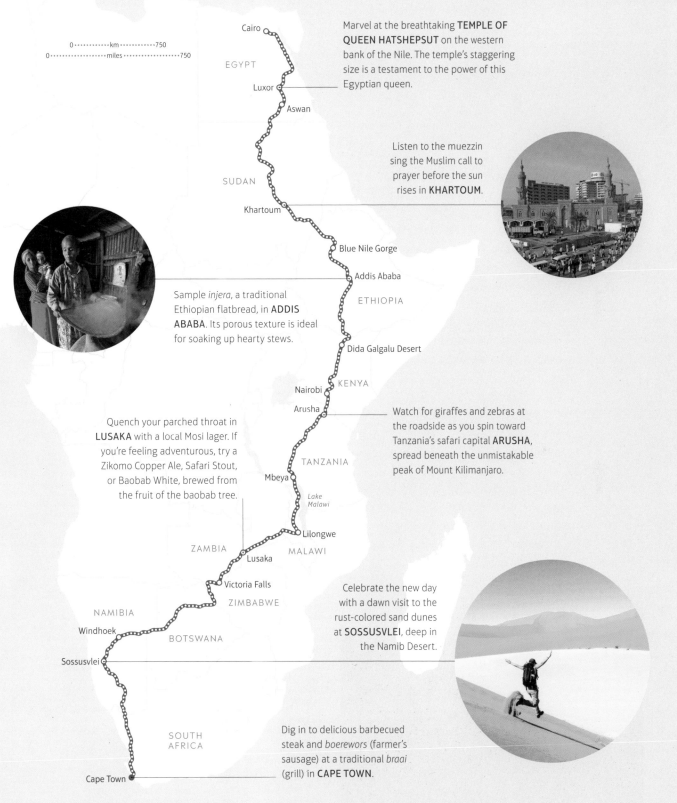

Cairo

EGYPT

0 ·········· km ·········· 750
0 ·········· miles ·········· 750

Luxor

Aswan

Marvel at the breathtaking **TEMPLE OF QUEEN HATSHEPSUT** on the western bank of the Nile. The temple's staggering size is a testament to the power of this Egyptian queen.

SUDAN

Khartoum

Listen to the muezzin sing the Muslim call to prayer before the sun rises in **KHARTOUM**.

Blue Nile Gorge

Addis Ababa

ETHIOPIA

Sample *injera*, a traditional Ethiopian flatbread, in **ADDIS ABABA**. Its porous texture is ideal for soaking up hearty stews.

Dida Galgalu Desert

Nairobi

KENYA

Arusha

Watch for giraffes and zebras at the roadside as you spin toward Tanzania's safari capital **ARUSHA**, spread beneath the unmistakable peak of Mount Kilimanjaro.

Quench your parched throat in **LUSAKA** with a local Mosi lager. If you're feeling adventurous, try a Zikomo Copper Ale, Safari Stout, or Baobab White, brewed from the fruit of the baobab tree.

TANZANIA

Mbeya

Lake Malawi

Lilongwe

ZAMBIA

Lusaka

MALAWI

Victoria Falls

ZIMBABWE

NAMIBIA

Windhoek

BOTSWANA

Sossusvlei

Celebrate the new day with a dawn visit to the rust-colored sand dunes at **SOSSUSVLEI**, deep in the Namib Desert.

SOUTH AFRICA

Dig in to delicious barbecued steak and *boerewors* (farmer's sausage) at a traditional *braai* (grill) in **CAPE TOWN**.

Cape Town

AFRICA AND THE MIDDLE EAST

The route itself sets off from the ancient Pyramids of Giza, beneath the timeless stare of the immortal Sphinx. As the morning mist rises, you begin your journey south along Egypt's Nile River Valley, across the forbidding sands of the Sahara Desert. Take advantage of the opportunity here to visit the Valleys of the Kings and Queens at Luxor—rest days off the bike not only are important to help to balance the physical challenges of this long ride but are a great opportunity to find out more about the local culture.

After crossing through unfailingly hospitable Sudan, you'll begin a long ascent into Ethiopia's biblical highlands, known as the Roof of Africa. These climbs are the highest you'll encounter en route, so you can take heart that you've already surmounted one of the ride's biggest challenges. Plus, the scenery brings its

IN FOCUS
The Naked Mile

For those cyclists on the Tour d'Afrique who are willing to risk sunburn in a tender spot, there's the option to ride the Naked Mile. What began as a dare has become a regular celebration of the flesh as participants strip down and roll (ever so carefully) along gravel roads in the remote Namibian desert, wearing nothing but a helmet and a smile.

own reward: the jagged peaks of the Simien Mountains lead to the breathtaking Blue Nile Gorge, which drops dramatically in a joyful 4,900-ft (1,500-m) downhill.

Leaving Ethiopia, the relentless heat of northern Kenya's Dida Galgalu Desert sets in. But there's another milestone to lift your spirits as you reach the equator, where you'll have the unique opportunity to stand in both the Northern and Southern Hemispheres at the same time. Continuing on past Mount Kilimanjaro, Africa's highest peak, you'll ride into verdant Tanzania, with a parade of giant baobab trees guiding you into the safari capital of Arusha. Congratulations—after two months of riding, you've managed to reach the halfway point in your journey. Celebrate by trading your saddle for a seat in a Land Cruiser, and spend a relaxing day exploring the nearby Ngorongoro Crater.

A cyclist with a fully laden bike looking out over the highlands of northern Ethiopia

Just 100 sq miles (260 sq km) in size, it's home to over 25,000 animals, including lions, zebras, buffaloes, and wildebeest.

The second half of the journey brings a change of pace as you pedal alongside the shores of Lake Malawi, dubbed the Lake of Stars—it's a tranquil stretch, with long, sandy beaches where you can rest and idly watch the fishing boats drift by. There's a sudden burst of drama in Zambia, as you ride through the swirling mist of the awe-inspiring Victoria Falls, before things switch back to a slower tempo in Botswana. The flat roads here follow the edge of the Kalahari to the Elephant Highway, where herds of pachyderms often stop traffic as they amble from one side of the road to the other. Rolling on through Namibia's eerie desert landscapes, punctuated by the bizarre silhouettes of quiver trees, you can quietly marvel at the fact that you've traveled 6,200 miles (10,000 km) under your own steam.

As you enter South Africa, your final, heavy-legged pedal strokes will take you to the finish point in the shadow of Cape Town's majestic Table Mountain. You'll have experienced every possible emotion over the past few months, from exhaustion to elation, and you'll find that the satisfaction of completing this singular journey is every bit as monumental as the challenge itself.

Elephants roaming through the tawny grasslands beneath Mount Kilimanjaro

MAKE IT SHORTER
Single Segment
The Tour d'Afrique is broken down into eight sectional rides, ranging from 7 to 22 days in length, so if you can't spare four months to cycle the whole route, then you can sign up to do a segment instead. You'll still get all the benefits of the full tour, including meals and transportation.

AFRICA AND THE MIDDLE EAST

Dodge camels, not cars, on the **AL QUDRA CYCLE PATH**. This 50-mile (80-km) traffic-free route takes you into the desert along a ribbon of smooth pavement slicing through the dunes.

Take a detour to **JEBEL SHAMS** if you're feeling intrepid (and fit). The highest mountain in Oman, it is also home to the spectacular Wadi Ghul, the "Arabian Grand Canyon."

Dubai
Al Qudra Cycle Path
Al Ain
UAE
OMAN
Jebel Shams
Ibri
Nizwa
Muscat

0 ········· km ········· 75
0 ········· miles ········· 75

67

Arabian Peninsula

DUBAI, UNITED ARAB EMIRATES,
TO MUSCAT, OMAN

Perfect for a winter cycling trip, this ride takes you across the desert from the bling of Dubai to the ancient forts and spice-scented souks of Oman.

Spend an afternoon in **NIZWA**, the old capital of Oman. Visit its famous souk to browse the wares and buy some lunch, then scale the walls of the old fort for the view.

Camels, sand dunes, and dazzling sunshine: this ride through Arabia has everything you might imagine. A remarkable traffic-free cycle path takes you out of Dubai and into the desert, where local Bedouin still live among the dunes. By the time you join the road, the city will be a distant memory as you pass camel ranches and race horses on the way to the Omani border.

Possessing just 6 miles (10 km) of paved road in 1970, Oman now has some of the newest, smoothest pavement in the world. And in contrast to the proud modernity of the UAE, there are ample reminders here of the region's history, with desert forts rising out of the sands and age-old souks offering their goods to passing travelers.

If the heat starts to get to you, simply pull over for fresh juice in the shade of a roadside shack. And remember: at the end of the ride lies the opportunity to wash away the dust with a dive into the glittering Indian Ocean.

407 MILES (655 KM) | 8,225 FT (2,507 M) | PAVED

170

ELEVATION PROFILE

3,000 ft
(914 m)

0

0   407 miles (655 km)

MAKE IT LONGER

Wahiba and the Wild Wadis

If you have a few extra days to spare, continue past Nizwa toward the east coast of Oman. Explore the dunes of the Wahiba Desert, cool off in the natural water holes of the wadis (Wadi Bani Khalid being the most famous), and enjoy turtle watching at the conservation center of Ras al Hadd.

68
Abarim Mountains

FEYNAN TO WADI MUSA, JORDAN

Uncover the treasures of the Jordanian desert as you pedal along a secret road to the ancient Nabataean city of Petra, carved from the very mountains through which you'll climb.

Top Tip
With nowhere to get water or food until after the climb, make sure that you carry supplies with you.

31 MILES (49 KM)

4,625 FT (1,410 M)

PAVED

Very few people—even Jordanians—know about the road that this ride follows up into the rugged Abarim range. Built by the military, it was originally closed to civilians, and the fact that it's now open to traffic has not been widely publicized. This seclusion only adds to the sense of adventure as you set off, winding through lifeless and harsh sand dunes, with the Abarim mountains erupting out of the desert ahead. Soon you're in their midst as the road climbs rapidly uphill, passing just below the peak of Jebel Proywe without giving you a chance to breathe.

Once you've reached the top, the hardest part of the ride is over, and the road turns south toward Petra, passing through a strangely lush and green plateau. This verdant paradise makes a stark contrast with the raw red face of the mountains and is a poignant reminder that, although a landscape may seem inhospitable, humanity has a knack for finding ways to exist and thrive almost anywhere.

ELEVATION PROFILE

5,000 ft
(1,524 m)

0

0   31 miles (49 km)

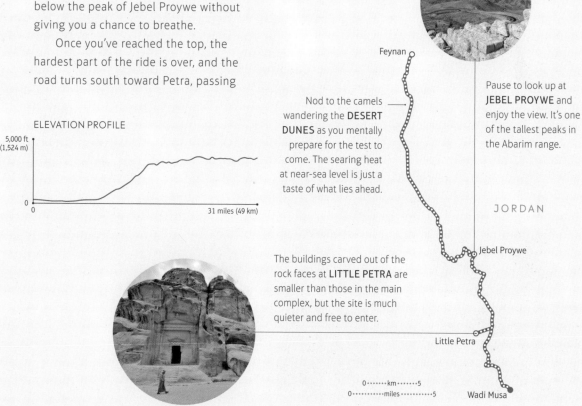

Feynan

Nod to the camels wandering the **DESERT DUNES** as you mentally prepare for the test to come. The searing heat at near-sea level is just a taste of what lies ahead.

Pause to look up at **JEBEL PROYWE** and enjoy the view. It's one of the tallest peaks in the Abarim range.

JORDAN

Jebel Proywe

The buildings carved out of the rock faces at **LITTLE PETRA** are smaller than those in the main complex, but the site is much quieter and free to enter.

Little Petra

0 ········ km ········ 5
0 ············ miles ············ 5

Wadi Musa

171

AFRICA AND THE MIDDLE EAST

69

Atlas Mountains

MARRAKECH, MOROCCO (LOOP)

Cycle through North Africa's crown jewel, the Atlas Mountains, on a spectacular route that offers a fun assortment of riding conditions and takes in Morocco's wonderful Berber hospitality.

567 MILES (912 KM)

44,439 FT (13,545 M)

PAVED / GRAVEL

172

The Atlas Mountains rise out of the Sahara, dominating the skyline of North Africa. These peaks have long been traversed by the local Berbers, who carved out trading routes across their dusty slopes. Today, those ancient pathways have been joined by a series of snaking modern roads, making the range a veritable playground for cyclists in search of a mountain-based challenge.

This ride is one for the all-rounders: it's got fast road segments, treacherous single-track, enticing gravel, and climbing—lots of climbing. Smooth pavement and switch-backs characterize the transition between Marrakech and the rocky wilderness of the mountains, while up in their heights, you'll find a haven of gravel pistes that wind precipitously through the steep terrain.

Scattered along the route are plenty of inexpensive *auberges* (hostels) and *riads* (traditional Moroccan accommodations), making it easy to do the ride as a fully supported tour—embrace the joys of traveling light and savor the generous local hospitality. The food that you'll get to sample at these stops is a reason in itself to do this ride. Expect hearty lunches of tagines and fresh salads and evening meals of couscous and Berber omelets. The only practicality you'll need to take care of is your water supply—between villages, there will often be no opportunity to fill your bottles, so make sure you've factored that into your setup.

ELEVATION PROFILE

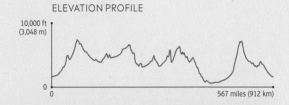

10,000 ft
(3,048 m)

0

0   567 miles (912 km)

Riding along smooth pavement toward the city of Ouarzazate

Get lost in the chaotic medina of **MARRAKECH**, a great place to shop for souvenirs at the end of your journey.

Catch your breath while admiring the 360-degree views at the top of **TIZI N'TICHKA**. On a clear day, you can see for miles over the Sahara.

Marrakech

Tizi n'Tichka Pass

Ouirgane

Ouarzazate

Stay a night in one of the small *auberges* near the top of **TIZI N'TEST**, all of which benefit from the most amazing sunset views in Morocco.

Tizi n'Test Pass

MOROCCO

Tazenakht

Taroudant

Aguinane Oasis

0 ·········· km ·········· 30
0 ·········· miles ·········· 30

Imi Mqourn

Issafn

Get some relief from the sun in the lush **AGUINANE OASIS**, a perfect place to rest in beautiful natural surroundings.

REFUEL

Berber Tea

Morocco's incredible food is a highlight for any rider exploring the country, but its tea culture really binds guests with Berber hosts. Expect to be invited to join many Berbers for sweet mint tea, made with black tea and fresh mint leaves picked from their own gardens and almost half a pot of sugar. It's the ultimate Atlas sports drink.

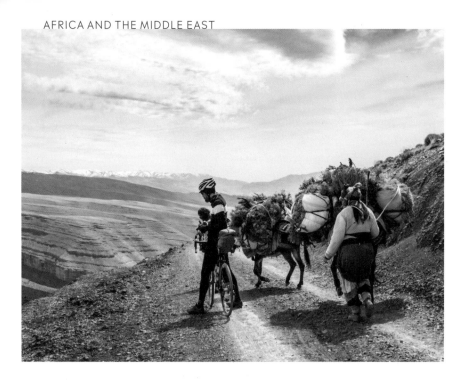

Sharing a trail with locals transporting goods by donkey

Your journey begins in Marrakech, a lively, colorful, and compact city. As you leave this bustling hub behind, the snowcapped peaks of the High Atlas rise suddenly and ominously from the desert before you. The ascent into the mountains is testing, leaving you gasping for air on the relentless gradients. Happily, there are plenty of roadside cafés where you can pause to catch your breath—like a local, request a *café noos-noos* (half-half): half coffee, half milk.

Your first serious climb of the journey comes in the form of the Tizi n'Tichka Pass, sitting 7,415 ft (2,260 m) above sea level. Thanks to continuing road improvements, it's a smooth, winding ride, snaking up the steep, rocky sides of the High Atlas. Don't think this means it's effortless, though—Tichka translates as "difficult."

Ouarzazate—the gateway to the Sahara—greets you at the bottom of your long descent. This ancient, red-hued city lies at the cross section of age-old trading routes, and its souks are a great place to work on your haggling skills. Fringed by hot, dry desert, the landscape here is in startling contrast to what's soon to follow in the foothills of the Anti-Atlas: the Aguinane Oasis. Verdant palm trees bedeck the floor of this rocky gorge, and you may well believe it's a mirage as you coast down the snaking road under the shade of the trees—the first relief from the Moroccan sun for a while.

Entering the Anti-Atlas themselves feels like stepping back in time. Ancient Casbahs dominate small dusty villages, and old colonial pistes stretch endlessly through the arid, rugged terrain. Some of these forgotten roads require small amounts of pushing the bike where the trail has been washed out and never rebuilt, but the benefit is no traffic—you'll feel like you are truly alone in the wide wilderness of Morocco, where your only company will be a few Berber shepherds and their flocks.

> You'll feel like you are truly alone in the wide wilderness of Morocco, where your only company will be a few Berber shepherds and their flocks.

A signpost indicating the way to a refreshment stop

The route back over the High Atlas takes you along the Tizi n'Test, perhaps the range's most famous road—and for good reason. Its serpentine switchbacks lead you from the heated desert floor to the incredible vista of the pass above. Your tired legs may lament over this last, unabating climb, but as you gain altitude, the air steadily cools, willing you onward and upward. At the top are several *auberges*, each claiming the best views of the Sahara. Stop and savor one last night in the mountains, before coasting downhill to Marrakech tomorrow.

MAKE IT LONGER

Edge of the Atlas

Transportation within Morocco is generally affordable and reliable, and finishing your ride in a different location and making your way back to Marrakech by bus (bikes are easily stowed in the hold) is easy for those wishing to go farther. At the western edge of the Atlas lies the holiday town of Agadir, which you can access by fast, paved roads leading down from the High Atlas to the coast.

The Tizi n'Tichka Pass, a difficult climb in the High Atlas mountains

70

Mountain Bike Safari in the Land of Giants

POINT DRIFT, BOTSWANA (LOOP)

Embark on an adrenaline-fueled wildlife encounter like no other, pedaling past lumbering elephants and majestic big cats on a thrilling mountain bike safari in Mashatu Game Reserve.

Known as the "Land of Giants," Mashatu Game Reserve is famed for its more than 1,500-strong population of wild elephants. But they're not the only large creatures you'll see as you explore this fenceless sanctuary. While cycling along migration trails elephants have trampled for thousands of years, you'll also clock up unsurpassed sightings of big cats, including lions, leopards, and cheetahs.

This might all sound a bit too close for comfort, but—as your mandatory park guide will tell you—if you stick together in single file, then the animals will see you as a very long shape rather than lunch. And because bikes are much quieter than jeeps, the wildlife isn't as easily spooked, which means you'll get closer to canopy-munching giraffes, balletic antelopes, and herds of pounding wildebeest. The chance to sleep out under the stars rounds off this unforgettable experience, which will leave you feeling infinitely closer to nature.

⊖ 49 MILES (79 KM)

⊙ 1,198 FT (365 M)

⊖ GRAVEL / DIRT

IN FOCUS
Conservation

Botswana is home to more than one-third of Africa's elephants, and the country is recognized globally for its conservation successes. Research suggests that elephants have a cognitive ability to understand areas of threat and safety, which may explain why they have increasingly sought refuge in Botswana.

Listen for the thrilling snap and crackle of the bush as you wait for elephants at **CHURCH TREE**, a popular sighting spot on the Pitsane River.

ELEVATION PROFILE

3,000 ft
(914 m)

1,500 ft
(457 m)

0   49 miles (79 km)

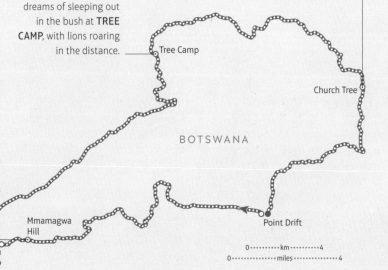

Fulfill your childhood dreams of sleeping out in the bush at **TREE CAMP**, with lions roaring in the distance.

Tree Camp

Church Tree

BOTSWANA

Point Drift

Watch the sun slide over the horizon while you sip a sundowner, perched on top of **MMAMAGWA HILL**'s massive sandstone ridge.

Mmamagwa Hill

Kgotla Camp

0 ·········· km ·········· 4
0 ·········· miles ·········· 4

Relax in **FREETOWN**. This chaotic city is close to some of Africa's most beautiful beaches, making it the perfect place to rest your tired legs.

Stop by Stylish's bike shop in **LUNSAR**. Stylish is one of the country's most dedicated cycling advocates and loves to show his homeland to visitors.

Head north toward the **MAYOSSO NATURE RESERVE** near Magburaka, one of the only parks in Sierra Leone that protects the threatened Dwarf Crocodile.

Makeni

Magburaka

Lunsar

Freetown

SIERRA LEONE

Bo

0 ·········· km ·········· 40
0 ·········· miles ·········· 40

71

Swit Salone

BO TO FREETOWN, SIERRA LEONE

Experience the riotous spectrum of life in "Swit Salone"— Sweet Sierra Leone—as you cycle from its verdant southern region to the thriving coastal metropolis of Freetown.

206 MILES (332 KM)

7,020 FT (2,140 M)

PAVED / DIRT

Setting off from the busy city of Bo, you're plunged wheelfirst into the heat and chaos of Sierra Leone. Prepare yourself for a friendly, sometimes frenzied, welcome when arriving in villages: you'll make quite a spectacle, as cycle tourists are rare in these parts. That said, the sport is on the rise in this tiny nation. Be sure to pause in Makeni, where Isata Mondeh, the women's national cycling champion, runs a bicycle repair shop, and keep an eye out for the multi-colored jerseys of the Lunsar Cycling Team—the country's biggest club—as you pass through their home town.

Traveling along a mixture of hard-packed mud and paved roads, this ride is an all-out attack on the senses. Bright-orange mud and lush green jungle foliage are never far away, even when you head into the towns, and the heady scents of thick humidity and roadside cooking will tantalize your nose. The Freetown finale offers something different again, with abundant traffic, plenty of noise, and a host of pristine beaches straight out of paradise.

177

Top Tip

Sierra Leone has 23 spoken languages, but *tenky* (thank you) and *howdebody?* (how are you?) are understood everywhere.

ELEVATION PROFILE

1,500 ft
(457 m)

0

0   206 miles (332 km)

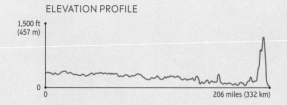

The idyllic sands of River Number 2 Beach, lying just outside Freetown

AFRICA AND THE MIDDLE EAST

72

Land of a Thousand Hills

RUHENGERI TO GISENYI, RWANDA

In a country known for its lush green landscapes and soaring mountains, there is no more jaw-dropping ride than this, from the slopes of Rwanda's volcanoes to the shores of one of Africa's Great Lakes.

44 MILES (71 KM) / 2,800 FT (853 M) / PAVED / GRAVEL / DIRT

Rwanda is a cyclist's paradise, with endless red dirt roads and smooth tarmac to explore, and—as implied by its nickname, the "Land of a Thousand Hills"—no shortage of climbs to test even the most accomplished riders. But the verdant, volcanic backdrop to this ride makes it one of the most special in the country, and perhaps in all of Africa. It's also largely downhill, making it accessible to all levels of cyclists, following a route that rises gently from Ruhengeri—a spartan frontier town that's the gateway to Volcanoes National Park—before making an exhilarating final descent into Gisenyi, beside Lake Kivu.

IN FOCUS

Adrien Niyonshuti

Adrien Niyonshuti was spotted at the age of 19 during Rwanda's first Wooden Bike Classic. He went on to become Rwanda's most successful cyclist, competing at the London and Rio Olympics and riding professionally for Team Dimension Data.

The events of 1994 have cast a long shadow over Rwanda's reputation. Between April and June of that year, more than 800,000 Tutsi and moderate Hutus were murdered by bands of Hutu militia in one of the most brutal genocides of the 20th century. These days, the country is safe, the leadership ambitious, and, as a result, travelers are beginning to flock to see its rain forests and game parks. Despite growing visitor numbers, you're likely to see very few cycle tourists, so be prepared for

Lush countryside near Gisenyi, overlooked by the peaks of Volcanoes National Park

178

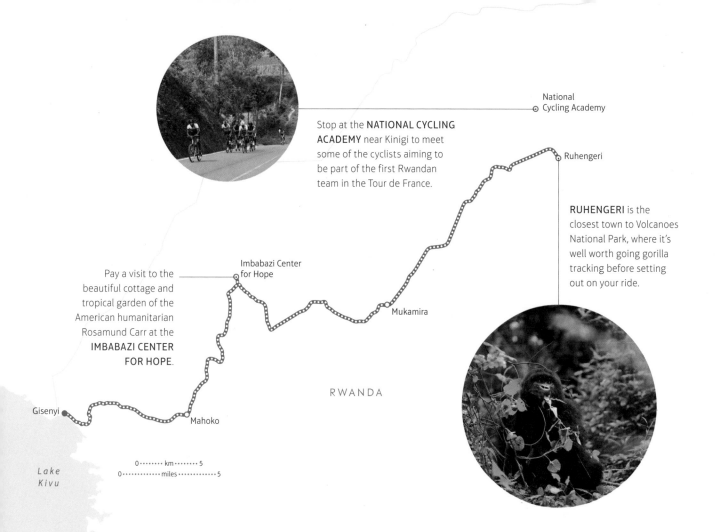

National
Cycling Academy

Stop at the **NATIONAL CYCLING
ACADEMY** near Kinigi to meet
some of the cyclists aiming to
be part of the first Rwandan
team in the Tour de France.

Ruhengeri

RUHENGERI is the
closest town to Volcanoes
National Park, where it's
well worth going gorilla
tracking before setting
out on your ride.

Imbabazi Center
for Hope

Pay a visit to the
beautiful cottage and
tropical garden of the
American humanitarian
Rosamund Carr at the
**IMBABAZI CENTER
FOR HOPE**.

Mukamira

R W A N D A

Gisenyi

Mahoko

0 ·········· km ·········· 5
0 ·········· miles ·········· 5

*Lake
Kivu*

plenty of cheering from locals as you pedal
through village after village in Africa's
most densely populated country.

The ride begins with a short stretch
on pavement toward Mount Muha Bura.
This peak and its neighboring volcanoes
form the border with Uganda and the
Democratic Republic of Congo and are
home to some of the last remaining
mountain gorillas on the planet. Keep
an eye out here for members of the
Rwandan national cycling team whooshing
past on training rides—their headquarters
are nearby, just south of Kinigi. As you
settle into a comfortable rhythm, you'll
begin traversing the volcanic plain, passing
through patchwork fields of banana and
bamboo plantations for much of the day.
Keep looking up from your handlebars—
the views around almost every corner
are scintillating, stretching south over
Rwanda's green patchwork of hills.

You can support the local economy
by hiring a guide for the ride, which is
well worth it for the insider knowledge.
Especially fun is to get translations of all
the things local people are saying about
you. You will, after all, be a rare cycling
visitor everywhere you go.

ELEVATION PROFILE

10,000 ft
(3,048 m)

3,000 ft
(914 m)

0

44 miles (71 km)

AFRICA AND THE MIDDLE EAST

Each deeply cut river valley forms its own pass, making for exhilarating, yet technical, riding. Expect it to be heavy on the legs and lungs on the ascents

73

Forest Passes of the Garden Route

MOSSEL BAY TO PLETTENBERG BAY, SOUTH AFRICA

With its magical mix of forested valleys, heart-pumping mountain passes, and glittering ocean views, this cycle through South Africa's Garden Route proves that the region is more than deserving of its evocative name.

145 MILES (234 KM)

13,057 FT (3,980 M)

PAVED / GRAVEL

180

Nowhere in South Africa can you cycle through as much indigenous forest as along the Garden Route, a spectacular coastal strip in the Western Cape province. It's a little while before you encounter it on this ride, though, as most of the first stretch away from Mossel Bay crosses undulating farmlands carpeted with grassy green fields. But the approach into George brings a glimmer of trees on the horizon, and soon you're right in the thick of them on the challenging climb up the iconic Montagu Pass. The oldest unaltered pass still in use in South Africa, its tight hairpin bends wind through forested lower slopes to emerge with sweeping vistas over the crumpled folds of the mountain.

It's from this point that you really get to immerse yourself in the dense, indigenous Afromontane Forest (local lore says it should be spelled with a capital "F" because it is considered a living, breathing entity with its own soul and personality). Taking the Seven Passes route between George and Knysna, the ride follows a 47-mile (76-km) tree-lined gravel road that crosses seven different rivers (it can be heavily potholed after rain). Each deeply cut river valley forms its own pass, making for exhilarating, yet technical, riding. Expect it to be heavy on the legs and lungs on the ascents, followed by tight corners on the downhills, accentuated by a loose-over-hard gravel surface—go easy on the brakes. Homtini Pass is undoubtedly the highlight, and it's here that you should take some time to hop off the bike and soak up the natural sounds and earthy scents of the Forest, full of towering trees with intriguing names like mountain waxberry, white stinkwood, and kamassi.

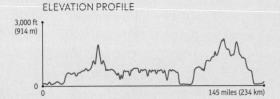

ELEVATION PROFILE

3,000 ft (914 m)

0

0   145 miles (234 km)

Be sure to stop at the delightful **HOEKWIL COUNTRY CAFÉ** to try the delectable cheesecake—it was once voted the best in South Africa.

Take a detour into the **GARDEN ROUTE TRAIL PARK**, a spectacular network of singletrack trails through a section of forest where wild elephants still roam.

0 ·········· km ·········· 15
0 ·········· miles ·········· 15

SOUTH AFRICA

Montagu Pass
Redberry Farm
George
Hoekwil
Karatara
Garden Route Trail Park
Homtini Pass
Phantom Pass
Knysna
Plettenberg Bay
Mossel Bay

Fuel up on various berry delights at **REDBERRY FARM**. There's lots of shade and plenty of places to sit and kick back.

Look out for the hauntingly beautiful moths after which **PHANTOM PASS** is named. These delicate gray and brown creatures arrive in the area each spring.

KNYSNA is well known for its oysters. Sample some of the town's freshest at O Pescador, on the Waterfront in Knysna Quays.

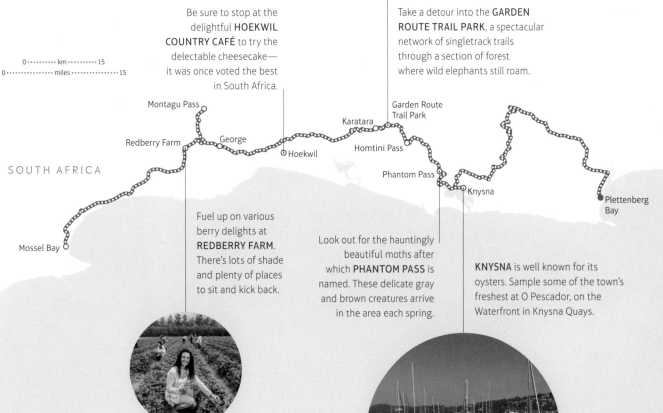

The final leg from Knysna to Plettenberg Bay starts out tough, with a long, steady climb under forest canopy. Distract yourself by looking out for shy antelope species, such as bushbuck and blue duiker, and see if you can spot the Knysna turaco after hearing its "kok-kok-kok." At the top, the trees thin out, leading into a pattern of verdant river valleys, pockets of forestry plantations, and pastoral farmlands on a high plateau. The descent into Plettenberg Bay ends the ride as it began: beside the inviting warm waters of the Indian Ocean.

MAKE IT LONGER
Harkerville Red Route

Stay in Plettenberg Bay an extra day and ride the famed Harkerville Red Route. It's a challenging 15-mile (24-km) MTB loop on forest trails and singletrack and features some spectacular clifftop riding. Expect rooty sections in the forest and blue gum plantations and then hardpack (muddy in the rainy season) in the fynbos (shrubland).

RUSSIA

KAZAKHSTAN

MONGOLIA

⊙ 74

UZBEKISTAN

⊙ 75
KYRGYZSTAN

TURKMENISTAN

TAJIKISTAN

78

AFGHANISTAN

NORTH
KOREA

SOUTH
KOREA

84

JAPAN

86 ⊙

CHINA

PAKISTAN

NEPAL

77 ⊙
BHUTAN

⊙ 83

76

TAIWAN

85

INDIA

BANGLADESH

MYANMAR

LAOS

79 ⊙   80 ⊙

THAILAND

82

VIETNAM

PHILIPPINES

CAMBODIA

SRI
LANKA

81

BRUNEI

MALAYSIA

SINGAPORE

INDONESIA

TIMOR-
LESTE

ASIA

74

Khangai Mountains Traverse

TSETSERLEG TO TARIAT SUM, MONGOLIA

Savor the serene expanse of the Mongolian steppe on this ride through the Khangai Mountains, winding from Tsetserleg to the shores of the mighty Terkhiin Tsagaan Nuur—the Great White Lake.

300 MILES (483 KM) 11,581 FT (3,530 M) DIRT

184

Located in the center of the country—some 250 miles (400 km) to the west of the capital, Ulaanbaatar—Mongolia's Khangai Mountains are beautiful and serene, promising a heady mix of rugged passes, lush forest, rolling grasslands, and crystal-clear streams. In a country as vast as Mongolia, the range is relatively compact in size, which makes the logistics for crossing it—the aim of this ride—relatively straightforward.

Following a horseshoe shape, the route runs from the populated settlement of Tsetserleg to Terkhiin Tsagaan Nuur (the Great White Lake). The scenery en route is best described as the Mongolia of popular imagination—mile upon mile of verdant, grassy steppe, speckled with *ghers* (yurts) and yaks. It's this sense of abundant, almost overwhelming space that really defines the ride. Land use across the country is shared, and with so many Mongolians still nomadic or seminomadic, it's a simple case of riding until you're out of energy, pulling over,

pitching your tent, and enjoying a blissful night's sleep wherever strikes your fancy.

Aside from the meditative grandeur of experiencing Mongolia's sheer sense of uninterrupted size, sights along the way include a remote set of "deer stones"—ancient megaliths carved with figurative symbols—and a series of *ovoos* (shrines), marking each pass. The route features a number of river crossings, depending on the season, and two high passes. Riders can also expect a few small and basic settlements in which rudimentary supplies can be bought—or, if you're lucky, a plate of meaty dumplings can be consumed.

Outside of these small settlements, there's not a fenceline to be seen, and traffic is similarly scarce—for the most part, it's rare to pass more than a few vehicles a day. Although it's important to be self-sufficient at all times, you're sure to encounter plenty of Mongolian hospitality during your ride. From every *gher* you pass, expect warm smiles and often a glass of fresh yak milk or a piece of jaw-breakingly dry cheese. Custom dictates that the latter will likely be washed down with a shot of homebrew vodka. And for the true Mongolian experience, always be prepared to swap a spin on your bike for a gallop on a horse.

ELEVATION PROFILE

10,000 ft (3,048 m)

3,000 ft (914 m)

0   300 miles (483 km)

Circling *Ovoos*

In Mongolia, mountain passes are marked by collections of tree trunks called *ovoos*. They reflect the country's spiritual duality: the surrounding animal skulls are clues to its Shamanistic traditions, while Buddhist prayer flags echo those found on the Tibetan plateau. Mongolians walk around each *ovoo* three times and add a stone to its base—or even milk and vodka—in reverence to the Sky God, Tingri.

Tariat Sum

Terkhiin Tsagaan Nuur

The route follows the northern flank of **TERKHIIN TSAGAAN NUUR**, offering your last chance for idyllic camping before reaching Tariat Sum.

Changia

MONGOLIA

Tsetserleg

Ease your way into your Mongolian experience by starting at the comfortable **FAIRFIELD GUESTHOUSE AND BAKERY** in Tsetserleg.

Deer stones

Around 100 miles (160 km) in, look out for a circle of **DEER STONES**, which date back to the Bronze and Iron Ages. There's no better picnic spot.

Jargalant

Zag

Stock up in **ZAG** if you're low on supplies. You'll also find classic meat and gristle dumplings on the menu at the restaurant here.

```
0 ········km········ 25
0 ········miles········ 25
```

It's this sense of abundant, almost overwhelming space that really defines the ride.

You'll either love or hate **SHAMSHY PASS**—it's likely to require some pushing, even on the descent. The views, however, are magnificent.

Bishkek

Tokmok

Shamshy Pass

Balykchy

Issyk Köl

KYRGYZSTAN

0 ·······km········ 50
0 ·········miles ·········· 50

Song Köl

Burkan Valley

Stay in a yurt at **SONG KÖL**: this high-altitude lake is the summer home for many nomad families and is also a great place to go for a swim.

Soak in the wild beauty of the **BURKAN VALLEY AND ARABEL PLATEAU**. This is a long, remote segment, and while a few nomads will invite you in for tea, you should be prepared not to see any civilization for a while.

75

Tien Shan Mountains

BISHKEK, KYRGYZSTAN (LOOP)

Ancient nomad trails take you deep into the Kyrgyz wilderness, where you'll find hospitable yurt villages and postcard-perfect alpine scenery on a ride that's epic in every sense of the word.

593 MILES (955 KM) 31,150 FT (9,495 M) GRAVEL / DIRT

Tien Shan translates as "Mountains of Heaven," and you will soon appreciate why the range was so named on this circular ride from the Krygyz capital of Bishkek. Embarking on a loop of staggering mountain passes, glittering turquoise lakes, and fertile alpine valleys, you'll experience soaring altitudes and divine views that will leave you breathless in more ways than one.

Much of the route is above 9,843 ft (3,000 m), and some of the "roads" have fallen into such disrepair that several of

the passes can only be conquered on two wheels. This remoteness makes you feel like you've stepped into a different world—and from the yurts, horses, and eagles that you'll see en route, it's clear that this is the nomads' world. Follow their lead on the ancient trails, camping under starry skies or staying in a welcoming yurt where you'll be treated like one of the family.

REFUEL

Kymyz

The nomads you meet on the trail are likely to offer you some *kymyz*—fermented horse's milk. This sour milk is an acquired taste, but is said by the locals to be good for your gut health.

ELEVATION PROFILE

13,000 ft
(3,962 m)

0

0   593 miles (955 km)

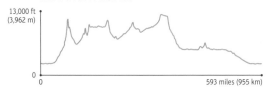

Get lost in the winding backstreets of **JAISALMER**. The sandstone architecture of this medieval city rises like a mirage out of the desert.

I N D I A

Absorb the complex spirituality of India in **PUSHKAR**, a city sacred to both Hindus and Sikhs. Home to over 400 temples, it abuts a holy lake where pilgrims bathe and make religious offerings.

Jaisalmer

Khimsar Fort

Pushkar

Jaipur

Agra

0 ········ km ········ 100
0 ········ miles ·········· 100

Learn about the history and culture of Rajasthan in **JAIPUR**, aka the "pink city," where there are multiple royal palaces and forts to explore.

76
Crossing Rajasthan

JAISALMER TO AGRA, INDIA

Pedal along ancient trade routes between the beautiful cities of Rajasthan, experiencing the best of the Indian desert, where peacocks roam free and cows rule the road.

525 MILES (845 KM)
4,775 FT (1,455 M)
PAVED

Cycling across this part of India means full immersion in all its colorful, noisy glory. Beginning in the "golden city" of Jaisalmer, next to its sprawling sandstone fort, the route leads you through the Thar Desert and on toward Agra, where it finishes at the world's most extravagant monument to love: the Taj Mahal.

In between, you'll wind your way through tiny desert settlements, pulling over for tooth-achingly sweet cups of cardamom-scented chai whenever you pass a roadside shack. Every couple of days, you'll emerge from the wilderness into the wall of sound and smells that is an Indian city. Join the complex chaos

of motorcyclists, cows, buffaloes, and rickshaws all competing for space on the road network, and enjoy the plentiful palaces, temples, and forts that speckle this part of the world—the Hawa Mahal palace and Amer Fort, both in Jaipur, are particular highlights. Embrace the mayhem, hang onto your helmet, and enjoy the ride.

Cycling along a narrow road through the desert in Rajasthan

ELEVATION PROFILE

3,000 ft
(914 m)

0

0

525 miles (845 km)

Soak up the local culture in capital city **THIMPHU**—if you can, time your visit for one of the famous *tsechus* (Buddhist festivals), when the city plays host to noisy and colorful celebrations.

Be blessed by a wooden phallus at **CHIMI LHAKHANG**, dedicated to so-called "Divine Madman" Lama Drukpa Kunley. Renowned for his sexual exploits, he's the inspiration behind the penises daubed on many houses.

77

Bhutan Demi-Traverse

PARO TO JAKAR, BHUTAN

Get a head for heights on a challenging ride halfway across the "Land of the Thunder Dragon," conquering breath-snatching Himalayan passes to explore mighty fortress-monasteries and remote mountain villages little changed in centuries.

205 MILES (331 KM)

26,775 FT (8,155 M)

PAVED / GRAVEL / DIRT

You don't saddle up in Bhutan expecting an easy ride—but in this long-isolated kingdom, guarded by Himalayan peaks soaring to over 24,600 ft (7,500 m), your exertions are guaranteed to be rewarded with an unforgettable adventure. This spectacular Buddhist land is bisected by an east–west road that links most of the country's biggest *dzongs*—huge fortress-monasteries—and offers an achievable, if challenging, roller-coaster ride into the country's heart.

But don't take our word for it: former king Jigme Singye Wangchuck, a keen biker who launched the 167-mile (269-km) Tour of the Dragon race between the Bumthang Valley and Bhutanese capital Thimphu, has often been seen pedaling around the latter. It's all part of his concept of Gross National Happiness, promoting the importance of physical and mental well-being over wealth. And boy, does it work.

You'll discover the benefits of biking by tackling a route that follows the Tour of the Dragon route in reverse, adding a stretch at the western end to begin near the only international airport at Paro. From that town, it's a day's ride east to the capital, giving you a relatively easy first leg. But that's just the warm-up for a succession of

ELEVATION PROFILE

13,000 ft (3,962 m)

0

0   205 miles (331 km)

188

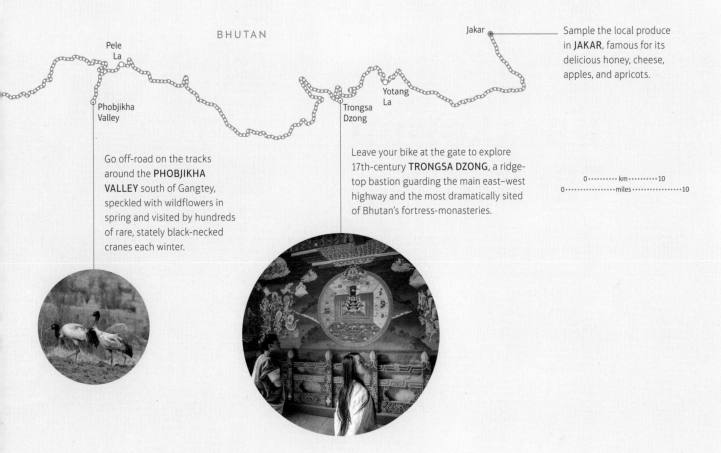

BHUTAN

Pele
La

Phobjikha
Valley

Go off-road on the tracks
around the **PHOBJIKHA
VALLEY** south of Gangtey,
speckled with wildflowers in
spring and visited by hundreds
of rare, stately black-necked
cranes each winter.

Jakar

Sample the local produce
in **JAKAR**, famous for its
delicious honey, cheese,
apples, and apricots.

Yotang
La

Trongsa
Dzong

Leave your bike at the gate to explore
17th-century **TRONGSA DZONG**, a ridge-
top bastion guarding the main east–west
highway and the most dramatically sited
of Bhutan's fortress-monasteries.

0 ········· km ·········10
0 ················· miles ·················10

passes, day after day topping 9,843 ft
(3,000 m) and more: Dochu La, Pele La,
and Yotang La, all marked by kaleidoscopic
prayer flags, a cluster of *chortens* (shrines),
and, with luck, panoramic views of snowcapped summits standing sentinel on the
northern horizon. Naturally, what goes
up must enjoy a thrilling downhill on the
other side, and you'll typically end up at
one of those hulking *dzongs*, invariably
with a comfortable hotel nearby.

Many sections of the highway also
traverse national parks, encompassing
broad, wildflower-strewn valleys and
hemlock, cypress and rhododendron
forests bustling with nutcrackers, and—
though you'd be lucky (or not) to spot
them—tigers and leopards. Cycling's the

ideal way to enjoy these verdant swathes,
giving ample opportunities to pause and
look around. And it's a great icebreaker
with the locals you'll meet at roadside
stalls peddling apples, chilies, and yak's
cheese. Sights, scenery, snacks, cycles:
it's a road map to nirvana.

MAKE IT LONGER
Tiger's Nest

As a warm-up before starting the main
journey, consider a side trip to Bhutan's most-
photographed sight, Taktsang Goemba, the
"Tiger's Nest Monastery," clinging improbably
to the side of a cliff. It's an undulating 7-mile
(11-km) ride north from Paro to the parking
area, followed by a steep 2-mile (3-km) hike.

The Karakoram Highway, winding through the dramatic Hunza Valley

78

Karakoram Highway

ISLAMABAD, PAKISTAN, TO KASHGAR, CHINA

One of the world's highest, hardest, and most scenic roads, the Karakoram Highway carves a path through Pakistan's high mountains and across the Xinjiang steppes to China's westernmost city.

805 MILES (1,298 KM)

64,250 FT (19,583 M)

PAVED / GRAVEL / DIRT

The Karakoram Highway (or KKH) has been a classic of cycle touring since it was first completed in 1979, a joint project between the governments of Pakistan and China. Linking these two very different countries, this challenging mountain road passes through some of Asia's finest scenery. Many will ride it as part of a larger transcontinental journey, but its rich variety, along with the fact that there are no boring stretches in between the good bits, means that it also checks all the boxes for a stand-alone trip.

Ride the KKH if you love vivid mountain scenery and want to discover a little-known and often misrepresented region of South Asia. Pakistan's tourist industry has dwindled over the last couple of decades due to security concerns, but in general, the northern area is safe, and foreign travelers pass through every year with relatively few problems. You'll often have the place to yourself and, as a rare visitor, will be treated to an extra-warm welcome.

ELEVATION PROFILE

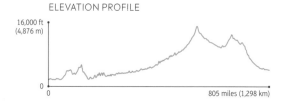

16,000 ft (4,876 m)

0

0   805 miles (1,298 km)

Top Tip

The best time to
cycle is April–May or
September–October,
when temperatures are
mild and passes are
free of snow.

Kashgar

Rent a yurt from the Kyrgyz yak herders who live around **KARAKUL LAKE**. On a clear day, you'll see the peaks of Muztagh Ata and Kongur reflected in its waters.

Karakul Lake

Ulugh Rabat

Tashkurgan

CHINA

Give yourself a rest day or two in **KARIMABAD**, the tourist capital of Gilgit-Baltistan. There are quiet cafés to refuel in and the magnificent Baltit Fort to explore.

Khunjerab Pass

Sost

Attabad Lake

Sip a chai at the **NANGA PARBAT VIEW HOTEL** as you gaze out over Nanga Parbat itself. It's the world's ninth-tallest mountain and Pakistan's second highest, after K2.

Ghulmet

Karimabad

Admire the turquoise waters of **ATTABAD LAKE**, formed in 2010 when a landslide dammed the Hunza River. The road was originally submerged but has now been diverted via several tunnels.

Gilgit

Nanga Parbat View Hotel

Indus Valley

Chilas

PAKISTAN

Chattar Plain

Mansehra

Abbottabad

0 ·········· km ·········· 100
0 ·········· miles ·········· 100

Before you leave **ISLAMABAD**, visit the city's Shah Faisal Mosque. This striking place of worship blends traditional architecture with ultramodern design.

Taxila

Islamabad

Take a lunch break to wander around the ancient city of **TAXILA**, a UNESCO World Heritage Site famed for its early Buddhist architecture.

It's in the Indus Valley that you'll find the KKH at its most vertiginous—in some places, it's little more than a narrow ledge

The lower stretches of the KKH take you north from the hubbub of the Indus plains around Islamabad, gradually ascending through leafy Abbottabad and Mansehra, before leaving the fertile Pothohar Plateau at Chattar Plain. From there, the route plunges down toward the river valleys that make up the next few hundred miles. Rich farmland and wooded slopes give way to rocky canyons as the road reaches the Indus Valley, whose increasingly steep sides may induce a feeling of claustrophobia. Travelers have been passing this way for millennia, as proven by the rock carvings left by Buddhist traders and pilgrims— you'll see some fine examples around Chilas.

It's in the Indus Valley that you'll find the KKH at its most vertiginous—in some places, it's little more than a narrow ledge, blasted out of the rock faces that overlook the churning Indus. Very little grows here, and in summer, the heat reflecting off the cliffs can make the place feel like an oven. Although the road is still relatively low at this point, the mountains you pass are some of the world's highest, and they're getting higher every year, as the Indian tectonic plate continues to thrust itself beneath the rest of Asia. This seismic instability makes the continued existence of the Karakoram Highway all the more impressive—every year, it has to be repaired after various earthquakes, landslides, and avalanches, and it's not uncommon for the road to be blocked for a few hours while fallen rocks are cleared.

The Hundred Year Diet

The unusually high life expectancy of the Hunza Valley's residents is usually attributed to their diet, which differs from the rich curries enjoyed elsewhere in Pakistan. Here the food is mostly vegetarian and features Hunza's famous apricots in sweet and savory dishes alike. Hungry cyclists will appreciate the pizzalike *chapsuro*, while anyone with gastric woes will be recommended *burus*, a local soft cheese.

You'll already feel like you're deep in the mountains when you reach Gilgit, but it's merely a preliminary sample. This small city is the gateway to the Hunza region, a stunningly beautiful series of green valleys set among crystalline mountain peaks that have long exerted a pull on visitors. It's rumored that the retreating armies of Alexander the Great passed through this area and that many of the soldiers liked it so much that they settled here, which would explain the blond hair and blue eyes of some of the Kalash people.

The glowering cliffs of the Indus will feel like a distant memory as you pedal along avenues of whispering poplar trees, returning the waves and smiles of brightly clad villagers as they tend to their orchards and vegetable gardens. You'll often be able to buy mulberries, cherries, and apricots by the side of the road and in some cases will even be given them for free. As you pass through Ghulmet, you're also greeted by the glistening snowy peak of Rakaposhi. Locals claim it is the most beautiful mountain in the world, and you'll struggle to disagree—at least until you see what's yet to come.

Roughly halfway along the KKH, you'll pass Karimabad, the main tourist center of the Karakoram region. Cobbled streets wind their way up through the old town to the spectacular Baltit Fort, which was home to the Mirs of Hunza until 1891 and commands breathtaking views of the river, the fertile valley that surrounds it, and the mountains beyond.

From there, the landscape opens dramatically as you make your way to one of Pakistan's newest wonders. In 2010, the Hunza River was dammed by a massive landslide, which submerged several villages and created the Attabad Lake. For a few years, the only way to reach the upper KKH was by boat, but the Chinese government—anxious to protect its access to the Persian Gulf—has worked with local authorities on a series of bridges and tunnels to bypass the newly formed lagoon, which is now itself an attraction.

IN FOCUS
Educating Hunza

As you ride through Hunza, you'll see regular billboards promoting the projects of the Aga Khan Development Network. This organization has been working in the area for many years, establishing clinics and water treatment plants and opening schools at which girls are taught alongside boys. As a result, the Hunza Valley has the highest literacy rate in all of Pakistan.

Beyond the lake you'll find Passu— which is where you'll revise your opinion that Rakaposhi is the most beautiful mountain in the world. Overlooking the town is Passu Cathedral (or Passu Cones), an intricate cluster of jagged triangular peaks whose sight has never failed to rejuvenate a tired cyclist. The road brushes past several glaciers here, and you may find yourself digging out long-neglected gloves and jackets as the temperature noticeably starts to drop.

Although the KKH is mostly uphill, it climbs fairly gradually until the border town of Sost, after which you'll gain as much elevation in 62 miles (100 km) as you did in the first 435 miles (700 km). The road finally leaves behind the Hunza River and zigzags its way through an increasingly barren landscape, animated by the occasional whistling marmot. The Khunjerab Pass is hard-won: the lack of oxygen at nearly 16,400 ft (5,000 m) will leave even the fittest cyclists gasping for breath.

The view over the
Hunza Valley from Baltit
Fort in Karimabad

Crossing into China is allowed only by bus, but this gives you a chance to rest and enjoy yet another dramatic change of scenery, as the intricate spires of the Karakoram mountains give way to the vast green steppes of western Xinjiang. You're allowed to cycle again from Tashkurgan, and the road crosses one more high pass—the 13,123-ft (4,000-m) Ulugh Rabat—before descending past the idyllic Karakul Lake and winding its way through the red sandstone of the Ghez Canyon.

The landscape becomes increasingly flat and arid in the final stretches of the ride, a reminder that the Taklamakan Desert isn't far off. But that's for another day; this cycle ends at Kashgar, a former crossroads on the ancient Silk Route, which has been welcoming tired travelers for thousands of years. You'll be greeted by the smell of kebabs and baking bread and can add your own tales of adventure to the cheer and cacophony of China's westernmost city.

Left A bread seller in the Old City bazaar in Kashgar

Above Cycling through a rocky landscape toward the Khunjerab Pass

MAKE IT SHORTER
Start in Gilgit

If you're pressed for time or would prefer not to cycle through Indus Kohistan due to changes with the security situation along the lower Karakoram Highway, you could follow the example of countless other travelers and take the bus to Gilgit from Islamabad, starting your ride on the doorstep of Hunza.

ASIA

79

Roof of Thailand

CHIANG MAI TO PAI, THAILAND

Take in waterfalls, strawberry fields, and stunning views from the highest mountains in Thailand on a steep and sinuous route connecting the country's twin capitals of outdoor adventure.

120 MILES (193 KM)

16,250 FT (4,953 M)

PAVED

This ride into the jungle-strewn mountains of northern Thailand sets off from ancient Chiang Mai. Climbing out of this walled city in a rhythmic pattern of steep–flat–steep gradients, you'll move from sticky jungle into the cooler air of the high mountains, passing elephants, roadside temples, and strawberry fields. At the ride's inflexion point, you're treated to the sight of Doi Inthanon, the country's highest peak, known as the "Roof of Thailand." Stunning views lie in every direction, as layers of deep-green mountains flow out to the horizon.

From here, glass-smooth pavement drops you into Pai, an outdoorsy town near the border with Myanmar, surrounded by waterfalls, caves, and hot springs. Enjoy the descent's perfect, slightly banked corners, with long sightlines that stretch through sun-dappled pine forest. It's one of the best 15 minutes you'll experience on a bike.

ELEVATION PROFILE

6,500 ft
(1,981 m)

0

0   120 miles (193 km)

Pai

Relax tired legs with a short, 1-mile (1.5-km) diversion off the main road to the **PAN NAM HOT SPRINGS**, a set of free geothermally heated pools.

Pan Nam
Hot Springs

THAILAND

Park and explore **KHUN KHAN NATIONAL PARK**, whose forests contain a plethora of flora and fauna, including bellowing gibbons.

Khun Khan
National Park

Chiang Mai

0 ········· km ········· 15
0 ········· miles ········· 15

Before you set off from Chiang Mai, grab a caffeine hit at **RIST8TO**, which serves the best coffee in town.

Twin pagodas sitting atop Doi Inthanon, with views of the landscape below

196

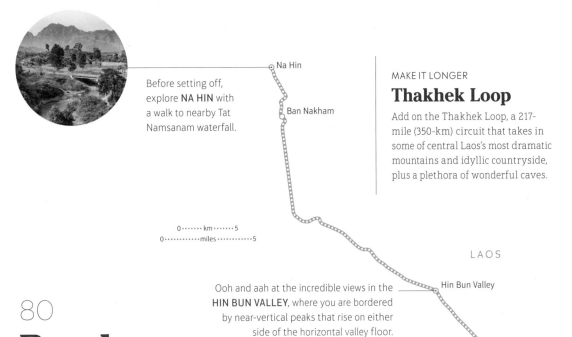

Before setting off, explore **NA HIN** with a walk to nearby Tat Namsanam waterfall.

Na Hin

Ban Nakham

MAKE IT LONGER
Thakhek Loop
Add on the Thakhek Loop, a 217-mile (350-km) circuit that takes in some of central Laos's most dramatic mountains and idyllic countryside, plus a plethora of wonderful caves.

0 ·······km······· 5
0 ·······miles·······5

LAOS

Ooh and aah at the incredible views in the **HIN BUN VALLEY**, where you are bordered by near-vertical peaks that rise on either side of the horizontal valley floor.

Hin Bun Valley

Kong Lor Cave

80

Road to Kong Lor Cave

NA HIN TO KONG LOR CAVE, LAOS

Backdropped by fantastically steep limestone mountains, this leisurely ride leads you along sleepy roads, past green paddy fields and forests that glitter with exotic butterflies, to the entrance of an extraordinary cave.

At **KONG LOR CAVE,** lock up your bike and take an underground river ride into the neighboring valley and back, spying stalactites and stalagmites along the way.

Southeast Asia is home to many of the world's most awesome caves, and even among these cathedrals of the underworld, Kong Lor Cave stands out. Nestled in a lush, leafy landscape, it can be reached via a scenic cycle from Na Hin, along a gentle road surrounded by soaring peaks. As you head south from the start, you'll wind your way around picturesque paddies, across the creaking wooden bridge at Ban Nakham, then on to a completely straight and level road where you can wander like you've never wandered before. The scenery improves at every turn as you enter the steep-sided valley of the Hin Bun River and amble along to Kong Lor, where a natural wonder awaits. This impressive cavern acts as an underground passageway for the river, so switch bike for boat and take a mesmerizing trip through the mountain, between the beautiful valleys on either side.

ELEVATION PROFILE

650 ft (198 m)

0
0   26 miles (42 km)

⊖ 26 MILES (42 KM)

⊗ 357 FT (109 M)

⊖ PAVED

Congratulate yourself on reaching **POINT PEDRO**—as the sign here proclaims, this is Sri Lanka's northernmost point.

Point Pedro

Jaffna

Elephant Pass

Kilinochchi

REFUEL

Idiyappam

Had enough rice and rotis? Try *idiyappam*, or "string hoppers." A tangle of thin white rice-flour noodles, they're a Sri Lankan staple eaten throughout the day. They make a splendid carbo-loading option in small-town canteens and come with a range of thin, spicy, savory sauces. Try them at breakfast with *kiri hodi* (a milk gravy) and the inevitable *sambol* (coconut, onion, and chili).

Explore the pools, temples, and huge shrines of the ancient city of **ANURADHAPURA**.

Anuradhapura

Climb the steps up to **SIGIRIYA**, an ancient fortress atop a rocky hill. It dominates the flat surroundings, with thrilling views over plains and peaks.

SRI LANKA

Sigiriya

Head up the hill from **KANDY** for a tour of a nearby tea plantation, finishing with a tea tasting in the café overlooking the city's lakes, temples, and mountains.

NUWARA ELIYA is peppered with remnants of Sri Lanka's colonial past, which can be glimpsed on a cycle around the town's lakes, gardens, and half-timbered houses.

Kandy

Nuwara Eliya

Haputale

Udawalawe

See elephant families and rainbow-coloued birds on a tour through **UDAWALAWE NATIONAL PARK**.

0 ·········· km ·········· 50
0 ·········· miles ·········· 50

Tangalle

Dondra Head

Before turning inland, take some time to appreciate the stunning southern coast with a beach stop in **TANGALLE**.

81

Sri Lanka
End to End

DONDRA HEAD TO POINT PEDRO, SRI LANKA

Lush, green, and compact, sunny Sri Lanka offers old-style cycle touring with an unhurried, low-tech charm. Ride away from the modern world to see ancient temples, colonial-style towns, and sleepy rural villages.

421 MILES (677 KM)

22,087 FT (6,732 M)

PAVED

A modest, avocado-shaped island in the warm shallow seas off southeast India, Sri Lanka is a delight to cycle around. This route explores all facets of the country, from south to north, immersing you in luxuriant tropical landscapes and offering intimate views of everyday villages and towns where it could still be the 1950s.

You'll get a strong feel for the two main cultures of the country—Sinhalese/Buddhist in the south and center and Tamil/Hindu in Hill Country and the north—from their different writing systems to the variations in cuisine. Tensions between the two sparked a civil war at the end of the last century, and the aftermath is sometimes still visible at the side of the road, particularly around Jaffna.

But today's peace makes Sri Lanka a calm, friendly place to cycle through.

It's safe, too: the only thing you're likely to have taken is your email address, and the fiercest thing you'll confront is a curry. (That said, watch out for buses lumbering toward you on your side of the road—the white lines in the middle of the pavement are more of a suggested guide than a boundary.) And while Hill Country deserves its name, with climbs up to 6,560 ft (2,000 m), the rest of the island is as flat as the rotis you'll have for breakfast.

Cycling past the colonial-style architecture found in the city of Jaffna

ELEVATION PROFILE

10,000 ft
(3,048 m)

0

0   421 miles (677 km)

MAKE IT LONGER
West Coast Extension

The resort of Negombo, site of Colombo's airport, makes an alternative starting point to Dondra Head. Adding about 124 miles (200 km), this extension follows old Dutch canals to Colombo and then continues down the beach-lined coast to Dondra Head via Galle, a gem of a fort town with a quaint old center.

You'll be on your way at dawn each day. Not just because it's cool—you won't want to cycle much after the noonday heat. And not just because the roads will be emptier then. It's mainly because there's something special about mornings in Sri Lanka. The sky transforms in minutes from starry black to cloudless blue, and unfamiliar birdsong fills the lemon-fresh air. Shopfronts are opened up and washed with buckets of water, while the aroma of baking flatbread and bubbling curries from nearby "hotels" (local canteens) wafts temptingly beneath your nose. Groups of giggling children in spotless white uniforms wave at you and say "hello" as they make their way to school. (They often say "bye!" because of a mistranslation.)

As the day gets going, you weave past men pedaling improbably loaded ancient bikes and ride through bright-green tea plantations, where women with baskets on their backs still pick the small leaves by hand. On one stretch of road, you might stop to admire a serene giant Buddha statue, while on the next, it's the riotously colorful carvings of a Hindu temple that catch your eye. You'll dodge chaotic but benign traffic through bustling towns, past old colonial buildings, aging cars, and exuberant games of street cricket with upturned crates as stumps.

Finding refreshment en route is no problem, whether you're in a tiny village or even in the middle of nowhere. Stop at the roadside to hydrate with the juice of a green coconut, plucked from a pile on a table, theatrically macheted open in front of you, and presented with a straw in the hole at the top. Or fuel up at a "cool spot" (cold-drink stall) with an energizing shake, prepared on demand from stacks of fresh fruit. Some of the ingredients may be familiar (banana, papaya, mango, pineapple), others not (custard apple, wood apple, rambutan, mangosteen), but you can be guaranteed that all are local—sometimes from the tree your bike is leaning against.

Arriving early at your accommodations, you'll enjoy that much-needed shower as you escape from the intensity of the afternoon heat. Home cooking is the heart of Sri Lankan cuisine and, come evening, big platters of jackfruit curry, rice, spicy fish, hot pickles, and sauces will soon send weary, perspiring, but happy cyclists off to sleep. You'll rise the next morning, relaxed, refreshed, and ready and raring to do it all over again.

Top Aerial view of a road winding through the Edinburgh Tea Estate in Sri Lanka's Central Province

Bottom left One of the bustling streets found in the city of Kandy

Bottom right Walking up steps toward the impressive Sigiriya fortress

Fuel up for the ride ahead in **HANOI**'s Old Quarter, where countless street-food stalls sell tasty treats like *pho* (noodle soup) and *banh xeo* (savory pancakes).

The Imperial City of **HUE** is utterly spectacular. The multiple layers of defenses in the Citadel here protected Vietnamese royalty in what was once the capital city.

Spend a day or two in **HOI AN**, known for its historic and atmospheric Old Town.

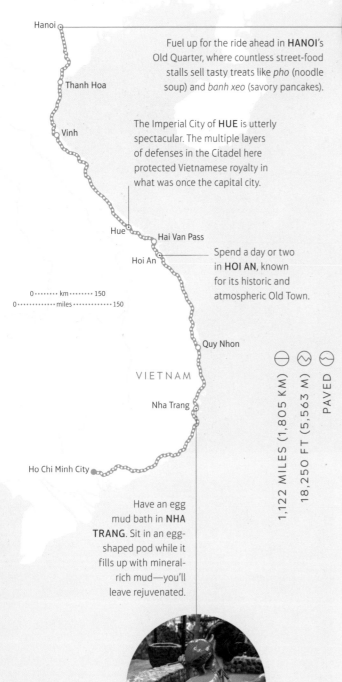

Hanoi

Thanh Hoa

Vinh

Hue

Hai Van Pass

Hoi An

0 ·········· km ·········· 150
0 ·········· miles ·········· 150

Quy Nhon

VIETNAM

Nha Trang

Ho Chi Minh City

Have an egg mud bath in **NHA TRANG**. Sit in an egg-shaped pod while it fills up with mineral-rich mud—you'll leave rejuvenated.

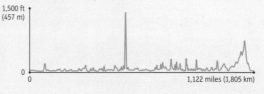

202

1,122 MILES (1,805 KM)

18,250 FT (5,563 M)

PAVED

82

Highway One

HANOI TO HO CHI
MINH CITY, VIETNAM

Seen as a symbol of national unity, the iconic Highway One follows Vietnam's stunning coastline via tiny hamlets, lush countryside, and sandy beaches.

Connecting the warring cities of Hanoi and Ho Chi Minh City during the Vietnam War, Highway One once represented a treacherous journey. Now, it's a popular route, both symbolically and physically linking the north and south of the country and buzzing with a stream of people and goods.

This is undoubtedly a route best appreciated by bike. At this slower speed, you can appreciate the steady transformation of the landscape, from cloud-frosted limestone cliffs in the north to idyllic stretches of sand in the south. Plus, you get to high-five the kids excitedly shouting *"xin chao!"* ("hello!") as you pass through each village.

The famous Hai Van Pass is a definite highlight of the route, although thanks to the at times 30 percent gradient, it might not feel like it. Power yourself up it, though, and you'll get to enjoy a perfect—and almost entirely traffic-free—4-mile (6-km) winding descent back to Highway One, complete with stunning ocean views.

ELEVATION PROFILE

1,500 ft
(457 m)

0

0   1,122 miles (1,805 km)

83

Lake Lugu

XICHANG TO LIJIANG, CHINA

This testing ride takes you into a remote yet ravishing corner of China, where the beautiful Lake Lugu lies surrounded by broad ranges of majestic mountains that stretch endlessly across the horizon.

Looking out over the tranquil Lake Lugu, surrounded by forested hills

308 MILES (496 KM) · 32,545 FT (9,920 M) · PAVED

Cycling through the mountainous provinces of Sichuan and Yunnan admittedly comes with some challenges. You'll face several demanding climbs, and the distances covered each day will make you long for your tent by nightfall. But in return you'll get an unrivaled glimpse into life in this sparsely populated part of China and full immersion in the rugged grandeur of its scenery.

Starting in Xichang in Sichuan, the route winds up lofty mountains on quiet roads, following turquoise rivers and passing through tiny mountain villages where farmers dry tobacco leaves on their rooftops. Serene Lake Lugu marks both the literal and figurative high point of the ride—stay a night here to witness dusk settling over

the distant mountains, while locals start fires against the cold. Your guiding beacon for the final stretch is the snowcapped Jade Dragon Mountain, standing sentinel over Lijiang and its beautifully preserved Old Town. It's an atmospheric spot to relax at the end of the ride, surrounded, as ever, by the presence of panoramic peaks.

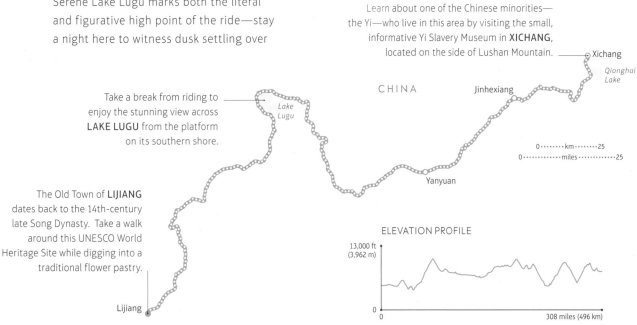

Learn about one of the Chinese minorities—the Yi—who live in this area by visiting the small, informative Yi Slavery Museum in **XICHANG**, located on the side of Lushan Mountain.

Xichang

Qionghai Lake

CHINA

Jinhexiang

Take a break from riding to enjoy the stunning view across **LAKE LUGU** from the platform on its southern shore.

Lake Lugu

0 ·······km······· 25
0 ·······miles········ 25

Yanyuan

The Old Town of **LIJIANG** dates back to the 14th-century late Song Dynasty. Take a walk around this UNESCO World Heritage Site while digging into a traditional flower pastry.

Lijiang

ELEVATION PROFILE

13,000 ft
(3,962 m)

0

0   308 miles (496 km)

84

Four Rivers Path

INCHEON TO BUSAN, SOUTH KOREA

Follow the flow of South Korea's longest waterways as you ride through dazzling modern cities and traditional agricultural villages on some of the best bike paths in the world.

366 MILES (590 KM) 12,575 FT (3,832 M) PAVED

The Four Rivers Path is probably the best bicycle network you've never heard of. Developed as part of a national dam project, it offers hundreds of miles of traffic-free cycle paths lined with temples, pagodas, and spas. The most popular section crosses South Korea from north to south, following its two longest rivers: the Hangang and the Nakdonggang.

Your journey begins in the city of Incheon; with its shiny office blocks and immaculate cycle lanes, this place oozes modernity. Be sure to pick up a "bike passport" at tourist information before you leave: if you collect enough stamps from the red telephone boxes that line the route, you'll earn a medal from the tourist information office at the end of your ride.

Cycling away from Incheon, you'll cross super-cool Seoul, home of K-pop and brimming with the latest fashion, before heading out along the Hangang River.

Riding through a park on the banks of the Hangang River in Seoul

The route's cycle lanes are well used—by speeding roadies, doting couples, and entire families on bikes—and the facilities are incredible, with public bike pumps, cyclist-only tunnels, clean toilets, and countless convenience stores offering free hot water for coffee and instant noodles.

Before long, you'll enter rural Korea, where rice paddy fields and traditional architecture offer a glimpse of the country's past. Riverside pagodas offer regular rest stops and provide sheltered camping spots for those riding self-supported. Roughly halfway into the journey, you leave the

ELEVATION PROFILE

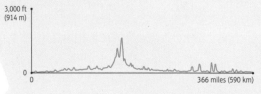

3,000 ft
(914 m)

0

0   366 miles (590 km)

Relish the cycling facilities along the path leading out of **SEOUL**. With regular water fountains, free hydraulic bike pumps, and immaculate self-cleaning toilets, this is what every cycle path should look like.

MAKE IT LONGER

River Run

A worthwhile detour, not long after leaving Seoul, heads along the Bukhangang River toward Chuncheon and back. You'll hug the edge of the river as it opens out into a lake, where wooden platforms built especially for cyclists are suspended over the water. Passing through rice paddy fields, the bright lights of Seoul feel a million miles away.

Learn more about the history of the Four Rivers Path at the **CHUNGJU DAM** exhibition and observatory, overlooking one of the largest dams on the route.

Incheon

Seoul

Join the hordes of cyclists celebrating their arrival at **IHWARYEONG**, the highest point on your journey.

Chungju

Suanbo

Soak your aching muscles in the spa town of **SUANBO**. It's the perfect place to try a *jjimjilbang* (public bathhouse).

Ihwaryeong

SOUTH KOREA

0 ········ km ········ 50
0 ········ miles ········ 50

Hangang to cross the mountains via the Saejae bike path. This is the high point of the route, at just over 1,640 ft (500 m), and is a shock to the system after miles of flat riding.

With the mountains out of the way, the final section follows the Nakdonggang River. Although it's now mostly flat, there are some short, sharp hills to get the lungs pumping before you eventually roll into bustling Busan. Waterfront cocktails on Haeundae beach offer a perfect end to your cross-country adventure—just don't forget to collect your medal first.

Busan

Pay a visit to Haedong Yonggungsa temple in **BUSAN**. Its oceanside location makes it unique among South Korea's places of worship.

205

ASIA

85

Cycle Route No 1

TAIPEI CITY, TAIWAN (LOOP)

This loop of Taiwan is truly a ride of two halves. Beginning as a leisurely cycle through pulsing urban cityscapes, it suddenly morphs into a rippling mountain route packed with unbelievably tough climbs.

603 MILES (970 KM)

24,590 FT (7,495 M)

PAVED

Home of the world-renowned bicycle manufacturer Giant, Taiwan has a proud passion for cycling that developed out of the stellar rise of the bike brand in the 1980s. The popularity of pedaling has only continued to increase since then, leading to large investment in bike-friendly infrastructure and the creation of the 603-mile (970-km) Cycle Route No 1 in 2015. This celebrated loop was inspired by the 2006 Taiwanese movie *Island Etude*, a fictional adventure about a young man who decides to embark on a cycle around the perimeter of Taiwan. The real-life journey—known in Mandarin as *huandao* (around the island)—has since become a well-known metaphor for freedom and good health and is considered a significant rite of passage in the local culture.

You have two main choices when deciding how to tackle Cycle Route No 1: clockwise or counterclockwise. The route described here follows the counterclockwise option, which, with its gentle start on the flat western seaboard, is the wisest strategy for easing your legs in. But if you're carved from granite and simply can't wait to get into the mountains, then you can hit the hard part first by venturing clockwise along the cliffs and gorges of the eastern coast. Either way, you'll need to be prepared for some of the toughest cycling climbs on earth: with 286 peaks cresting 9,843 ft (3,000 m), this mountainous island has a number of ascents that will seriously test your mettle.

ELEVATION PROFILE

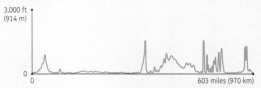

3,000 ft
(914 m)

0

0

603 miles (970 km)

Cycling along a smooth road beneath a forest canopy on the island of Taiwan

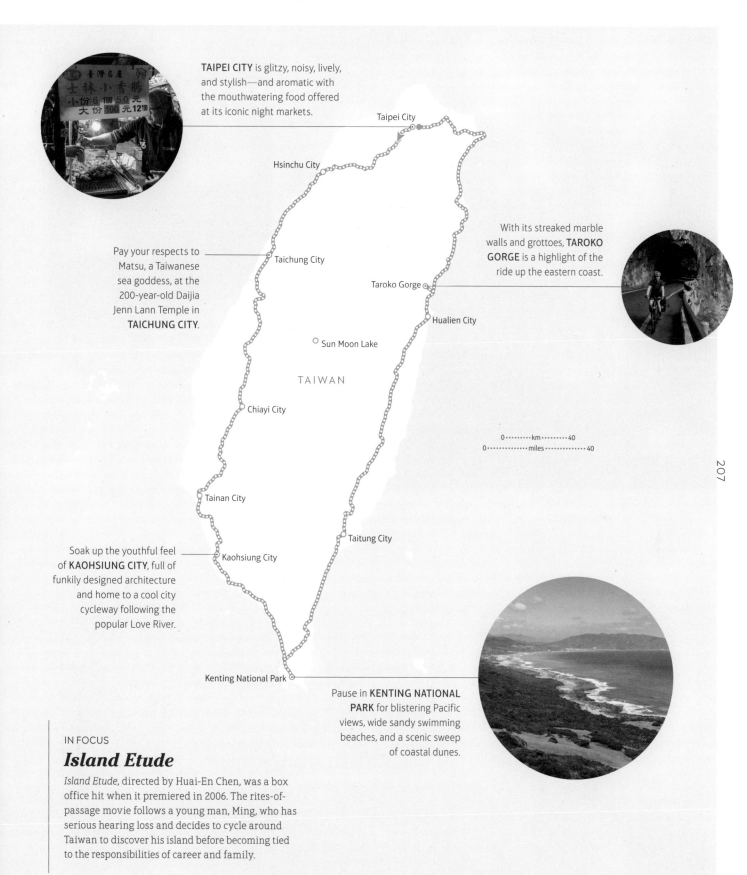

TAIPEI CITY is glitzy, noisy, lively, and stylish—and aromatic with the mouthwatering food offered at its iconic night markets.

Taipei City

Hsinchu City

With its streaked marble walls and grottoes, **TAROKO GORGE** is a highlight of the ride up the eastern coast.

Pay your respects to Matsu, a Taiwanese sea goddess, at the 200-year-old Daijia Jenn Lann Temple in **TAICHUNG CITY**.

Taichung City

Taroko Gorge

Hualien City

○ Sun Moon Lake

TAIWAN

Chiayi City

0 ·········· km ·········· 40
0 ·········· miles ·········· 40

Tainan City

Taitung City

Soak up the youthful feel of **KAOHSIUNG CITY**, full of funkily designed architecture and home to a cool city cycleway following the popular Love River.

Kaohsiung City

Kenting National Park ○

Pause in **KENTING NATIONAL PARK** for blistering Pacific views, wide sandy swimming beaches, and a scenic sweep of coastal dunes.

IN FOCUS
Island Etude

Island Etude, directed by Huai-En Chen, was a box office hit when it premiered in 2006. The rites-of-passage movie follows a young man, Ming, who has serious hearing loss and decides to cycle around Taiwan to discover his island before becoming tied to the responsibilities of career and family.

Above Pedaling along one of the tree-lined roads that make up Cycle Route No 1

Left Looking out over Taipei City, both the start and end point of the route

Setting off with packed panniers amid the frenetic hubbub of Taipei City can feel overwhelming. Just stick to the cycle lanes, eyes focused on the road, and all will be fine. The roads are hectic down the flat western seaboard, and you'll make rapid time. Much of this early section skirts through and around urban settlement and industry, in the shadows of futuristic skyscrapers—but there are moments of eye-catching inspiration sprinkled in between. Stretches of dedicated seashore cycleways provide spectacular vistas of the Pacific Ocean—as well as a welcome break from the traffic—while some of the inland roads are lined with emerald-green rice paddies. Look out along this coast for the ornate temples dedicated to Matsu, a Taiwanese sea goddess.

Before the route slingshots around the island's southern tip, it enters Taiwan's youthful second city, Kaohsiung. Prepare here for the Herculean labors ahead by harmonizing your yin-and-yang with a reflexology foot massage and loading up on carbs at the bustling Liuhe food night market. Local delicacies to look out for at the latter include fermented stinky tofu, which tastes a little like overly mature cheese.

REFUEL

At Your Convenience

Convenience stores such as 7/11 and Family Mart are scattered along the length of Route No 1 and are little treasure troves of well-earned treats. Just as your reserves are waning, there they appear, full of temptations: cold drinks, chocolate, egg tarts, ice cream, sushi, and bento boxes packed full of carbs.

Following golden beaches and the dunes through Kenting National Park, with seemingly endless seascapes of the boisterous Pacific Ocean, you veer onto the east coast and point your handlebars north. The fun begins with a bang on the brutish climb into Taitung County, beyond which lies a fortress of forested mountains. At times the roads are chiseled from sheer cliff faces, and you may find yourself pedaling tensely with one eye on the road and the other looking down at dizzying drops. The crescendo comes along the dramatic Su'ao Highway, where there are several long mountain tunnels shared with automobiles—these can be a little nerve-wracking, so make sure your bike lights are well charged.

Sun Moon Lake

Cycle Route No 1 allows for a number of scenic deviations inland. The nicest of these is a tough yet picturesque cycle to the iconic Sun Moon Lake, an ethereal body of water surrounded by subtropical forest and townships rich in Taiwanese folklore.

The road emerges into the light to bring you out at Taiwan's greatest natural wonder, Taroko Gorge. Here, a series of little waterfalls and milky streams scythe through fairy-tale grottoes forged from the glistening marble canyon. The climb feels more Tour de France than Taiwan, and your legs will soon be aching, so avail yourself of the revitalizing hot springs that occur on this volcanic coast.

You're nearly there now, so keep going. The scent of victory ahead is as sweet as the fragrant oolong tea that grows in the hills of Yilan County. As Taipei City's vertical cityscape appears on the horizon, the smell of fumes and food stalls returns, along with the noise of traffic and trash collectors piping out classical music. Amid the bustle, pause for a moment of pride at completing your circumnavigation: many Taiwanese, both young and old, cherish the dream of embarking on the feat you've just accomplished.

A section of the spectacular Taroko Gorge, cut through by a gurgling river

REFUEL
Brilliant Bento

Ubiquitous throughout Japan and wrapped up like joyful presents, bento boxes are the ultimate packed lunch for hungry cyclists. Varying in cost depending on the contents, they often feature compartments of meat or fish, pickles, rice, cooked vegetables, and sweets.

Step into the slightly surreal **KOSANJI TEMPLE** on Ikuchi Island, and see how many of the buildings you recognize from Japan's other renowned religious sites.

Visit **OYAMAZUMI SHRINE** to admire its impressive collection of samurai weaponry, which is one of the finest in Japan.

Honshu Island

Onomichi

Mukaishima Island

Innoshima Bridge

Murakami Suigun-jo Castle

Innoshima Island

The **MURAKAMI SUIGUN-JO CASTLE** on Innoshima Island houses a fantastic museum with exhibits on a 14th-century pirate clan.

Konsanji Temple

Ikuchi Island

Oyamazumi Shrine

Tatara Bridge

JAPAN

Omishima Island

Hakata Island

0 ·········· km ·········· 5
0 ········· miles ········· 5

Oshima Island

Kurushima-Kaikyō Bridge

The gigantic **KURUSHIMA-KAIKYŌ BRIDGE** offers amazing views of the Seto Sea's emerald-green islands and shimmering silvery tide, alive with boats.

Imabari

Shikoku Island

ELEVATION PROFILE

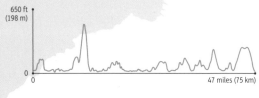

650 ft (198 m)

0

0   47 miles (75 km)

210

86

Shimanami Kaido

ONOMICHI, HONSHU, TO IMABARI, SHIKOKU, JAPAN

The remarkable Shimanami Kaido takes you over land and sea through a microcosm of Japan, where cutting-edge modernity is strikingly juxtaposed with a zenlike reverence of nature and tradition.

47 MILES (75 KM)

3,320 FT (1,012 M)

PAVED

Connecting the major Japanese islands of Honshu and Shikoku, the Shimanami Kaido transports cyclists across the inland Seto Sea in style. Opened in 1999, the route follows the Nishiseto Expressway along a series of futuristic-looking suspension bridges with segregated cycle paths, peeling off at regular intervals to explore six small, traditional islands on quiet, scenic roads.

Get into the spirit of the ride by renting a cruiser-style *mamachari* ("mom bike")—complete with a front basket for your bento box—in Onomichi, your starting point on Honshu. There's no need for lots of gears, as the route is mostly flat, and once you arrive on the islands, your pace will naturally become more sedate as you slow down to soak up the atmosphere. Each isle possesses a character of its own, and you'll want to take time to admire the traditional fishing villages and explore inland forests rich with the earthy fragrance of maples and pines. Be sure to stop at the quirky

Konsanji Temple on Ikuchi, built in the 1930s by a businessman-turned-monk in honor of his mother. If you think some of the structures in this complex look familiar, then you're right—many of their designs have been appropriated from famous buildings in temples and shrines across Japan. Don't miss the Oyamazumi Shrine on the forested island of Omishima, either; its serene setting is the surprising location of Japan's finest collection of samurai weaponry, offered up by warlords in thanks for success in battle.

But let's not forget how you'll get from island to island—acting as modern stepping-stones, the precision-engineered bridges you cross are striking reminders of Japan's technological prowess. There's the triple-span Innoshima Bridge—on which you'll have the surreal experience of riding along a cycle lane suspended beneath the main roadway, with the sound of cars driving above—and the majestic Tatara bridge, whose 720-ft- (220-m-) tall towers are reminiscent of inverted wishbones. The very best is saved for last: your final push to the island of Shikoku spans the Kurushima-Kaikyō, one of the world's longest suspension bridges. Unfurling to an impressive 2 miles (4 km) in length, this soaring bridge makes for a suitably satisfying grand finale.

> Once you arrive on the islands, your pace will naturally become more sedate as you slow down to soak up the atmosphere.

AUSTRALIA

87 88

AUSTRALASIA

PAPUA
NEW GUINEA

SOLOMON
ISLANDS

VANUATU

FIJI

92 ⊙

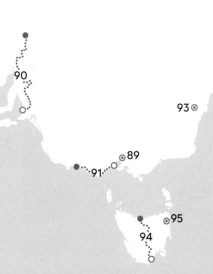

90

93 ⊙

⊙ 89
91

⊙ 95

94

100 ⊙

99

98 ⊙

NEW
ZEALAND

⊙ 97

⊙ 96

87

Rottnest Island

THE SETTLEMENT, ROTTNEST ISLAND, AUSTRALIA (LOOP)

Jump on your bike for this stunning circuit around a rugged island paradise, where the golden coastline is fringed with turquoise shallows and the inland undergrowth is dotted with quokkas.

Top Tip
Avoid traveling to "Rotto" during Western Australia's "schoolies" week (late November)—it gets very busy.

18 MILES (29 KM)

1,017 FT (310 M)

PAVED

214

Although it lies just 12 miles (20 km) offshore from Perth, Rottnest Island—or "Rotto"—feels a world away from the city. Known by the local Whadjuk people as Wadjemup, the island got the name "Rottnest" in the 17th century, when Dutch explorer Willem de Vlamingh mistook the native quokkas (mini kangaroolike marsupials) for giant rats.

You'll have plenty of opportunity for quokka-spotting on this rough loop around the island's perimeter; just be careful to keep your brakes covered—like their mainland wallaby cousins, these cute critters haven't got much road sense. Keep an eye out for dugites, too, as you're pedaling along—these venomous snakes love to bask on the hot black pavement, curled atop the road like brown moustaches. Luckily for quokkas and snakes—and for cyclists as well—the blissfully smooth paved roads are virtually car-free, other than the odd service vehicle or bus.

The ride starts by the ferry terminal at the Settlement, a quaint hamlet in Thomson Bay. Stock up on water and any last-minute supplies before setting off—aside from here and Geordie Bay, there are very few refreshment options en route. Minimal shade makes this ride tougher than it looks, and you'll soon work up a sweat as you roll up and down the undulating hills.

The sun may be strong, but the beauty of an island ride is that there are plenty of beaches where you can cool off with a refreshing dip. Parker Point is a particularly good snorkeling spot—look for rainbow-colored moon-wrasse fish among the seagrass and pinky-purple cauliflower

ELEVATION PROFILE

300 ft
(91 m)

0

0   18 miles (29 km)

One of the many white-sand beaches lining this circuit around Rottnest Island

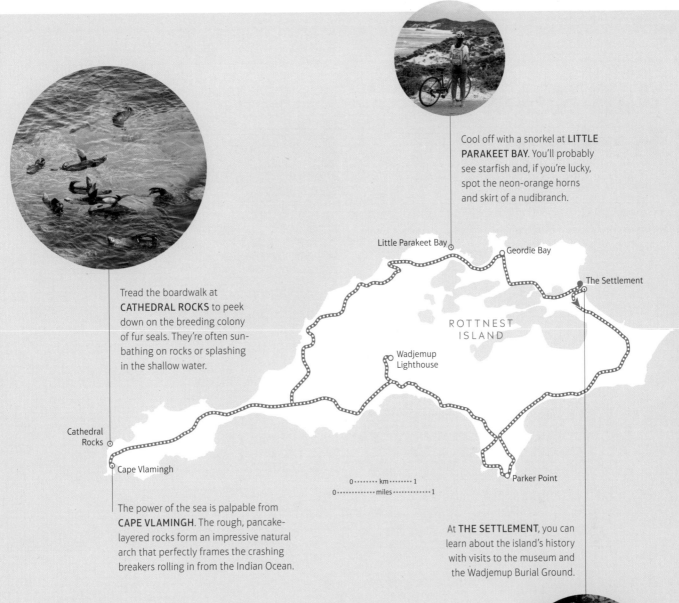

Cool off with a snorkel at **LITTLE PARAKEET BAY**. You'll probably see starfish and, if you're lucky, spot the neon-orange horns and skirt of a nudibranch.

Tread the boardwalk at **CATHEDRAL ROCKS** to peek down on the breeding colony of fur seals. They're often sunbathing on rocks or splashing in the shallow water.

The power of the sea is palpable from **CAPE VLAMINGH**. The rough, pancakelayered rocks form an impressive natural arch that perfectly frames the crashing breakers rolling in from the Indian Ocean.

At **THE SETTLEMENT**, you can learn about the island's history with visits to the museum and the Wadjemup Burial Ground.

Little Parakeet Bay
Geordie Bay
The Settlement
ROTTNEST ISLAND
Wadjemup Lighthouse
Cathedral Rocks
Cape Vlamingh
Parker Point

0 ······· km ······· 1
0 ······· miles ······· 1

coral. Other highlights include Wadjemup Lighthouse, with a 360-degree view that stretches all the way to Perth, and Cathedral Rocks, where you can watch New Zealand fur seals practicing their "yoga."

The final stretch takes you past several inland lakes near Geordie Bay. You might wonder at this point if the heat is causing you to hallucinate, but fear not—the lakes' sometimes-pink color and wind-whipped foam edges are the result of an unusual algae and high salinity. Thankfully, it's not too much farther to the Settlement, and time for a well-earned drink in the shade.

IN FOCUS
Rottnest's History

Once connected to the mainland, Rottnest was a key ceremonial meeting place for the Whadjuk. However, rising sea levels cut off access to the site around 7,000 years ago. The Whadjuk did not return until the 19th century, and then only as prisoners, forced by British colonialists to construct many of Rotto's current buildings.

88

Rail Reserves Heritage Trail

PERTH, AUSTRALIA (LOOP)

Looping through the Perth Hills on former train tracks, this easy-going ride is perfect for soaking up a unique mix of railway nostalgia and stunning outback landscapes.

26 MILES (41 KM)

1,262 FT (385 M)

PAVED / GRAVEL / DIRT

It was a major challenge for 19th-century engineers to find a railway-friendly route through the steep granite of the Perth Hills, but their past struggles are your gain. Combining two old train lines, this heritage trail uses former trackbeds to create a mostly off-road loop through Perth's outskirts.

Underwheel, you'll have deep ocher-hued ironstone and relatively sparse pea gravel, which together create a firm, if

The tumbling Hovea Falls, one of the highlights of John Forrest National Park

slightly corrugated, surface. Ahead, there's a mix of long, hot straight paths with azure-blue cloudless skies and gentle bends through shadier rock-hewn cuttings. Jarrah woodland lines much of the route, but don't rely on it for shade—the sun's heat sneaks down through the tall green trees and shorter-growing wattles. Be sure to take plenty of water, and—better still—cool yourself with ice cream from the historic townships en route.

216

ELEVATION PROFILE

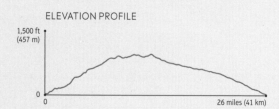

1,500 ft (457 m)

0

0   26 miles (41 km)

You'll need a flashlight to venture down the **SWAN VIEW TUNNEL**, a 1,115-ft- (340-m-) long passage that is reputedly haunted.

Visit **JOHN FORREST NATIONAL PARK** to spy the burnt-orange rock of Hovea Falls, plus kangaroos and wallabies.

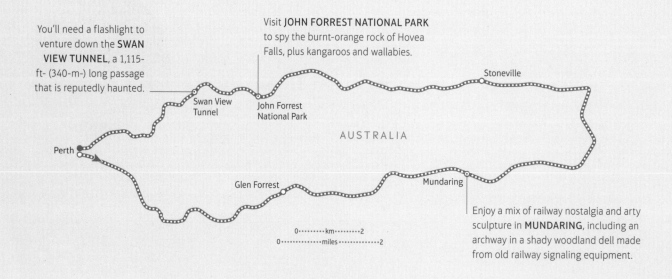

Swan View Tunnel

John Forrest National Park

Stoneville

Perth

AUSTRALIA

Glen Forrest

Mundaring

0 ········· km ········· 2
0 ··········· miles ··········· 2

Enjoy a mix of railway nostalgia and arty sculpture in **MUNDARING**, including an archway in a shady woodland dell made from old railway signaling equipment.

Royal Park

Yarra Bend Park

Flinders Street
Station

Docklands

Royal
Botanic Gardens

Port
Melbourne

People-watch at historic **FLINDERS STREET STATION**—every moment a microcosm of Melbournians passes through what was once the busiest rail station in the world.

Snack on fish and chips on the beach at **PORT MELBOURNE**, one of the city's coolest areas.

Port
Phillip Bay

Albert Park

St Kilda

| 0 ········· km ········· 2 |
| 0 ········· miles ········· 2 |

89

Capital City Trail

MELBOURNE, AUSTRALIA (LOOP)

Roll from city to beach on a laid-back ride through the heart of Melbourne, an effortlessly vibrant city that oozes Southern Ocean chill.

25 MILES (40 KM)   770 FT (235 M)   PAVED

Let the sun kiss your skin as you glide past iconic city sights on this relaxed ride, which follows Melbourne's Capital City Trail before looping down to the coast. You'll taste the best coffee in the world and share the route with commuters, sports fanatics, and leisure cyclists in Australia's number-one cycling city. Along the way, you'll pass by the futuristic architecture of Federation Square and the leafy avenues of Victorian-era Fitzroy Gardens. Every bend offers a new experience—there's the graceful flow of the Yarra River and the heady scent of the eucalyptus trees, the gleaming towers of the modern Docklands neighborhood, and the salty tang of the seaside of Port Phillip Bay and St. Kilda. The outdoorsy vibe here is addictive—once you're tuned in, you'll want to see more of Australia's cultural capital.

Little penguins waddle out of the sea at sunset to find their burrows along **ST. KILDA**'s breakwater— these cuties make quite a spectacle (and noise).

217

MAKE IT LONGER
Beyond the City

Explore beyond the city to reach bush, ocean, or vineyard using the bike routes that intersect the Capital City Trail. Two of the best are the oceanside Bay Trail, which takes you past secluded coves, rolling dunes, and coastal scrub, and the Main Yarra Trail, following the meandering Yarra River along leafy green paths.

ELEVATION PROFILE

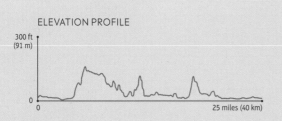

300 ft
(91 m)

0

0   25 miles (40 km)

Aerial view of cyclists rolling through the stunning Ikara-Flinders Ranges National Park

90

Mawson Trail

ADELAIDE TO BLINMAN, AUSTRALIA

Pack your bike for a world of challenge and awe. From the coastal, green city of Adelaide to the fossil-littered seabeds of ancient gorges, the Mawson Trail captures iconic Australia in all its glory.

545 MILES (880 KM) 22,015 FT (6,710 M) PAVED / GRAVEL / DIRT

Let's not beat around the bush: you'll have to be as tough as an old pair of boots to take on the Mawson Trail self-supported. But for riders ready to be humbled by the true soul of "Down Under," this trail promises a passage into the heart of a country like no other.

Named after adventurous geologist Douglas Mawson, the trail is a ride through history, from Australia's modern-day wine regions to the planet's earliest formations. The deeply spiritual land of the ancient Ikara-Flinders Ranges, formed 800 million years ago, is the route's crowning glory.

You'll have to be well prepared to undertake this ride. While well-spaced towns offer good rest and refuel options for the first half of the trail, things get trickier after that. Be prepared to carry enough supplies for two days on remote parts of the trail, including water—lots of water—and expect to spend several nights rough camping.

ELEVATION PROFILE

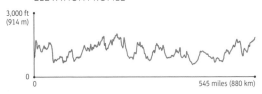

3,000 ft (914 m)

0

0   545 miles (880 km)

219

AUSTRALASIA

The Mawson Trail is open all year, but from January to March, it can be fiercely hot and is usually best avoided. Even during spring (August to October), daytime temperatures can exceed 86 °F (30 °C)—before plummeting into single figures after sunset, particularly in the outback. This is a place where it's possible to have both sunstroke and hypothermia within the same day.

While the ever-changing temperatures might be something to think about, you won't have to add cars to the list. Thankfully, this waymarked route is largely traffic-free, with any asphalt stretches generally on little-used country roads. In fact, the trail is mostly made up of gravel, double tracks and dirt, with a couple of fun whoop-whoop single trails thrown in as a surprise here and there. It's not all smooth sailing, though: you'll need to keep your wits about you, as there are some sketchy, washed-out sections en route. Plus, if it rains, parts of the trail are almost guaranteed to turn into a sticky fudge, which collects on your bike and makes riding—and often even pushing—near enough impossible.

Your Aussie adventure begins in coastal and cultured Adelaide. A quiet cycle path runs from the city along the tranquil Torrens River, popping out close to the official start of the Mawson Trail at the foot of the vine-covered Adelaide Hills. But don't let this lull you into a false sense of security—there's no polite introduction to the trail itself. Instead, you'll immediately be subject to a testing set of killer climbs that wind up through the ruggedly beautiful landscape.

The good news is that, from here, the toughest ascents of the whole journey are

already behind you. Now's the time to marvel at giant red gum trees, with trunks big enough to hollow out for a livable home (as some early European settlers actually did). Then, enjoy a fast white ribbon of dirt, which billows between infantries of vines marching down into the Barossa Valley. Happily for wine connoisseurs, three of South Australia's divine wine regions—Adelaide Hills, Barossa Valley, and Clare Valley—are all found within the first 124 miles (200 km) of the trail. Set aside some time to hop off your bike, take a break, and enjoy a tasting session or two—you're definitely going to earn it.

REFUEL
Bush Food

Humble bush food has come a long way in recent years. En route, you might want to try an emu egg omelet, kangaroo tail soup, and camel sirloin. Warm quandong tart with ice cream is a dessert must. Quandong—also known as "wild peach"—is a tiny, bright-red native bush fruit that packs twice the vitamin C of an orange and is a fraction of the size.

Cyclists on the final section of the Mawson Trail, surrounded by the dramatic rock formations of the Ikara-Flinders Ranges

Blinman

In **BRACHINA GORGE**, you can seek out the "Golden Spike," a disc that marks the first rock layer of the Ediacaran period.

Razorback Lookout

Brachina Gorge

Ikara-Flinders Ranges National Park

Gaze back in wonder from the **RAZORBACK LOOKOUT**, where the trail cuts a scythelike spectacle through the rugged Heysen Range.

Walk into **IKARA** and be awestruck by this natural amphitheater—one of the most impressive features of the Ikara-Flinders Ranges National Park.

Hawker

Quorn

Stop for a few days in the mountain bike mecca of **MELROSE**, which has an extra 62 miles (100 km) of trail to play on.

Wilmington

Melrose

Grab some award-winning Golden North ice cream in **LAURA**. Made here since 1923, this sweet treat is recognized as a Heritage Icon by the National Trust of South Australia.

Laura

Spalding

Burra

Check out the "monster mine" in **BURRA**—it is one of Australia's most significant mining heritage sites.

AUSTRALIA

Clare Valley

Auburn

Barossa Valley

Adelaide

Adelaide Hills

ADELAIDE HILLS is one of Australia's best cool-climate wine regions. It's followed on the trail by the Barossa Valley, a haven for red aficionados, and Clare, which is known for its exceptional whites.

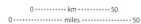

0 ·········· km ·········· 50
0 ·········· miles ·········· 50

AUSTRALASIA

Powering on, you'll hit immense grassy pastures split by dirt roads, which disappear into a heat-shimmering hazy horizon. Here, if you're lucky, a solitary wedge-tailed eagle or mob of emus might keep you company for a bit. You'll probably also spy troops of grazing kangaroos, but watch out—they can sometimes bounce across the road in front of you. In fact, you should expect to do quite a bit of wildlife dodging, especially at sunset, when animals are drawn to the roadside by the water run-off. While reptiles really won't want to bother you, it's a good idea to give them a chance to shimmy away—they could be dangerous.

As you continue on through the vast grasslands, the story of Australia's more recent history is told by the townships you pass through and the quintessential Aussie characters you meet, whose ancestors

IN FOCUS

Adnyamathanha People

The Adnyamathanha people are the traditional custodians of the Ikara-Flinders Ranges National Park. Their connection with the land stretches back many thousands of years—*Ikara* means "meeting place." Ancient rock paintings and engravings in the park at Arkaroo Rock depict the Yura Muda (creation stories specific to the Adnyamathanha people) of Ikara.

came in search of precious metals, rich pastures, and a new life. Many in these remote communities won't even have heard of the Mawson Trail, so don't be surprised if locals wonder how your saddlesore self ended up here.

Exactly where the outback starts is a subject of great debate, but there's a noticeable transition on the trail after the town of Quorn. Grassy fields give way to rust-colored earth, trees morph into stocky shrubs, and the occasional whiff of a rotting carcass gets up your nose. Mythical, mysterious, and greatly misunderstood, the outback bewitches with an absurd natural beauty. Nestled in its southeast is Ikara-Flinders Ranges National Park, a glorious example of what happens when two continental plates collide. The result is a crumpled mountain range of towering cliffs, deep craters, and plunging gorges, which hold the secrets of Earth's origins. Fossils found in the park forced scientists

A mob of emus standing in Ikara-Flinders Ranges National Park

Riding alongside fields near the town of Hallett, with a row of windmills in the background

to rethink Earth's geological timeline, and a brand-new period—the Ediacaran—was named after the sun-baked hills you'll ride through here.

The last 62 miles (100 km) through the park and into the tiny town of Blinman is billed as the best riding of the trail. Skirt round the edge of the mighty Ikara—a gigantic natural amphitheater—and bash through countless stony creeks, watching out for the endangered yellow-footed rock wallaby as you go. Listen for the cackle of the kookaburra while zipping between silvery gums, and be awestruck by the legendary "Razorback" slice of the trail, which strikes like lightning through the mauve and ocher mountains.

The First Peoples of this nation say everything in the environment, from the stars to the red dust, is related to people. When you have given your all to the Mawson Trail, you will leave a little of your soul on this land.

ANOTHER WAY
Go Supported

Don't want to lug all your gear along the length of the route? Bicycle SA's Outback Odyssey *(bikesa.asn.au/ outbackodyssey)* is a fully supported journey, with all your luggage, transportation, meals, and camping taken care of. Just rock up with your bike and daypack and ride.

91

Great Ocean Road

TORQUAY TO WARRNAMBOOL, AUSTRALIA

There are a lot of ocean roads in the world, but only one they call Great. Hugging the southeastern corner of the country, this route provides a quintessential snapshot of Australia and more than deserves its iconic status among cycle tourists.

156 MILES (251 KM)   7,175 FT (2,185 M)   PAVED

A roller-coaster ride of exhilarating views, taxing ascents, and Australian icons, the Great Ocean Road has it all. It starts in Torquay, 62 miles (100 km) southwest of Melbourne, and ends at Warrnambool—although the Australian tourist board will try to persuade you to carry on to Nelson, at the border between Victoria and South Australia. With scenery like this, you may as well take them up on the invitation and go the distance.

The only catch is that this route is firmly on the beaten path: tourist traffic can be heavy, so cyclists are generally better off attempting the ride mid-week or during the off-season. But even the ubiquitous tour buses can't spoil the view—it really is one of the finest roads in the world and should be on every ambitious cyclist's bucket list.

The best-known attraction on the Great Ocean Road is the Twelve Apostles, a group of striking limestone stacks, images of which adorn many a postcard—but there are plenty of other gorgeous sights to drool over. Surrounded by crashing waves and screeching gulls, a rock arch shares its name (but nothing else) with London Bridge, while the verdant rain forest found

Top Tip

Magpies are known for dive-bombing cyclists on this route. Attach cable ties to the top of your helmet to ward them off.

Warrnambool   Allansford

If you're lucky, you might spot calving southern right whales at Logan's Beach in **WARRNAMBOOL**. The best time to catch them is between June and September.

ELEVATION PROFILE

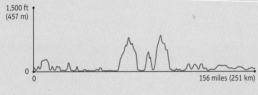

1,500 ft (457 m)

0

0   156 miles (251 km)

The Great Ocean Road winding along the verdant coastline, near the town of Lorne

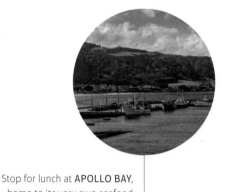

AUSTRALIA

Stop for lunch at **APOLLO BAY**, home to its very own seafood festival. You can't spend this long riding along the coast without pausing to try some fresh lobster or calamari.

0 ·········· km ·········· 20
0 ·········· miles ·········· 20

Torquay

Anglesea

Lorne

Port Campbell

London Bridge

Twelve Apostles

Apollo Bay

Great Otway National Park

Swap your bike for a surfboard in **TORQUAY**, the undoubted surfing capital of Australia.

Join the tour buses at the **TWELVE APOSTLES** to marvel at these famously photogenic limestone stacks.

Take a walk on the wild side in **GREAT OTWAY NATIONAL PARK**. A quick stop at Mait's Rest will reward you with a beautiful boardwalk amid giant ferns and ancient rain forest.

225

just inland is somewhat unexpected for those who consider Australia to be a sun-baked continent.

The beauty of following such a popular route is that whenever hunger strikes, you're never far from a range of rest stops and refuel options. For a quick bite to eat, snack on cheap-and-cheerful Aussie pies or freshly fried fish and chips— or, if you fancy treating yourself, head to one of the upscale seafood restaurants that line the coast. Whatever you choose, wash it down with a selection from one of the local vineyards found along the road.

IN FOCUS

The World's Largest War Memorial

Part infrastructure, part memorial, the Great Ocean Road was built by soldiers returning from World War I and is dedicated to all those who didn't make it home. Started in 1919, the road took 3,000 soldiers 13 years to build. Intended to provide a connection for isolated villages and support local industries, it remains the world's largest war memorial.

Aerial shot of the Great Ocean Road tracing the scenic coastline

The ride officially starts at Torquay, the country's effortlessly cool surfing capital. In fact, the whole stretch of coast west of the town is known as the "Surf Coast," with miles of world-class beaches to tempt you away from the saddle. But don't get too distracted—there's a challenge ahead. Oscillating up and down, the twisting road climbs and falls over stunning clifftops. At

> It's not just climbs you have to watch out for: the Great Ocean Road is also renowned for its wildlife.

least there are plenty of opportunities to ease aching muscles in the ocean.

But it's not just climbs you have to watch out for: the Great Ocean Road is also renowned for its wildlife. Kangaroos litter the golf course at Anglesea, and you can hang out with koalas near Apollo Bay—so there's definitely no mistaking the country you're pedaling through. If you're lucky, you may even spot migrating whales as they cruise up and down the coast.

After Apollo Bay, the road takes you inland, through the Great Otway National Park. If you've got time, spend an extra day here and use the opportunity for a detour. Take a loop through the national park to explore the rain forest in more depth or wander down to the coast to visit

MAKE IT LONGER
Go West

If the Great Ocean Road leaves you thirsty for more, why not continue west toward Adelaide? Spend a night behind bars in Mount Gambier, where the old jail is now a popular hotel *(theoldmountgambiergaol.com.au)* and camp in the company of pelicans at Meningie, on the edge of the Coorong National Park.

Looking out over the seaside city of Warrnambool, the final stop on the ride

the famous lighthouse at Cape Otway. Whichever way you go, prepare your legs: the climbs can be fairly brutal, so you'll be grateful for a comfortable bed at the end of the day.

As you return to the ocean, the Surf Coast becomes the Shipwreck Coast, with over 600 known shipwrecks strewn along the rocks between Cape Otway and Port Fairy. It's easy to see why, with mile after mile of treacherous cliffs and sea stacks offering danger for sailors but a welcome distraction for passing cyclists. Flatter

gradients mean you can enjoy the views even more as you coast along the home straight toward the end of the ride.

The route eventually finishes near the coastal city of Warrnambool, the perfect spot to rest and recuperate from all of those miles you've clocked up. Take some time to explore its nature trails and Botanic Gardens or put your feet up and enjoy a well-earned rest on the beach while watching for whales. When you're done, you can jump on a train to cool and cultured Melbourne. Or, better still, continue the adventure—and check yet another quintessential Aussie experience off your list—by riding home via the country's iconic outback.

Pausing for a break with a view

92

Rainforest to Reef

MOUNT MOLLOY TO PORT DOUGLAS, AUSTRALIA

Power down a fast-and-furious mountain bike trail that connects two of Australia's most unique biospheres: the lush rain forest of the Wet Tropics and the rainbow-colored Great Barrier Reef.

22 MILES (35 KM)

980 FT (299 M)

PAVED / GRAVEL / DIRT

Downhill demons: buckle up. Part of a vast network of trails in Queensland's north, this adrenaline-filled route will take you on a wild ride down an undulating dirt track all the way to the ocean.

The ride starts deceptively with a long gentle climb through the rugged Great Dividing Range. You'll be treated to an eye-popping panorama of the highland savanna and verdant Wet Tropics World

Heritage Area before plunging down, down, down into the ancient rain forest. Tens of millions of years older than the Amazon, the Wet Tropics is crammed with flora that dinosaurs once munched on. Check your brakes before you barrel down the 4-mile (6-km) Bump Track—first an Indigenous trail and later a wagon road, it was once the only link between the highlands and the sea. Laced with waterfalls and creeks, this roller-coaster descent is now a favorite among downhill riders.

The track pops out at Four-Mile Beach before rolling along its hard-packed sand to swanky Port Douglas. Here, switch bike for boat and set off to explore Australia's iconic natural wonder—the Great Barrier Reef.

228

ELEVATION PROFILE

1,500 ft
(457 m)

0

0   22 miles (35 km)

Pick up big speeds on the hard-packed sands of **FOUR-MILE BEACH**.

Port Douglas

Four-Mile Beach

Craiglie

AUSTRALIA

Keep your eyes peeled for the **SOUTHERN CASSOWARY**, a huge flightless bird, at the creek crossing on Black Mountain Road.

Bump track

Mount Molloy

0 ·········· km ·········· 5
0 ·········· miles ·········· 5

End your ride at the surf club at **PORT DOUGLAS**, where you can change into your swimsuit and take a dip in the ocean or jump on a boat to head off and explore the Great Barrier Reef.

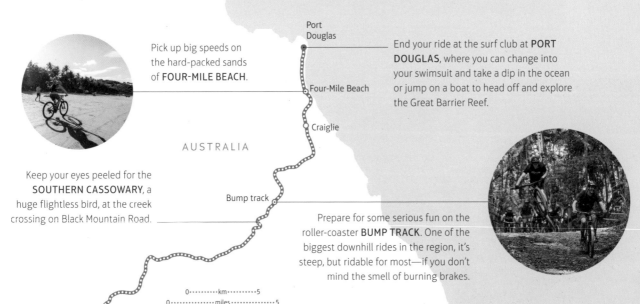

Prepare for some serious fun on the roller-coaster **BUMP TRACK**. One of the biggest downhill rides in the region, it's steep, but ridable for most—if you don't mind the smell of burning brakes.

93

Narrow Neck Trail

KATOOMBA, AUSTRALIA (ROUND-TRIP)

Winding through the eucalyptus-scented air of Australia's Blue Mountains, this invigorating route blazes a trail between two yawning valleys, where the expansive views have remained unchanged for millennia.

14 MILES (23 KM)   1,985 FT (605 M)   GRAVEL / DIRT

Here, in this rugged realm of New South Wales, the scent of gum trees hangs in the air. Their fragrant oils create an indigo haze that gives Australia's Blue Mountains their name—and their scent refreshes cyclists who tackle the Narrow Neck Trail.

Winding along a hilly plateau, the route sails between the Jamison and Megalong Valleys, offering views of both from the narrowest parts of the trail. There's a varied pace to this bumpy gravel ride: around 2 miles (4 km) in, a thrilling downhill is swiftly followed by a thigh-burning incline. The final uphills are gentler, and the flat to Tarros Ladder is a welcome relief.

At Tarros Ladder, drink in views across an amphitheater of sandstone cliffs. The land's traditional owners, including the Gundungurra and Darug peoples, have spent millennia learning the Blue Mountains' secrets. As you cycle back, you'll realize that you've only scratched the surface of what this magical landscape has to offer— but that's just all the more reason to return.

ELEVATION PROFILE

4,000 ft (1,219 m)

2,000 ft (610 m)

0   14 miles (23 km)

Make a day of it by taking a detour on foot down the **GOLDEN STAIRS**, following a challenging, steep trail to the "Ruined Castle" rock formation.

Car park

Golden Stairs

AUSTRALIA

Take a breather at the **NARROW NECK FIRE TOWER**, a lofty rest stop capped by a radio mast. Fringed by gum trees, it's a great place to picnic or to photograph sweeping views.

Narrow Neck fire tower

Secure your bike and climb up **TARROS LADDER**, gripping the hand-holds fixed to the rock face. At the top, survey sublime views of the Wild Dog Mountains and Lake Burragorang.

0 ·····km·····1
0 ··········miles··········1

Tarros Ladder

MAKE IT LONGER

Leura Cascades

Starting your ride at Leura Cascades adds 4 miles (7 km) and more wow-factor views. The road from these tiered waterfalls winds southwest to the Narrow Neck trailhead, passing lookouts over the Three Sisters rock formations and picnic spot Katoomba Falls.

Taking in the spectacular view over Australia's rugged Blue Mountains

94

Tasmanian Trail

DOVER TO DEVONPORT, TASMANIA, AUSTRALIA

Cycle the length of Tasmania on the path less traveled. This adventurous trail will take you on an off-road ride through the remote interior of this still-wild state.

289 MILES (465 KM)

28,850 FT (8,793 M)

PAVED / GRAVEL / DIRT

Top Tip

The route's official website *(tasmanian trail.com.au)* is a great planning resource.

Dissecting the island almost right down the middle, the Tasmanian Trail stretches all the way from Dover (just south of Hobart) to Devonport, sans asphalt. On the way, it passes through the stunning heart of the "Apple Isle," taking in dense, ferny forests; the expansive subalpine Central Plateau; vast swathes of farmland; and shimmering lakes and lagoons.

Linking together rural settlements, the route is made up of a collection of off-road trails, logging routes, and gravel country roads. It might be off the beaten track, but thankfully over 90 percent of it is clearly marked, and it's almost completely ridable—almost. At points, you'll encounter some brutal climbs, so expect to spend some sections slowly pushing your bike uphill, legs on fire. One of the trickiest climbs can be found on the way up to Jeffries Track, where the gradients push 20 percent and you'll have long sections of bluestone to navigate—but there's a silver lining. Once you make it

onto the track, through deep ruts left behind by trail bikes and 4WDs, the route careens down through pastoral landscapes on a sweeping gravel descent—one of the most enjoyable you're ever likely to find.

You'll need to prepare in advance to tackle this route. There are limited food and water stops along the way, so make sure you plan ahead and carry plenty of supplies with you, or you may end up bartering with a friendly farmer (almost everyone here is friendly). Plus, you'll likely experience all four seasons on the island—sometimes in one day; be sure to pack plenty of layers and sunscreen.

Powering along through dense forest on one of the trail's gravel tracks

ELEVATION PROFILE

5,000 ft (1,524 m)

0

0   289 miles (465 km)

Make sure you have a little something left in your legs for the grueling twin climbs of Needles and (ironically named) Paradise as you approach **DEVONPORT**.

Devonport

Railton

Sheffield

Pull in at the tiny town of **RAILTON** to enjoy a locally made pint or two at artisan brewery Seven Sheds.

TASMANIA

Stop off at **TODS CORNER POWER STATION**, a striking brutalist concrete silo by the Great Lake. Built in 1965 and still operational, it is a truly surreal sight.

Tods Corner

Great Lake Hotel

Ouse

The **DERWENT RIVER** is a great place to drink in the view of sheep-dotted fields and leafy vineyards.

Derwent River

New Norfolk

Jeffries Track

Dover

0 ········· km ········· 50
0 ········· miles ········· 50

When it comes down to it, half the fun of the Tasmanian Trail is not knowing exactly what to expect. Each day offers something new: a different landscape to soak in, different riding conditions to push through, or, seemingly, a different climate to endure. Whether you're tackling steep, rocky climbs or trying to outrun the scorching Australian sun (or sideways rain), the reward is in triumphing through the day and heading to the campfire or pub that night to recount your many tales of adventure.

REFUEL

Great Lake Hotel

One of the few places to stop for a meal along the way, the Great Lake Hotel (*greatlakehotel.com.au*) serves up much-needed hearty fare. Even better, all the meals are made with locally sourced ingredients. Try the heavenly Powerhouse steak or mouthwatering chili cheese bread.

AUSTRALASIA

TASMANIA

Look up from the **BLUE TIER** mountain plateau and see if you can spot an endangered wedge-tailed eagle soaring through the sky above.

Blue Tier

Go for a swim in the pristine turquoise waters of the **BAY OF FIRES**, framed by bright-orange lichen-splattered boulders.

0 ········ km ········ 5
0 ········ miles ········ 5

Bay of Fires

Mount Pearson

Take a break while traversing **MOUNT PEARSON** and get your camera out to snap your first clear view of the sparkling seascape panorama that marks the end of the trail.

95

Bay of Fires Trail

BLUE TIER TO BAY OF FIRES,
TASMANIA, AUSTRALIA

Clear air, pristine natural wilderness, swathes of native rain forest, and sparkling coastlines: Tasmania has it all. Experience the full package on a thrilling mountain-to-sea journey, riding world-class flow trails.

232

26 MILES (42 KM)   2,067 FT (630 M)   GRAVEL / DIRT

Bordering the Blue Derby network, the Bay of Fires Trail starts on the heather-blanketed heights of the stony Blue Tier mountain plateau. Take a moment here to soak up the views of the forested Tasmanian wilderness—and maybe, if it's a clear day, the turquoise waters of the East Coast. Then, gulp down some of the planet's cleanest air before plunging wheelfirst into the aniseed scents of the dense, native Tasmanian rain forest. Mother Nature is very much in charge here: monolithic granite boulders guard tunnels of giant tree ferns, branches drip with nearly fluorescent moss, and shards of ethereal light pierce dark volcanic dirt.

Savor the joys of the flow zone—a section of heart-leaping bumps and high-pitched, sweeping, tacky corners. All too soon the trail bleaches to pure white sand as you arrive at the pristine Bay of Fires. Here, float or paddle in the crystal-clear waters and dream of doing it all over again—you'll want to, for sure.

IN FOCUS

Blue Derby

The largest single mountain bike project ever undertaken in Australia, the Blue Derby is a custom-built, 78-mile (125-km) single-trail network through Tasmania's pristine natural environment. Catering to all skill levels and riding styles, the project has single-handedly revived the struggling local economy.

Passing through the Bay of Fires Trail's "Gardens Lookout," with views of the coast

ELEVATION PROFILE

3,000 ft (914 m)

0

0   26 miles (42 km)

Enjoy a drink in the welcoming **CHATTO CREEK TAVERN**, once the watering hole for hundreds of hopeful gold miners.

Oturehua

Poolburn Gorge

Omakau

Chatto Creek

Clyde

Alexandra

Ranfurly

Stop off in **RANFURLY**, formerly a busy railway town, to admire its stunning Art Deco architecture.

Pop into **GILCHRIST'S GENERAL STORE** in Oturehua. Built in 1899, this old-school establishment is filled with nostalgic mining memorabilia.

Hyde

```
0 ·········· km ··········20
0 ·········· miles ··········20
```

Middlemarch

Spend a couple of days in the historic town of **MIDDLEMARCH**, using it as a base for hikes in the Rock and Pillar Range or for visiting Sutton Salt Lake, New Zealand's only saline lake.

96

Otago Central Rail Trail

CLYDE TO MIDDLEMARCH, NEW ZEALAND

Get ready to journey into Otago's wild heartland—this relaxed ride traces the route of a former railway, whose trains once ferried eager miners in search of gold.

95 MILES (152 KM)

2,337 FT (712 M)

GRAVEL

This is a truly spectacular route. Not because of long, lung-busting climbs; heart-racing descents; or thigh-aching distances—you won't find any of these on this relatively short and flat gravel trail. No, the enduring attraction of this route—the original of the 22 Great Rides that criss-cross the country—lies in the sense of freedom you'll feel from wandering through a tawny-hued landscape beneath vast, blue skies, while folded hills encircle you on every side. Along the way, you'll pedal across soaring viaducts, roll past tiny wayside stations, and ride—or, to be on the safe side, walk—through inky tunnels blasted out of the schist rock, all evidence of the route's past life as a railway. Have your camera at the ready for the dramatic Poolburn Gorge, whose two imposing tunnels and sweeping 121-ft- (37-m-) high viaduct were painstakingly constructed by a band of 300 weather-beaten men. Eventually the trail will lead you toward one old gold-rush town or another, where Wild West–style pubs offer you welcome helpings of famous Kiwi hospitality.

ELEVATION PROFILE

3,000 ft (914 m)

0

0

95 miles (152 km)

233

97

Alps 2 Ocean Cycle Trail

TAKAPŌ/LAKE TEKAPO TO ŌAMARU, NEW ZEALAND

Take a leisurely journey through the South Island's scenic heart. Passing through snowy alpine vistas, golden tussock plains, and rolling emerald farmland, the Alps 2 Ocean offers breathtaking views of some of New Zealand's loveliest landscapes.

178 MILES (287 KM)

6,200 FT (1,890 M)

PAVED / GRAVEL

234

Tracing its way from tiny Takapō/Lake Tekapo to historic Ōamaru, the Alps 2 Ocean Cycle Trail takes you on an amazing tour of the South Island's stunning, ever-changing landscapes. One day you'll be cycling beside turquoise-tinged lakes in the shadow of soaring mountain peaks, the next rolling alongside winding ribbonlike rivers edged with emerald-hued farmland.

The best part about this scenic ride? Apart from a handful of climbs, the trail is mainly downhill, dropping 2,339 ft (713 m) from Takapō/Lake Tekapo to Ōamaru; there are no mountains to haul yourself over, or anything that takes you too far

from a hot meal and comfortable night's lodging. This makes the ride suitable for everyone, whether it's bikepackers carrying their own gear, e-bikers confident on gravel, or families looking for a challenge.

With mostly easy riding, it can be tempting to enjoy the speed and knock the ride out quickly—but resist the urge. This is a ride to savor, to appreciate the changes in the landscape as they open up around you: sit and let the alpine beauty of the high country soak into your bones, linger over your picnic at the side of a turquoise lake, or explore a walkway that winds through golden grassland.

The easy-going nature of the ride is reflected in the chilled-out Kiwis you'll meet along the way. Expect to encounter cheerful farmers eager for a chat, bed-and-breakfast hosts keen to introduce you to their corner of New Zealand, or café and shop owners who welcome the extra life that the Alps 2 Ocean cyclists breathe into their villages.

Cycling toward
Duntroon on the
Waitaki plains

IN FOCUS

Work in Progress

One of New Zealand's 22 Great Rides, the Alps 2 Ocean has been built in stages as part of the New Zealand Cycle Trail initiative. It opened in 2013, and since then it has progressed with moving its on-road sections off-road to make the trail even safer. The whole route is now on purpose-built off-road tracks or quiet country roads.

Spend an awe-inspiring evening stargazing at the acclaimed **MOUNT JOHN OBSERVATORY**, situated in the Aoraki Mackenzie International Dark Sky Reserve, with vast, clear views.

Stop to photograph sparkling **LAKE PUKAKI**, scenically backdropped by the peak of Aoraki/ Mount Cook.

Marvel at the turquoise hue of **TAKAPŌ/LAKE TEKAPO**, whose distinctive color is due to the glacial "flour" (ground-up rock) found in the water.

Aoraki/Mount Cook Village

Takapō/ Lake Tekapo

Mount John Observatory

Lake Pukaki

Takapō/ Lake Tekapo

Lake Ōhau

Twizel

Lake Benmore

Ōmarama

Wharekuri

Explore the ghost town of **WHAREKURI**, where in 1865 the hotel was held up. Local lore has it that the robbers abandoned their stolen loot in the nearby hills.

Lower your tired muscles into a private wood-fired hot tub of fresh mountain water at **HOT TUBS ŌMARAMA** and then lie back and admire the wide Mackenzie sky.

Elephant Rocks

Ōamaru

NEW ZEALAND

Wander around **ELEPHANT ROCKS**, a valley scattered with huge, pachydermlike limestone boulders.

235

0 ·········· km ·········· 40
0 ·········· miles ·········· 40

ELEVATION PROFILE

3,000 ft (914 m)

0

0   178 miles (287 km)

AUSTRALASIA

You'll start your laid-back ride in tourist hot spot Takapō/Lake Tekapo, situated on the banks of the eponymous lake. Linger to take a look at the famous Church of the Good Shepherd, a simple stone building spectacularly positioned by the edge of the turquoise lake, and then get pedaling. From here, easy riding under big skies takes you through the tawny grasslands of the Mackenzie Basin and along the lupin-lined shores of Lakes Pukaki and Ōhau, behind which loom the ever-present Southern Alps. This is South Island high country, rugged and beautiful, painted in tones of blue and gold—it's home to tough merino sheep and even tougher farmers.

You'll encounter one of the few ascents on this ride along the section from Lake Ōhau to the tiny town of Ōmarama. The longest climb of the trail, it's a steady 1,148-ft (350-m) upward haul. But take heart—the views from the top are well worth the slog, with shimmering Lake Ōhau, the angular Ben Ōhau Range, and the Mackenzie Basin spread out below you. Plus, from this point, it's pretty much downhill all the way.

As you spin gently past the willow-fringed lakes of Benmore, Aviemore, and Waitaki, the high country slowly gives way to rolling valleys. For the next while, the route follows the flow of the looping Waitaki River, passing through fresh green farmland that's framed by folded, arid hills. The tiny towns that line this section will attempt to lure you from the trail— and it's a good idea to let them. Enjoy a traditional meat pie in rural Kurow or go fossil-hunting in diminutive Duntroon.

Top left The stone Church of the Good Shepherd, overlooking Takapō/Lake Tekapo

Bottom left One of the signs marking the way along the Alps 2 Ocean route

236

Riding away from
Lake Ōhau and the
snowcapped peaks of
the Ben Ōhau range

Leaving the river behind, you'll amble
through eroded limestone valleys and past
closely grazed fields dotted with softly
mooing cows. Two of the few climbs on
the route sit between you and the historic
town of Ōamaru, your journey's end.
But whatever weariness you might feel
at the peak of the second ascent is offset
by jaw-dropping views over rolling green
hills and sparkling sea. It's a slightly
bittersweet feeling as you roll through
Ōamaru's Victorian-era harbor precinct,
coming to the end of your ride on the
shores of the Pacific—but the expansive
views of this peaceful, never-ending ocean
help to make up for it.

ANOTHER WAY
Aoraki/Mount Cook Village Start

Instead of starting at Takapō/Lake
Tekapo, you can begin your ride
1 mile (2 km) from Aoraki/Mount
Cook Village and then take a short
helicopter ride across the Tasman
River. From there, it's a 27-mile
(43-km) cycle down the shore
of Lake Pukaki to join the Takapō/
Lake Tekapo branch of the trail.

AUSTRALASIA

98

Old Ghost Road

LYELL TO SEDDONVILLE, NEW ZEALAND

Thunder through the remote valleys and native forests of New Zealand's South Island on a back-country wilderness adventure. On the way, you'll be spellbound both by the rugged landscapes and glimpses of gold-rush history.

53 MILES (85 KM)

6,970 FT (2,125 M)

GRAVEL / DIRT

Following a former gold-mining trail from Lyell to Seddonville, the Old Ghost Road is an adrenaline-soaked route through the pristine wilderness of New Zealand's least-populated region, the South Island's West Coast. Snaking through some truly breathtaking scenery, including ferny forests and high-mountain saddles, the route's testing ascents and white-knuckle descents will leave you exhilarated, if more than a little saddlesore.

As a Grade 4 (advanced) mountain biking trail, the Old Ghost Road is only for fit, experienced off-road cyclists. Up to eight hours of cycling per day is required to reach the spartan huts that break up this multi-day ride. You'll sweat through extended uphill climbs, pedal across sections of trail as narrow as 3 ft (1 m), dodge rocks (and hikers), and careen across narrow suspension bridges. Occasionally, when the terrain gets too

rough or you encounter one of the staircases sprinkled along the route, you'll switch roles with your bike, hopping off your saddle and carrying it over your shoulder. You'll also navigate unbridged crossings—with an eye on the weather forecast, in case of flooding.

But this ride is just as much about the history and scenery as it is about the adventure and adrenaline kicks. As you cycle, you'll spy glimpses of the area's short-lived mid-19th-century gold rush, which saw a deluge of hopeful miners flock to the West Coast. Historical remnants,

Negotiating a narrow section of trail on the Old Ghost Road

ELEVATION PROFILE

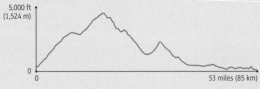

5,000 ft (1,524 m)

0

0   53 miles (85 km)

IN FOCUS

A Golden Past

After learning that the Māori had found gold, European settlers poured into the West Coast in the 1860s. Prospectors established settlements and mining trails, hoping to strike it rich—but gold fever quickly fizzled out, and by the 1870s, roads were left abandoned. Between 2006 and 2015, some of these gorge-side walkways and overgrown paths were painstakingly transformed by volunteers into New Zealand's longest single-track cycling route—the Old Ghost Road.

Rejoin the old mining road at **MŌKIHINUI GORGE** for the final 11 miles (17 km), skirting sheer cliffs on one side and the rushing river on the other.

Celebrate the end of your adventure with a pint in the welcoming **SEDDONVILLE HOTEL**.

Seddonville

Mōkihinui Gorge

NEW ZEALAND

Pedal hard uphill to reach **THE BONEYARD**, a vast, rocky realm, and snap photos of the uniquely named lakes Grim and Cheerful.

Whiten your knuckles along **SKYLINE RIDGE**, a vertiginous section of the trail, before carrying your bike down the steep wooden steps.

The Boneyard

239

Ghost Lake

Skyline Ridge

0 ·········· km ·········· 5
0 ·········· miles ·········· 5

Lyell Saddle

including an old graveyard and the remains of long-abandoned shelters, emerge from the surrounding forest, evidence of the trail's once-golden past. What's more, at every turn you're rewarded by views of forest-cloaked valleys, thundering rivers, and the occasional weka—flightless birds that scamper through the bush. You'll pedal past the diminutive Ghost Lake and navigate the soaring Skyline Ridge; power through the expansive, earthquake-sculpted Boneyard wilderness area; and skirt along the thrillingly sheer-sided Mōkihinui Gorge.

By the time you reach the end of this epic back-country cycle, tired yet elated, the South Island's raw beauty will be forever imprinted on your memory.

Crash at the 3,937-ft (1,200-m) **GHOST LAKE HUT**, an overnight stop high above the tree line, with sweeping alpine views.

Lyell

Aerial view of a winding road leading through Waipoua Forest on the North Island

Top Tip

Start planning at the Tour Aotearoa website *(touraotearoa.nz)*. It's full of maps, practical info, and blogs to inspire you.

99

Tour Aotearoa

CAPE REINGA TO BLUFF, NEW ZEALAND

This long-distance bikepacking odyssey takes intrepid cyclists on a New Zealand end to end. It showcases the islands' huge scenic variety along many of the country's greatest off-road trails.

1,880 MILES (3,025 KM)

52,457 FT (15,989 M)

PAVED / GRAVEL / DIRT

The geographical range of New Zealand, or *Aotearoa* in Māori, is astonishing. The North Island has tropical forests, volcanoes, and hot springs; the South Island has glaciers, mountains, and fjords; wilderness blankets both. The Tour Aotearoa (TA) leads you through these landscapes along dedicated off-road trails and quiet back roads.

For a long time, New Zealand's clean'n'green, laid-back outdoors were better known for long-distance walks than long-distance bike routes: the often busy roads aren't great for touring. But this all changed in 2016, when Kiwi cyclist and guidebook writer Jonathan Kennett created the TA by linking together some of New Zealand's most celebrated cycling trails. Stretching from Cape Reinga in the north to Bluff in the south, the route soon established a reputation as a mighty end to end.

ELEVATION PROFILE

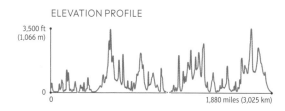

3,500 ft (1,066 m)

0

0   1,880 miles (3,025 km)

Stand on the tip of **CAPE REINGA**, known traditionally as the point from which the spirits of deceased Māori return to their ancestral home.

Cape Reinga

Stroll around the ancient **WAIPOUA FOREST** to admire native trees, such as the kauri. Look out for huge Tāne Mahuta, the biggest kauri in New Zealand.

Waipoua Forest

Auckland

Explore the vibrant, personable city of **AUCKLAND** on handy cycle paths, making sure to pedal up to Mount Eden for great views over the center.

Matamata

NEW ZEALAND

Taumarunui

Admire the giant kiwi statue in **EKETĀHUNA** and maybe see real kiwis on a night tour at the nearby Pūkaha National Wildlife Centre.

Palmerston North

Eketāhuna

Follow the Great Taste Trail in **NELSON** to sample world-class wines from Marlborough's famous vineyards.

Nelson

Picton

Wellington

Lake Rotorua

Greymouth

Take a break from cycling alpine roads to admire the bright-blue ice of the retreating **FOX GLACIER**.

Fox Glacier

Haast

Makarora

Wanaka   Hāwea

Arrowtown

Queenstown

Get your adrenaline going in **QUEENSTOWN**, New Zealand's outdoors capital. Go jet-boating, zip-lining, bungee-jumping, or skydiving before taking a boat across the lake to resume your ride.

Invercargill

Bluff

0 ·········· km ·········· 100
0 ·········· miles ·········· 100

Photo Stops

In case you need an excuse for selfies, the TA website lists 30 photo checkpoints along the route to provide proof that you've done the trail. Snap the start of the route at Cape Reinga and its end at Bluff, along the way taking pics of Waikato cows, *Lord of the Rings*'s Hobbiton™, a giant kiwi, and much more. They'll form quite an album of your Kiwi cycling adventure.

A group of riders pedalling along Ninety-Mile Beach on the North Island

Roughly a third of the distance is on pavement, a third on gravel roads, and a third on gravel trails, but with a fair chunk of mud-track mountain biking too. You'll need a sturdy machine with a bikepacking setup, plus plenty of stamina and self-reliance: in several places, you're on your own for a day or more with no amenities, so camping and cooking gear are essential. The TA can be ridden independently at any time (although wintry June to October is best avoided), but the summer Brevet—a free, annual event—lets you take part in a memorable group ride. Its fastest participants take 10 days to complete the full route, the slowest 30; independent riders could easily take a whole summer. Just make sure that you're fit before you set off—you hit the ground (or rather the sand) pedaling from day one.

There's no doubt that this ride is a major challenge, but there's no better way to experience the country's extraordinary range of nature and scenery: bathe in natural hot pools, picnic in pristine forests, crest half-mile mountain passes and ride alongside glacial lakes. You'll find the soul of New Zealand in the rural towns and villages, where the country's unpretentious small-town hospitality shines at its best. Kiwis are an inclusive, down-to-earth, practical lot, and their culture mixes 21st-century open-mindedness with an old-style love of nature and simplicity. This laid-back lifestyle is mirrored by the trail itself. You might spend your nights camping in a bowling club, remote school, or fire station; lying down in a remote hut; or drying out in a cozy backpacker hostel. Your food stop might be gourmet coffee and organic regional specialities in a stylish local café, a pie and mug of tea, or maybe a bottle of beer in a woody local bar. If you take part in the Brevet, locals will welcome you—and hundreds of your fellow riders—with food and drink, friendly chats, and cheers to encourage you on your way.

You'll find the soul of New Zealand in the rural towns and villages

Riding through
lush native forest
on the North Island

What's great about the Tour Aotearoa is that the scenery gets even better the farther you go, with the section from Haast to Queenstown—near the end of your journey—one of the most spectacular parts of the ride. The sweeping views of mountains, forests, and lakes—with gritty shades of sandstone and mudstone set against vivid greens and deep blues— are as good as any you'll get from from a saddle anywhere in the world.

REFUEL
Roadside Rest Stop

One of the best-known food stops on the TA is the roadside caravan at Bruce Bay, 50 miles (80 km) south of the Haast junction. Enjoy pulled pork, coffee, and cakes; use the Wi-Fi; and look out for penguins, dolphins, and whales in the Tasman Sea.

Leaving behind the coastal town of Haast (and hopefully the West Coast's notorious sandflies), the road climbs gently up the river valley to the narrow bridge at the Gates of Haast. As you cycle along, the slow, broad waters gradually become bright-turquoise torrents; steep hills on either side appear likely to close in at any moment; and deafening waterfalls gush out of the forests. Roads only got this far in 1965, and reaching the densely wooded summit of Haast Pass—one of the country's highest at 1,850 ft (564 m)—it's easy to understand why.

After an exhilarating 12-mile (20-km) descent down the river valley, alongside the ribbonlike waters, you'll have worked up an appetite. Happily, the café in Makarora is a great place to do something about that. Stretch out your legs on the beanbags on the wooden terrace, surrounded by lush mountainscapes, and fuel up on cake.

As you cycle onward, there's no doubt that this is glacier country; here, roads squeeze between water's edge and cliff's bottom. Between Lake Wanaka and Lake Hāwea, the pavement vaults through a nick in the mountains to Hāwea town, where a glorious shorefront campground is served by food trucks with options from healthy to guilty—another excellent excuse to stop for a snack.

After gravel paths to Wanaka comes the long, steady climb up to the Crown Range—the country's loftiest sealed-road pass, at 3,530 ft (1,076 m). En route is the white-clapboard Cardrona Hotel, an iconic survivor of New Zealand's 19th-century gold rush. The top is the TA's high point in every sense: a place for triumphant picnics amid alpine peaks and glimpses down to distant ranges and lush valleys through the gaps between them.

MAKE IT SHORTER

A Ride of Two Halves

The route is split across the North and the South Island in roughly equal halves, offering two shorter routes of around 930 miles (1,500 km) each. For either half, allow at least one week (very fast) or up to three weeks (time to explore).

The descent toward Queenstown is fast and thrilling, smooth roads slicing through hills to the Terraces—and then an equally thrilling, but rough and steep, track that plunges down to Arrowtown. From there, flat riverside roads and paths lead to Queenstown, New Zealand's outdoors capital, stunningly set on Lake Wakatipu—scenery doesn't get any better than this.

Make no mistake, this is a strenuous, challenging, high-status adventure for capable, independent riders. But those who've done it rate it as life-changing and revelatory, whether first-time visitors or locals. As a way to experience the natural, genuine heart of one of the world's most spectacular—and welcoming—countries, it's something very special.

Below left
The striking exterior of the gold rush–era Cardrona Hotel

Below right
Stopping for a photo on the Arrowtown-to-Queenstown section of the Tour Aotearoa

100
Timber Trail

PUREORA TO ONGARUE, NEW ZEALAND

The Timber Trail has a real back-country feel, but the riding's mellow as you trace former logging tramways on a journey through the lush and rugged terrain of the North Island's Pureora Forest Park.

The Timber Trail is all about regeneration. The native forest, once devastated by intensive logging, has been given space to flourish, while local communities that lost their economic mainstay when the timber industry declined have found a new lease on life. You might even find some rejuvenation of your own on the trail: feel your spirits lift as you spot local wildlife, cross soaring suspension bridges, or admire the Southern Hemisphere's star-studded night sky from a remote lodge or campsite.

Your starting point is Pureora, a tiny settlement that's once again prospering thanks to the trail. You'll face a 1,476-ft (450-m) climb within the first 8.7 miles (14 km) to reach the route's highest point, standing tall at 3,185 ft (971 m), but don't worry—it's steady rather than steep. Even better news: from here you're heading—mostly—downhill.

Whether it's up or down, gradients are gentle on the old logging trails and tramways that form the backbone of the route. This means that you'll be free to appreciate the sights and sounds of this revitalized forest: dappled light on the understory, the lavish growth of moss and lichen on the trees, or the chiming call of the tūī, a bird with blue-green iridescent wings that's more often heard than seen.

Zooming through the native bush on the Timber Trail in Pureora Forest Park

ELEVATION PROFILE

3,000 ft
(914 m)

0

0   53 miles (85 km)

Ongarue

That said, you might get jelly legs when crossing one of the trail's suspension bridges. Spanning up to 463 ft (141 m), these thin ribbons vault across steep-sided valleys, offering bird's-eye views of the forest below—some of them have replaced the crumbling wooden trestles of the original tramways. You'll also find evidence of the route's past life scattered along the trail, including the impressive Ongarue Spiral, which sees the track loop round in an arc via two bridges and a curved tunnel.

Eventually, thick forest gives way to the broad golden pastures of the Mangakahu valley as you roll toward historic Ongarue. Today, this old timber town is back to its bustling self, thanks to the cyclists who've just completed their rides. It's a final nod to the Timber Trail's regenerating powers.

IN FOCUS

Hoz Barclay

A key figure in establishing the Timber Trail was Hoz Barclay, whose grandfather once ran the timberyard at Ongarue. Hoz conceived the idea of a modern trail linking the original tramways and spent many arduous days tracing trackbeds buried deep in the bush before eventually overseeing the final construction of the trail.

Pureora

Mount Pureora

Take a side trip on foot from the trail's highpoint, found at 3,185 ft (971 m) on the shoulder of **MOUNT PUREORA**, to reach the peak's 3,822-ft (1,165-m) summit.

NEW ZEALAND

Spy traces of the trail's origins at **HISTORIC NO. 10 CAMP**, including a loading platform and the remains of huts.

Piropiro

Maramataha Suspension Bridge

Gawk at **MARAMATAHA BRIDGE**. At 463 ft (141 m) long and 174 ft (53 m) high, this is the Timber Trail's most impressive suspension bridge.

Historic No. 10 Camp

0 ·······km······· 3
0 ·······miles········ 3

Ongarue Spiral

Prepare to be impressed by the **ONGARUE SPIRAL**, a highly unusual feat of engineering. Here, the trail makes a tight 270-degree turn and descends 141 ft (43 m), partly in a tunnel.

Index

Acknowledgments

DK Eyewitness would like to thank Patrick Bareham, Matthew Coates, Fraser Duff, Saul Harris, Mike King, Ed Steele, Geoff Turner, and Rob Winter, whose help and assistance contributed to the preparation of this book, plus the following authors for their words:

Rob Ainsley writes about touring, leisure, and everyday cycling, and researches routes for *Cycling Plus* magazine. He collects international End to Ends, and has cycled all Britain's rhyming coast-to-coasts. Rob lives in Yorkshire, UK, and won't stop going on about it at *yorkshireridings.blogspot.com.*

Robert Annis spent nearly a decade as a newspaper reporter before becoming an award-winning outdoor-travel journalist. His work appears in numerous publications and websites, including *Outside, National Geographic Traveller, Afar, Bicycling, Men's Journal,* and *Popular Mechanics.*

Paul Bloomfield is a writer and photographer specializing in active adventures, wildlife, and history. He's cycled, hiked, kayaked, rafted, and run thousands of miles on six continents, writing travel features for newspapers, magazines, websites, and books including the *Telegraph,* the *Times, Wanderlust, National Geographic Traveller,* and *BBC Wildlife.*

Oli Broom is the founder and managing director of travel company The Slow Cyclist. Previously he spent 14 months cycling from London to Brisbane to watch a cricket match, followed by two years running a charity in Rwanda.

Emily Chappell is an author and long-distance cyclist, whose journeys have taken her across several continents, and whose words have appeared in numerous cycling and travel publications. She has written two books, one about her years as a cycle courier, and one about her racing exploits.

Lee Craigie was an outdoor instructor and therapist before becoming a full-time mountain bike racer, representing Team GB in World Championships and Scotland in the Commonwealth Games. She established Velocity Bike Workshop and The Adventure Syndicate and is currently the Active Nation Commissioner for Scotland.

Tracey Croke is an award-winning travel journalist addicted to rough-and-tough adventures and galavanting on her mountain bike. She has a special talent for following whims and getting lost. Luckily, her woeful map-reading skills are overlooked as long as she brings back a good story.

Anne Cunningham is a writer, marketing copywriter, and editor living in Toronto, Canada. In her spare time she enjoys learning about nature, hiking, and bicycling, and exploring her beautiful country and other destinations around the world.

Chiz Dakin is proud to call England's Peak District National Park her local playground, but has visited all seven continents in her quest to explore the natural world. She is the creator of the Tour de Peak District cycling route, and loves exploring quiet backways, semi-technical bridleways, and awesome long descents.

Lisa Drewe, author of *Islandeering* and founder of *Islandeering.com,* travels the globe seeking out walking and cycling routes, wild spaces, and great coffee. She's a committed ocean conservationist and chair of the global Whale and Dolphin Conservation.

Caley Fretz's work as a cycling reporter has sent him around the world, from the Tour de France to the Rio Olympics and more. He always brings his own bike along to explore. He once rode a unicycle down a set of stairs; it remains his crowning achievement.

Jason Frye is the author of travel guides to North Carolina, the Blue Ridge Parkway, and Great Smoky Mountains National Park. From his home on the North Carolina coast, he writes about food and travel in the US and around the world.

Neela Gerken has been hooked on bike touring since she cycled solo from Shanghai to Singapore in 2015. When she's off the bike, she writes, dreams, and gives talks about bike touring, solo traveling, and feminism. While touring, she shares her experiences on *www.naiveorbrave.com.*

Cass Gilbert has been embarking on two-wheeled explorations for over 20 years. He's crossed Asia and the Middle East, ridden dirt roads from Alaska to Ushuaia, bikepacked his way around the southwest US, and run a guiding business in the Indian Himalaya. Catch up with his travels via Instagram: @whileoutriding.

Margie Goldsmith has biked, run, paddled, and climbed in 140 countries. She has written over 1,000 articles for countless publications and has published three books.

Sam Haddad writes about cycling, adventure travel, and the outdoors. Aside from the seafront in her home town of Brighton, the best places she's ever cycled are San Francisco, Bali, and Helgeland in Norway. You can keep up with her on Twitter: @shhhaddad.

David Houghton has cycled the Tour d'Afrique, Tour du Canada, Race Across America, Ruta Maya, and Magical Madagascar. He is the author of several books and his writing has appeared in *Bicycling* magazine, *Boneshaker, Cycling Plus,* and *Endurance Sport,* among many others.

Anita Isalska is a writer specializing in France, Eastern Europe, Australia, and the US, with a focus on outdoor travel, technology, and historical oddities. An expat Brit currently based in California, Anita is happiest on her bike (or skis). Read her stuff on *www.anitaisalska.com.*

Simon "Esjay" James is a Sydney-based photographer and designer who founded the Over Yonder website in 2015 as an excuse to explore the Australian outdoors. Many years and not enough adventures later, Esjay still enjoys finding new ways to turn a bike ride into a near-death experience.

Darryl Kotyk is a Canadian-born writer with a huge passion for cycling. He has lived and cycled in several countries around the world, and has published bicycle-related articles in books and magazines, and on his site *www.lovingthebike.com.*

Carol Kubicki is a travel writer and blogger with a blue camper van. Her writing focuses on walking, cycling, and history in the UK and mainland Europe. She's a regular contributor to motorhome and camper van magazines, and in 2018 won the Caravan Writer's Guild Douglas King Award.

Jazz Kuschke is a writer and editor based in South Africa's Garden Route region. He has written (and ridden) extensively on cycling in South Africa. He was the one-time deputy editor on *RIDE* magazine and has covered the ABSA Cape Epic and Cape Town Cycle Tour (among others) for many years.

Becky Lomax is an award-winning writer of guidebooks about US national parks. She lives in Montana, near Glacier National Park, where she joins other locals each spring to cycle the Going-to-the-Sun Road before it opens to cars.

Felix Lowe is author of *Climbs and Punishment: Riding to Rome in the Footsteps of Hannibal.* A columnist and regular contributor to *Cyclist* magazine, he also heads Eurosport's online coverage for all the major pro-cycling races and writes the popular Blazin' Saddles blog. He can be found on Twitter: @saddleblaze.

Colleen MacDonald is author of the popular Let's Go Biking blog *(letsgo biking.net)* and has written guides to cycling in Vancouver and the Okanagan. Colleen has cycled all over the world and still thinks British Columbia is one of the best places to explore.

Laurilee McMichael is a journalist and avid mountain biker. Her idea of the perfect holiday is loading up the bikes with tent, sleeping bags, and camp stove, and setting off to explore New Zealand's cycle trails.

Shafik Meghji is an award-winning travel writer and co-author of more than 40 guidebooks to destinations across Latin America, Asia, Europe, Australasia, and North Africa. Based in South London, he writes and takes photos for publications like *BBC Travel, Wanderlust,* and the *Guardian.* He can be found on Twitter and Instagram: @ShafikMeghji.

John Metcalfe is an award-winning writer based in the UK. His interests include travel and adventure sports. John's bestselling book, *Dividing the Great,* is a humorous account of his ride along the Great Divide mountain bike route.

Laura and Tim Moss spent 16 months cycling around the world and have visited over 30 countries on two wheels. They spend their free time organizing the UK's Cycle Touring Festival and running The Next Challenge website *(thenextchallenge. org),* which encourages people to live more adventurously.

Tom Owen is a cycling writer who loves riding bikes in new places. He has a particular proclivity for scaling Spanish mountains, discovering Macedonian monuments, and sleeping under hedges in a "bivvy bag." He lives in Cambridge in the UK and dreams of cycling up Mauna Kea in Hawaii.

254

Christina Palassio writes about cycling, culture, and causes for a variety of publications. She and her bike have been all over Canada, from the Rockies to Haida Gwaii. Prince Edward Island's Confederation Trail is the only ride she's done twice, and she can't wait to go back.

Richard Peace took to outdoor writing and photojournalism after qualifying as a lawyer and working as a teacher. He has written over 20 cycling titles, including the best-selling *Ultimate C2C Guide* and guides to the Avenue Verte (London to Paris) and Veloscenic (Paris to Mont-Saint-Michel).

Vicky Philpott is a travel and festival blogger at *www.vickyflipfloptravels.com*. She loves a bit of adventure, particularly when it involves sampling local food and drink, and will try anything once.

Chris Scaife lives on the edge of the English Lake District and spends most of his time walking, cycling, and exploring caves. He is a member of the Outdoor Writers and Photographers Guild and is at his happiest heading out into the wild with a heavily laden pannier rack.

Kimberly L Simmons is a historian, educator, and author. She is an advisor to the Underground Railroad Bicycle Route and a partner with the US National Park Service Underground Railroad Network to Freedom.

Jon Sparks has been riding bikes all his life, and photographing and writing about them for most of it. Mountain, road, or gravel bike; close to home in Lancashire or on the other side of the world—if there's a bike involved, it's all good.

Mark Stratton has written and recorded for the British national press for 20 years, with a focus on off-the-beaten track and a love of nature. On the rare occasions he is home, he lives in the wilds of Dartmoor National Park.

Joanna Styles is a freelance writer based in Malaga, Spain. Her writing covers a range of topics, including everything and anything about Spain. When she isn't typing at her keyboard, Joanna loves to explore Europe's waterways on two wheels.

Jenny Tough has pedaled road, gravel, and singletrack in over 40 countries. Between exploring, she also competes in long-distance bikepacking races and was the first woman to finish both the inaugural Silk Road Mountain Race and Atlas Mountain Race.

Claire Tyrrell is an avid cyclist from Australia, who believes there is no better way to see the world than by bicycle. In her professional life, Claire is an accomplished journalist with a passion for writing about her experiences on the bike.

The publisher would like to thank the following for their kind permission to reproduce their photographs:

(Key: a-above; b-below/bottom; c-centre; f-far; l-left; r-right; t-top)

123RF.com: inkdrop 18-19t; ossiridian 146tl.

Rob Ainsley: 68cla.

Alamy Stock Photo: 192tl; The Africa Image Library 179cr; agefotostock / Christian Goupi 119c,/ Javier Larrea 136clb; Dorothy Alexander 23bc; All Canada Photos / Barrett & MacKay 26cl,/ Mike Grandmaison 25cl,/ Steve Ogle 70-71, 75b,/ Leanna Rathkelly 16br,/ Rich Wheater 17cr; Anyisa 81tl, 81cb; Arterra Picture Library / Collection Clement Philippe 111b, 115br; © Bill Bachmann 25br; Andrew Bain 142bc, 233tl, 234bl; Martin Bennett 115ca; blickwinkel / M. Woike 68cra; blphoto 20tr; David Broadbent 143cra; D. Callcut 113br; Cavan / Aurora Photos / Keri Oberly 68br; Cavan Images / Aurora Open RF / Kennan Harvey 46ca; Thornton Cohen 157bc; Gary Crabbe / Enlightened Images 33tl; Tim Cuff 239tc, 239cla, 239bc, 242cl; Richard Cummins 37cb, 106cr; Mark Daffey 221cr; Luis Dafos 132br, 152cb; Ian Dagnall 23cr; Ian G Dagnall 98bc; Max Dominik Daiber 197crb; Daniel Dempster Photography 47tr; Danita Delimont / Russ Bishop 41bl,/ ,/ Michael DeFreitas 21crb,/ Chuck Haney 42; dbimages / Jeremy Graham 63bc; Design Pics Inc / Brand B / Lorna Rande 18tl; Kathy deWitt 30cla; dmac 54cr; Stephen Dorey ABIPP 110cl; Alan Douglas 17tl; Randy Duchaine 26bc, 53cra; Joe Dunckley 107tr; Adam Eastland 126cr; eye35 245bl; Alex Fieldhouse 109br; David Flanagan 103br; Stephen Fleming 93c, 142tc, 245br; FLPA 95clb; Peter Forsberg 202tc; Rob Francis 65bl; Chris Frost 194bl; Richard Green 106tl; H. Mark Weidman Photography 38br; James Hackland 22br, 24cra; Urmas Haljaste 98tc; John Hayward 109clb; Hemis.fr / Bertrand Gardel 23tc,/ Michel Gotin 195cl,/ Christian Guy 125tc,/ Pierre Jacques 100bl; Camille Moirenc 124cr; Grant Henderson 88bl; Cindy Hopkins 189cl; Horizon Images / Motion 210br; Peter Horree 135bl; Rilind Hoxha 152cr; Image Professionals GmbH / Roetting / Pollex 207cra;

imageBROKER / Harald von Radebrecht 87crb,/ Martina Katz 188tl,/ Reinhard Marscha 171cr,/ Robert Seitz 79bc,/ Stefan Kiefer 131cra; Images By T.O.K. 38bl; Imaginechina Limited / Tuchong 203tr; Jeffrey Isaac Greenberg 1+ 54bc; ITPhoto 79cl; Ivoha 123cr; Jeffrey Isaac Greenberg 3+ 49cr, 50tl; Dennis K. Johnson 53cb; Jon Arnold Images Ltd 124tc, 242cla,/ Alan Copson 46tr; Ronald Karpilo 67tr; John Kellerman 127crb, 132cr; Matthew Kiernan 34crb; Olga Kolos 186cla; Jason Langley 173tr; Nick Ledger 177br; Frans Lemmens 117tr; Andrew Lloyd 108cr; Luxy Images Limited / L Collection 123tr; Fabrizio Malisan 145bc; Itsik Marom 19tr; master2 77bl; Matthew Williams-Ellis Travel Photography 149bc; mauritius images GmbH / Walter Bibikow 106ca,/ ClickAlps 171bc,/ Werner Dieterich 134br,/ Nicolas Marino 168bl,/ Novarc Images / Nicolás Marino 178bl; Aliaksandr Mazurkevich 152cl; Minden Pictures / Pete Oxford 72bl; Mira 58tl; MLouisphotography 31tr; David Moore / Victoria 217tl, 225cr; Rupert Sagar-Musgrave 192crb; National Geographic Image Collection / Jim Richardson 167cla; NatureByDarrellYoung 48bl; Jaak Nilson 99bl; Sérgio Nogueira 185cra; Samantha Ohlsen 225tc; Robert K. Olejniczak 58cr; oneworld picture / Achim Oberhauser 103cr; Joris Van Ostaeyen 135cra; Paul Thompson Images 51b,/ Chris Ballentine 181crb; J. W. Philpot 52br; Robert Preston 192bc; Prisma by Dukas Presseagentur GmbH / Heeb Christian 57tl; Paul Quayle 208tr; rabh images 48c; M Ramírez 98cr; RnDmS 132tl; Robertharding / Jean-Pierre De Mann 167cra,/ Markus Lange 130cla, 134cl,/ Ben Pipe 199br; Alexandre Rotenberg 73cla; Boaz Rottem 179tl; Oleksandr Rupeta 10b; Peter Schickert 65cr; James Schwabel 17br, 45cb, 48tc; Alex Sipetyy 186cr; Keith Skingle 139cl; Witold Skrypczak 64ca; Kumar Sriskandan 73br; Stephen Frink Collection 59cr; Stockimo / SteveFleming 92bl, 122br; Tasfoto 116bl; Terry Smith Images 34br; Tetra Images / WalkerPod Images 229br,/ Mike Kemp 9t,/ Sam Diephuis 155t; TMI 37cla, uskarp 207tl; Visual360.co.uk 85crb; Sebastian Wasek 94cr; Alan Waterman 21tl; Geoff Waugh 105br; Karl W. Wegmann 185bc; Jim West 62cr; Westend61 GmbH / Gemma Ferrando 167br,/ JLPfeifer 128-29,/ Stefan Sch√ºtz 85cla; Jan Wlodarczyk 147cla.

Alps 2 Ocean Cycle Trail: Cindy Mottelet 235bc, 236bl.

Black Cabin Coffee: 41crb.

Paolo Ciaberta: 172bl.

Chiz Dakin: 215tl.

Depositphotos Inc: phb.cz 114bc.

Dreamstime.com: Leonid Andronov 119br; Valery Bareta 95cra; Maciej Bledowski 198bl; Delstudio 79tc; Oliver Foerstner 80tc; Franky 20cl; Pierrette Guertin 37tr; H368k742 139cra; Ina Hensel 127tc; Thanayu Jongwattanasilkul 196br; Gennadiy Karasev 149clb; Kotenko 94tl; Jesse Kraft 157clb; Chris Labasco 59clb; Lunamarina 138bl; Zdeněk Matyáš 158ca; Cj Nattanai 205br; Outcast85 207crb; Paop 78bl, 86bl, 195tr; Marek Poplawski 197tl; Rolf52 236cl; Saiko3p 157tc; Shaiith 221bl; Smontgom65 56bl; Calin Stan 147br; Steveheap 33tr; Michal Stipek 119tr; Tsvibrav 222bl; UlyssePixel 170cr; Michele Ursi 100cl; Wallixx 240-41; Anastasia Yakovleva 216br; Robert Zehetmayer 146crb.

Elfis Sjostuer: 93tr.

Experience Montenegro: www.3etravel.me 150-51.

Fairfield Guesthouse, Cafe and Bakery: 185crb.

Josh Firth: 9b.

Caley Fretz: 76br.

Garden Route Trail Park: 181tc.

Getty Images: 500px / Thomas H. Mitchell 117cl,/ Wen Wen 226t; Cavan Images 10t, 35tl; Corbis Documentary / Merrill Images 30bl; EyeEm / Carlos J Ripoll Carmona 198cl,/ Daniela Simona Temneanu 153br,/ Li Lín Yi 148tl,/ Ratima Sritangwong 208tl,/ Tsvi Braverman 224br; The Image Bank / Heath Korvola 35ca,/ John Coletti 45tl,/ Michael Hall 175b,/ Franz Marc Frei 120tl; LightRocket / John S Lander 210tc; Moment / Boy_Anupong 198crb,/ Frank Chen 206br,/ Matteo Colombo 66br,/ Jack Hoyer 32bl, 118cb,/ John Crux Photography 225cl,/ Gw. Nam 204cr,/ @ Didier Marti 156cr,/ Morten Falch Sortland 189c,/ Neal Pritchard Photography 214br,/ Alexander Spatari 96-97,/ Angel Villalba 139tl,/ Peter Zelei Images 104, 144cr,/ photography by p. lubas 173cla,/ Sasipa Muennuch 209bl, / Sebastián Crespo Photography 73cr,/ Seiman Choi photography 205tl,/ Shehzaad Maroof 190-91,/ Paul Biris 201br; National Geographic Image Collection / Pete Ryan 44bl; Photodisc / Jeremy Woodhouse 201t,/ Karl Weatherly 87cra; Stone / Alan Majchrowicz 44crb,/ Andrew Peacock

Project Editor Elspeth Beidas
Editor Rachel Laidler
US Editor Heather Wilcox
Senior Designer Ben Hinks
Designers Nell Wood, Van Le
Illustrator Ben Spurrier
Proofreader Kathryn Glendenning
Indexer Helen Peters
Picture Researchers Adam Goff, Ben Hinks, Sumita Khatwani, Vagisha Pushp
Senior Cartographic Editor Casper Morris
Jacket Designer Ben Hinks
Jacket Picture Research Adam Goff, Ben Hinks
Senior Production Editor Jason Little
Technical Prepress Manager Tom Morse
Senior Production Controller Stephanie McConnell
Managing Editor Hollie Teague
Managing Art Editor Bess Daly
Art Director Maxine Pedliham
Publishing Director Georgina Dee

First American Edition, 2021
Published in the United States by DK Publishing
1450 Broadway, Suite 801, New York, NY 10018

Copyright © 2021 Dorling Kindersley Limited
DK, a Division of Penguin Random House LLC
21 22 23 24 25 10 9 8 7 6 5 4 3 2 1
001–322270–Apr/2021

All rights reserved.

Without limiting the rights under the copyright reserved above, no part of this publication may be reproduced, stored in or introduced into a retrieval system, or transmitted, in any form, or by any means (electronic, mechanical, photocopying, recording, or otherwise), without the prior written permission of the copyright owner.

A catalog record for this book is available
from the Library of Congress.

ISBN 978-0-7440-2885-0

DK books are available at special discounts when purchased in bulk for sales promotions, premiums, fund-raising,or educational use. For details contact: DK Publishing Special Markets, 1450 Broadway, Suite 801, New York, NY 10018
SpecialSales@dk.com

Printed and bound in Malaysia.

www.dk.com

This book was made with Forest Stewardship Council ™ certified paper—one small step in DK's commitment to a sustainable future. For more information go to www.dk.com/our-green-pledge

The rapid rate at which the world is changing is constantly keeping the DK Eyewitness team on our toes. While we've worked hard to ensure that this edition of *Ride* is accurate and up-to-date, we know that roads close, routes are altered, places close, and new ones pop up in their place. So, if you notice we have something wrong or left something out, we want to hear about it. Please get in touch at travelguides@dk.co.uk

CANADA

ICELAND

NORWAY

SWEDEN

DENMARK

U.K.

IRELAND

GERMANY

POLAND

UNITED
STATES

FRANCE

SPAIN

MOROCCO

WESTERN
SAHARA

ALGERIA

LIBYA

TUNISIA

MEXICO

CUBA

BELIZE

NICARAGUA

COSTA
RICA

PANAMA

VENEZUELA

GUYANA

SURINAM

COLOMBIA

ECUADOR

PERU

BOLIVIA

PARAGUAY

BRAZIL

CHILE

URUGUAY

ARGENTINA

MAURITANIA

MALI

NIGER

CHAD

SENEGAL

GUINEA

BURKINA
FASO

NIGERIA

CENTRAL
AFRICAN R

SIERRA
LEONE

CÔTE
D'IVOIRE

LIBERIA

GHANA

CAMEROON

CONGO

GABON

DEM.
OF CO

ANGOLA

NAMIBIA

BOTS

SOU
AFR

1 2 3 4 5 6 7 8 9 10 11 12 13 14 15 16 17 18 19 20 21 22 23 24 25 26 27 28 29 30 31 32 33 34 35 37 38 39 40 41 42 43 44 45 46 47 48 49 50 51 52 53 54 55 56 57 58 59 61 62 63 64 69 71 73

ITALY

GREE